GROWING UP IN ˙

G000153513

Growing Up in Transit
The Politics of Belonging
at an International School

Danau Tanu

berghahn
NEW YORK · OXFORD
www.berghahnbooks.com

First published in 2018 by
Berghahn Books
www.berghahnbooks.com

© 2018, 2020 Danau Tanu
First paperback edition published in 2020

Front cover illustration by Mona Schlapp
Front cover design by Claire Molloy
Figures illustrated by Claire Molloy

Library of Congress Cataloging-in-Publication Data

Names: Tanu, Danau.
Title: Growing up in transit : the politics of belonging at an international
school / Danau Tanu.
Description: New York : Berghahn Books, 2017. | Includes bibliographical
references and index.
Identifiers: LCCN 2017037771 (print) | LCCN 2017043322 (ebook) | ISBN
9781785334092 (ebook) | ISBN 9781785334085 (hardback : alk. paper)
Subjects: LCSH: International schools—Indonesia. | International education—
Social aspects—Indonesia. | Third-culture children—Education—Indonesia.
| Educational anthropology—Indonesia. | Eurocentrism.
Classification: LCC LC46.94.I64 (ebook) | LCC LC46.94.I64 T36 2017 (print) |
DDC 370.116—dc23
LC record available at https://lccn.loc.gov/2017037771

British Library Cataloguing in Publication Data

A catalogue record for this book is available from the British Library

ISBN 978-1-78533-408-5 (hardback)
ISBN 978-1-78920-795-8 (paperback)
ISBN 978-1-78533-409-2 (ebook)

To my father, mother, and sister

Contents

Figures

Please note that the diagrams are not representative of relative group sizes.

Foreword

In recent years, the number of international schools throughout Asia has grown rapidly. Often very well resourced, these schools attract students not only from expatriate communities, but also increasingly from the elite sections of the local community. Students from both of these two groups are globally mobile and networked, with experiences that are transnational and transcultural, and aspirations that are cosmopolitan and internationally-minded. Many of them are often referred to as "Third Culture Kids," and they are familiar with and can relate to more than one set of cultural traditions. International schools are places where such students can be expected to feel most comfortable, where they can escape the parochialism and poverty of life outside their educational setting, and where they can experiment with a diversity of cultural expressions. In this sense, international schools are transnational learning spaces where cultural hybridization is the norm rather than an exception. Yet they are also highly complex and contradictory places where global forces often conflict with local and national imperatives, where it is possible for students to experience lives that are divorced from the pressures of life outside the walls of their school.

This wonderful book takes us inside one of these schools, in Indonesia. The author, Danau Tanu, attended international schools herself and then immersed herself in a similar school as an ethnographer. This enabled Danau to occupy a unique vantage point from which to observe the ways in which global forces, connections, and imaginations play out at the school; the ways in which experiences at the school are interpreted and negotiated by both teachers and students; and the ways in which the school attempts to work with and reproduce the privileges that it and its students enjoy. Through a wide variety of narratives—many drawn from deep conversations with students—this book compellingly and beguilingly shows that while there are a diverse range of intercultural practices enacted at the school, they are internal to a relatively closed milieu, often divorced from the broader relations of power. It shows how the school's ideology of "being international" is linked to the ways in which national and international class structures are produced and reproduced, through their location within the socio-economic hierarchies that are often obscured by its discursive rhetoric of inclusivity and internationalization.

While the school promotes values of intercultural understanding, and of "engaging peaceably with others across difference," Danau convincingly argues that this engagement is largely informed by a set of assumed norms that maintain a distance from the local by embracing all things Western. The form of cosmopolitanism that is thus promoted and practiced at the school is largely Eurocentric, displaying a high degree of continuity with the traditions of Western colonialism. This is not to say that the students at the school are not interested in finding alternative ways of imagining and practicing cosmopolitanism. Rather, Danau shows delicately how alternatives available to them are highly constrained by various transnational discourses and organizational practices associated with global mobility, and the processes of internationalization.

Danau points to the colonial and transnational capitalist discourses that shape the subjectivities of transnational mobile youth at such schools. The use of English as a global language features prominently in their cultural formations, establishing a marker of distinction in both national and transnational contexts. Student subjectivities are also affected by the ways the school engages with the local Indonesian cultural traditions, often encouraging a social distance from them. From the perspective of the school, the local community is represented as unfamiliar, alien and even dangerous.

At the same time, the parents and students at the school aspire to Euro-American cultural capital. They are mindful of cultural capital associated with Western education and the ability to speak English, and consider these qualities to be essential for gaining access to higher education in the West. In this way, the social spaces in the school are often structured in order to perpetuate the cultural affinity with Euro-American values. Accordingly, the relationship of the students to the normative idea of cosmopolitanism is deeply ambivalent, especially in view of their hybrid identities—often of being Eastern and Western at the same time. To develop in students a cosmopolitan imaginary, the school encourages diversity but also assumes colonial precepts of race, gender, and class upon which it is defined.

This is a wonderful book—well-structured and beautifully written. Perhaps the most attractive aspect of the book is the ways in which it uses student voices most skillfully to support its various theoretical observations, and to develop its overall argument. Also impressive is the level of self-reflexivity that it displays. In a remarkably skillful manner Danau weaves her own biography into the arguments she presents. This is indeed a rich book, not only in the stories it offers its readers but in its highly nuanced analysis.

Fazal Rizvi
The University of Melbourne

Preface

"What makes you angry?" asked a visiting professor as we stood in the hallway of the university's limestone buildings. I had casually told her that I had been mulling over a possible research topic for three long years. But it only took a split second for me to answer her: "The question, 'Where are you from?'" I said. One gut reaction to a simple question set the course for the next few years of my life. A trusted friend once said, "You talk about 'identity' ad nauseam." This was because my answer to the question was never straightforward and rarely left unchallenged.

I was born in Canada to a Chinese Indonesian father and a Japanese mother.[1] I learned to speak four languages as a child. I had lived in four countries by the time I was eighteen and six by age twenty-two. Sometimes I moved because I was tagging along with my parents, who were serial migrants; at other times I moved on my own for study. I attended local schools in Indonesia and Japan for a year each, but mostly attended international schools in Indonesia and Singapore.

My mobile upbringing is typical among young people who attend international schools and who are popularly referred to as "Third Culture Kids" (TCK). Much has been said of their experiences of many childhood hellos and goodbyes as well as the cultural displacement that comes with an intensely mobile lifestyle, and the impact that these experiences have on a child's sense of identity and belonging. David Pollock and Ruth E. Van Reken wrote the seminal book on the topic, *Third Culture Kids: Growing Up Among Worlds*. Among those in the know, it is dubbed "the TCK bible."

But there are many aspects of my experiences of mobility and English-medium international schools that are missing from the literature on privileged international mobility and schooling. My own experiences of mobility and the gap that I felt between my home culture and that of the international schools I attended raise questions about the cultural hierarchies embedded within the social worlds of so-called cosmopolitan elites and the way these hierarchies shape the way children interact with one another across difference. I share my own story here to give some background on how I came to self-identify as a Third Culture Kid (for a brief while anyway, until I got it out of my system), yet abandon the term as an analytical concept in writing this book with the intention of focusing on the diversity of this cohort.

Hereditary Transnationalism

The transnationality of my story did not begin with me. It began at least three generations prior with my great grandfather on my father's side. According to family stories, my Chinese grandfather's father had worked as a bodyguard on a ship and died on Borneo island, where the ship had stopped over for trading. My grandfather's mother also died some time later, leaving my grandfather and his younger brother orphaned. At nineteen, my grandfather boarded a boat for the Dutch East Indies, now Indonesia. He was part of the exodus of Chinese emigrants in the early 1900s, who left for various European colonies as indentured workers to escape impoverishment in a country torn by political turmoil. In the Dutch East Indies, my grandfather worked to pay off his passage and help his fiancée (they had been betrothed as infants) and younger brother to join him from China. My grandparents then saved money to begin street-side peddling in markets, which eventually grew into several successful businesses.

By the time my father was born in the mid-1950s, his parents spoke fluent Indonesian and were financially comfortable. Grandfather had only studied until the second grade, but was able to read and write Chinese, and became fluent and literate in Indonesian through self-study. Dad was sent to an elementary school in Jakarta where the language of instruction was Mandarin. When Dad was in sixth grade, the school was closed down along with other Chinese schools across Indonesia as part of the aftermath of the attempted coup of 1965, which was allegedly carried out by communists. The ethnic Chinese in Indonesia were used as political scapegoats during the subsequent purge of communism in the young republic that saw Suharto rise to power. Public use of Chinese languages was discouraged, importation of printed materials in Chinese prohibited, and diplomatic ties with the People's Republic of China frozen (Hoon 2008). Sino-Indonesian diplomatic relations were gradually restored in the early 1990s, but the ban on Chinese printed material was only lifted in 2001, three years after Suharto's downfall in 1998.

When his Chinese school was closed down, Dad moved to an elementary school where the language of instruction was Indonesian. After three or four years, he was sent to Singapore with some of his siblings to study at a local school whose language of instruction was English. Sending children overseas to study in a more developed country is still a common practice among middle- and upper-class Indonesians as a means to provide them with high-quality education (Yeo 2010). Today Dad speaks English fluently with an "Asian" accent whose specific origins are unidentifiable; he prefers to read books on certain topics in English; he feels most comfortable speaking Indonesian; he spoke Mandarin to Mom when they first met because that was their only common language at the time; and he is now fluent enough in my mother's native language to crack jokes in Japanese. It is clear from my family history on my father's side that my own disposition for cosmopolitan engagement was transmitted to me through the family (Bourdieu 1986).

My mother's story also illustrates that acquiring a cosmopolitan disposition is a generational project. Mom, who is older than my father, grew up in the immediate aftermath of Japan's defeat in World War II, and came of age in the 1960s during Japan's rapid economic growth. Both of my maternal grandparents were from a village and only had a few years of elementary school education. My grandmother left her village in Niigata Prefecture as a young woman to work in a factory in Tokyo for several years before returning to the village for an arranged marriage. My grandfather was a carpenter who built workboats for the Shinano River, which runs through my mother's village.

While their lives were not luxurious by any means, Mom remembers that her family lived more comfortably than some of her poorer neighbors by the time she was in elementary school. Grandmother liked to try new, foreign things (perhaps due to her exposure to Tokyo during her youth), such as introducing meat to the family diet in a country where fish was the staple source of protein, introducing my mother to the Western tradition of Santa Claus (minus the Christianity), and serving coffee to guests. The coffee was diluted to the color of tea because it was an expensive imported good, and because my grandmother did not know how to properly prepare the exotic foreign drink. Mom later became the first woman in her village to attend university where she studied Chinese literature. After completing university in Tokyo and working for several years, she left for Singapore to study

Mandarin. Little did she know that she would then spend the rest of her life abroad.

My parents met in Singapore in the 1970s. They were later married in Canada. They have both since moved countries multiple times, along with their children and a couple of suitcases. Though my father does not self-identify as a Third Culture Kid, he fits the profile. If nothing else, he became what I used to jokingly call a "serial migrant" (long before it was turned into an academic term).

It is evident that my own transnational experiences are a result of the cross-border engagements that began in previous generations in my family. A similar pattern emerges among those I interviewed for this book—the transnational engagements of previous generations in the family facilitated their own cosmopolitan dispositions. My parents' transnational exposure and financial capability ensured that both my sister and I learned to speak fluent English. This secured our privileged position in the changing linguistic landscape of Indonesia, where the middle and upper classes are increasingly using English in daily speech and business communications, much like the elites who spoke Dutch during colonial times.

Like a Second-Generation Immigrant

By all appearances, my transnational background should have predisposed me to being "international," a supposedly cosmopolitan way of being that is lauded among the globetrotting population of expatriates, their children, and their children's international school educators. I am a native speaker of English, Japanese, and Indonesian, and conversational in Mandarin. Everyone in my immediate family speaks these four languages to different levels of fluency, largely determined by our schooling. My parents and I left Canada and went "back" to Indonesia after I turned three. My younger sister was born in Japan during a temporary visit. I spent a year at a local school in Indonesia before my parents moved me to an international school in Jakarta where I did most of my schooling to prepare me for our intended return to Canada (a trip we never made).

Despite my mixed background, I did not have sufficient cultural knowledge and skills, which Pierre Bourdieu (1973) refers to as "cultural capital," to fit in comfortably at my international school. The international school I attended used English as its main language of instruction and prided itself on the myriad nationalities that were represented on campus, but culturally speaking it was predominantly North

American. I remember being puzzled as an elementary school student that it was considered normal to have mothers who knew how to bake brownies while mine made sushi, and that my schoolmates had access to popular American sweets and toys, such as Nerds, licorice, and Cabbage Patch dolls, none of which were available at the local shops in Jakarta in the 1980s. My classmates had access to them because their parents purchased them on furloughs home to the United States or in stores and country clubs in Jakarta that were frequented by the Western expatriate population. I experienced a sense of cultural dissonance vis-à-vis the dominant school culture. I was like a second-generation Asian immigrant in a Western industrialized country (Foner and Kasinitz 2007). International schools are marketed as the nurturing bed of cosmopolitan transformation, but the social spaces that they offer are not free of cultural inequalities as they are imagined to be.

English and Linguistic Imperialism

As I was growing up, I felt a sense of superiority for speaking English.[2] I remember arguing with Mom in my teens when I switched from Japanese to English mid-argument. I spoke fast, using English expressions that I knew were too difficult for my Japanese mother to understand due to her limited English. She asked me to speak in Japanese. I talked back, telling her something to the effect that English was my first language and she was going to have to deal with it. My outburst was a combination of genuine frustration at not being able to express myself in Japanese as well as I could in English, and arrogance at being able to speak English better than her. Mom was furious. She threatened to withdraw me from the international school. Mom said in Japanese, "I would rather have an uneducated child who has a good heart than an educated child who lets their education ruin them on the inside!" I eventually apologized after she tried to throw my thick, heavy American textbooks in the trashcan. It was one of the best lessons she taught me.

According to Charlotte Burck (2005), language issues among migrant families can disrupt relations of power in families. Colonial and capitalist discourses about language and culture have imbued English with such power that even a child can use language as cultural capital to maintain or challenge relations of power with adults. The tension between parents' desire for their children to retain their home language and culture while acquiring the linguistic and cultural skills to operate in the global economy and their children's desire to acquire the same skills to succeed in their social milieu is a recurring theme in this book.

Cultural Reproduction in Schools

I cannot overemphasize the role that schools play in shaping the cultural disposition of children. Although my sister and I have much in common—we both speak the same four languages, we grew up mostly in Indonesia, and we made similar international moves—we are different in our cultural orientation largely because we went to different schools. I am a Canadian citizen who was educated mainly at an international school in Indonesia, and I speak English as my first language. My sister is an Indonesian citizen who grew up in Indonesia and went to an Indonesian school for the most part, and she speaks Indonesian as her first language. Within the family, we share similar values and can culturally relate to one another on the most part. Cultural differences become apparent when our varied levels of language ability and acculturation affect the way we relate to others outside the family.

I struggled greatly with my sense of identity, while my sister did not seem to. This was partly due to differences in personality, but not entirely. Her educational milieu corresponded to the cultural context of the country we were living in, while mine did not. My international school was Americanized. I learned how to count American coins (the penny, nickel, dime, and quarter) in elementary school long before I ever visited the United States. In the early 1990s, they set up a television outside the high school office that aired CNN's daily reports on the presidential election between Bill Clinton and George Bush. The Americanized international school environment led me to subconsciously think of myself as American until my mid-twenties. Educational milieus can shape a person's sense of identity so as to reproduce the dominant culture that they represent (Levinson and Holland 1996; Willis 1977). International schools are no different.

Mobility and Cultural Displacement

My family moved to Japan for a year when I was eleven and about to start sixth grade. The different academic calendar that Japan used meant that I had to complete fifth grade all over again at a public school in Tokyo. At the time, I had a rudimentary grasp of written Japanese and failed most of the weekly *kanji* (Chinese/Japanese character) tests that the teacher set. This did not bother me much, owing perhaps to the fact that I could speak English—I was aware that English was an internationally valued language and thus felt emotionally compensated for my failed tests, at least temporarily.

However, I did not fit in well in my new social environment due to my gender and different cultural upbringing. I was neither able nor willing to participate in the strictly hierarchical social relations prevalent among my female classmates. My male classmates had a less defined sense of hierarchy that seemed to almost disappear once they hit the soccer field. I longed to join them as I was a tomboy and usually played with the boys in my old international school, but it seemed taboo to engage in mixed gendered play at the new school. There was another girl in my class who also did not belong to any social group and was sometimes verbally bullied and once slapped by one of the popular girls. I did not have the courage to do anything about it at the time. I kept my distance from her at school because I feared being stigmatized by association, but I used to engage her in conversation on our long walk home from school. Hierarchical relations and gender restrictions were less pronounced outside the confined grounds of the school campus.

I spent a year having no friends at school (though I had plenty of friends at church) and began to show signs of *tōkōkyohi*[3] or "school phobia" (Yoneyama 2000: 77). *Tōkōkyohi* is a Japanese term that describes a social phenomenon where school-aged children develop psychosomatic symptoms that prevent them from attending school. I loved studying, and while I was living in Indonesia I refused to miss school even when I was unwell. But Mom recalls that toward the end of our stay in Japan, I would get stomach aches as I was about to put my shoes on to go to school. By then I had spent many recesses walking slowly up and down the school hallways to kill time. Though I had many friends later in life, the childhood pain from this period of isolation remained with me until I began this research, which turned out to be self-therapeutic.

When we returned to Indonesia to my old international school, I thought things would return to normal. On the contrary, I had become "too Japanese." I dressed awkwardly—different from my Americanized classmates back at the international school. I no longer knew how to relate to my old friends and, I presume, vice versa. I found new friends of various backgrounds, a few of whom were Dutch. I also made Japanese friends.

I was introduced to the Japanese students through my mother, who had met their parents. My links to the Japanese community on campus was subsequently partially maintained through my mother's links with my Japanese friends' mothers. Social networks on campus are facilitated by off-campus networks between parents, which Bourdieu (1986) refers to as hereditary social capital. But I did not have the cultural capital to fully engage in the Japanese social group. Had I tried to do so, I would have had to play the cultural chameleon and consciously perform and accentuate my "Japaneseness" at the expense of playing down my other cultural influences. Neither was I keen on being fully identified with a group that was considered "ESOL" (English for Speakers of Other Languages). Many of the Japanese were enrolled in ESOL classes because they were still struggling with English and had fewer opportunities to interact with students in the mainstream classes. As a result, ESOL students were often invisible to the mainstream Anglophone[4] students and seen as inferior in the school's social hierarchy. One Anglophone Indian graduate, with whom I later got in touch, could not even recall the presence of a large contingent of ESOL students at our former school. So I hung out mainly with my new British, Dutch, Malaysian, and American friends and would only drop in to see my Japanese friends briefly during the course of the school day.

However, as middle school turned into high school and high school progressed, my non-Japanese friends moved away one by one. The transient nature of the highly mobile student body that characterizes international schools disrupted my social network. Around this time, student cliques became increasingly defined by language and cultural orientation—a pattern that I did not notice about my own experience until after I began this research and heard of similar patterns through the interviews I conducted. My Dutch friends increasingly hung out with their Dutch peers, likewise my Indian friends with other Indians, and my Korean friends with other Koreans. It became more difficult each year to replace my social network.

I found myself shifting in and out of a few language groups without feeling at home in any. This was not surprising with regard to the Korean and Dutch groups, considering that I could not understand anything beyond a few swear words. But I was neither at home in the English- nor Japanese-speaking groups even though I was fluent in both languages, partly because my social skills did not develop as fast as those of my peers, nor were they accompanied by the appropriate cultural capital. At the end of ninth grade, the number of Japanese students grew when students from the Jakarta Japanese School moved en masse to my international school. I befriended many of them because by this time my view of the Japanese students had changed and I had become infatuated with Japan. However, despite my interest in them I was still unable to fully immerse myself in the Japanese student groups. This sense of infatuation with the "home" country in their teen years was also common among the participants in my research. Likewise, the influence of cultural capital upon the formation of social groups and campus dynamics features prominently among the students I researched.

Then at sixteen I moved. I moved ten times over the next eleven years between seven cities in six countries for various reasons, sometimes with the family and sometimes without. Many envied me for having lived "overseas"—an elusive place whose location changed in relation to where the speaker was from—and for being multilingual and able to move fluidly between different cultural milieus. I was fully aware that it was a great privilege and adventure to live in so many countries at a young age. Nevertheless, by the end I was emotionally exhausted. I experienced many of the symptoms that characterize those who make many moves while growing up—rootless, restless, and unable to reconcile my seemingly fragmented identities. I felt as though nobody knew who I was as I had to reestablish myself and build new relationships with each move. I also felt I had to *perform* different identities to suit each cultural context in order to accommodate the fact that others could only relate to certain fragments of my identity—North American, Japanese, Indonesian, and so on. Still, considering the privileges that came with a transnational upbringing, I assumed I was making a big deal out of nothing.

This changed when I began the preliminary research for this book in 2008. I read about a range of topics relating to identity, from migration to mixed-race children as well as Third Culture Kids. To my naïve surprise, "identity" was a major issue for many. The dissertations and academic articles that I read—the kind of writing that is usually considered dry and boring—often conjured up emotional responses in me. In particular, the literature on Third Culture Kids helped me to narrate my own story of repeated cultural displacement. But I still had qualms about using the term "Third Culture Kids" myself because it seemed better suited to describe the "Western expat kids" with whom I had gone to the international school and to whom I could not fully relate.

Between Local and Expat, Asian and Western

I often visited Jakarta as an adult and drove past my old international school campus on numerous occasions. Each time, I experienced a strange, fleeting, and unsettled feeling, which I did not understand until more than a decade later. All my classmates had been foreign nationals, making me a local who was acculturated into a nonlocal, mainly Western expatriate culture. I was trained to see Indonesia through foreign eyes from a perceptual distance that ran contrary to my family's close affiliation with the country. W. E. B. Du Bois (2007 [1903]: 8) describes this feeling as the "peculiar sensation" of "double-consciousness, this sense of always looking at one's self through the eyes of others, of measuring one's soul by the tape of a world that looks on in amused contempt and pity."

There were times when I heard my classmates speak about Indonesians or Asians in a condescending way, though this rarely happened at a school that had zero tolerance for overt racism. It was the less obvious but systemic omission of Indonesia from campus life that trained my gaze. Indonesia, and the entire world outside of Western civilization for that matter, was all but absent from our textbooks. The non-Western world appeared only in tokenistic or traditional forms: the Saharan desert in geography class and the Egyptian pyramids and Great Wall of China in ancient history class. Modern history was Western history, literature was Western literature, mythology was Greek mythology, and science was invented by Westerners. The rest of the world was invisible and exotic (Said 1985 [1978]).

Indonesia was inferior to the West. The Indonesian staff was mostly employed in support positions such as teaching assistants, library assistants, clerical staff, cleaners, and security guards. In contrast, the teaching and other positions of authority were almost always filled by foreign staff, who were mostly white. Apart from my first grade teacher who was Indonesian, the compulsory Indonesian language, society, and history classes were the only classes I remember being taught by Indonesians. But by the time I reached high school, my first grade teacher had also been transferred to high school to teach only Indonesia-related subjects.

Even as students, some of us were aware through the adult conversations that we overheard both at home and in school that multinational companies, international organizations, and international schools used a three-tiered pay scale. Indonesian teachers occupied the bottom rank of the pay scale for teachers. The middle rank was for the locally hired foreign teachers, including one of my Japanese teachers who openly complained about the system in class. She seemed bitter that she was paid less than the other foreign teachers despite being a foreign national herself. As students, we did not know how to respond to a teacher's outburst against the school, so we listened quietly. The top rank was reserved for foreign teachers who were hired overseas. The pay scale system was similar at the international school where I did my fieldwork. The locally hired foreign teachers who I interviewed were most critical about it. The system assigned less economic value to the "local," which had implications for how the "local" was perceived socially and culturally. As a child, I internalized these hierarchies, which I later had to unlearn as an adult.

Even positive words spoken about Indonesia were said from a place of distance and power. My white North American teacher once said, "I love Indonesian culture, it's beautiful." I reasoned that I should be happy that she had said something nice about Indonesia. But she spoke as an outsider about a "culture" that to her was exotic and to be tasted like ethnic cuisines in a multicultural society. Seeing Indonesia as an exotic "Other" induced a strange, unsettling feeling of double-consciousness in me. I was partly a local, but I was complicit in exoticizing Indonesia by virtue of participating in the school.

On the other hand, I saw white people through Indonesian eyes. In fifth grade our teacher took us to an orphanage to deliver second-hand books in an act of charity. A group of us, from what was one of the most expensive schools in the archipelago, were bussed to the main road near a maze of Jakarta alleyways. We got off and walked a little in our branded sports shoes and casual wear on an unmaintained, decrepit lane to reach the classroom, where the Indonesian students were waiting in their red and white—also the color of the national flag—elementary school uniforms. It was a tiny, hot classroom ventilated only by the half-opened slats of the louvre windows facing the dusty lane. This was in stark contrast to our carpeted, fully air-conditioned classrooms. The host teacher welcomed our teacher and they spoke in front of the classroom as we sat on the wooden chairs watching. I only have a vague recollection of our visit. I do not recall the language they spoke in. It is possible that both teachers had some command of the other's language. But I do remember being struck by the way the host teacher, who looked as though she had made a lot of effort to dress well for the occasion, spoke to our white teacher—who towered over her—with awe as though she had been visited by semi-royalty. Though I was economically far more privileged than the Indonesian teacher, I found myself caught between two vastly unequal worlds, unsure where to locate myself in the relationship between local and expatriate (Fechter 2007; Fechter and Walsh 2010; Leggett 2003).

Looking back, I had a strong desire to become and be perceived as "Western," while never quite achieving it (Bhabha 1984). My mother did a great job of reprimanding me for overtly using English to exert power, but battling the hidden desire to do so continued long after. I internalized the cultural hierarchies that privileged the West. Writing this book helped dismantle the racist views that I had internalized by identifying the discourses that shape cultural inequalities in transnational spaces. The themes of double-consciousness and cultural hierarchies are pertinent to international schools.

Self-Identifying as a Third Culture Kid

In 2008, despite some reservations, I signed up for the mailing list of the first online community for Third Culture Kids, TCKid.com. Brice Royer, whose father is Vietnamese-French and mother is Ethiopian and who lived in seven countries before he turned eighteen, created the site to provide a space for TCKs to connect with each other. At the time, I was struggling with issues of identity and a sense of not being able to "integrate" into Australian society, where I was living. I soon found an email in my inbox from Brice with a short essay attached, "TCK Relationships and Grief." It was written by Ruth E. Van Reken (n.d.), a white American who was raised for thirteen years in Nigeria, about the emotional impact of being repeatedly uprooted through multiple international moves while growing up. Her writing resonated with me.

No sooner had I realized that her words described my own experience, I found myself on the floor, sobbing. Recognizing my own story in her words resolved deep-seated issues that I personally had with regard to identity and belonging, and my experience is not uncommon. The Third Culture Kids concept can evoke powerful emotional responses. I subsequently immersed myself in the literature and the online community, and actively sought out other self-identifying TCKs in my city. I later found that it is common for members of minority groups within a society to immerse themselves within that community for a finite period of time until they have come to terms with their sense of identity.

Situating the Researcher

I write about my experiences here because it influences the way I relate to the field (the participants and transnational social spaces) and the gaps I notice in the literature. Nearly a century has passed since Bronisław Malinowski (1922) wrote of himself as a white researcher arriving on the shores of a native beach to start his ethnographic work, thus cementing a "radical separation between 'home' and the 'field'" as well as the researcher Self and the native Other (Bunzl 2004: 435). Much has since been said of the changing nature of the ethnographer's role in a postcolonial world as the lines between outsider and insider researcher increasingly blur (e.g., Amit 2000; Narayan 1993). Nevertheless, anthropology is traditionally the study of the Other from an outsider perspective and, as Matti Bunzl (2004: 338–339) argues, even critiques of fieldwork approaches based on "a Malinowskian fetishization of cultural alterity" have scarcely overcome the entrenched "epistemological separation" between the ethnographic Self and native Other. This separation requires the researcher to locate with precision their position in the complex grid of relations of power and meaning in the field.

But this form of separation is problematic because relations of power and meaning are situational. Instead of defining cultures as fixed entities to which one does or does not belong, I treat culture as a sense of mutual intelligibility based on shared experiences that offers a framework for interpreting those experiences. This sense of mutual intelligibility is momentary and shifts depending on the sociohistorical context. In this sense, I share a sense of mutual intelligibility with different participants to varying degrees, as they do with each other. To some, I am an insider, to others I am an outsider, and to still others I may be both. The insider/outsider status is situational, especially in transnational spaces.

My experiences suggest that the existing research on Third Culture Kids is valuable, but my research indicates that it is insufficient as an analytical concept. It addresses well the impact of mobility and multiple cultural exposure on individuals, and the nature of TCK relations with the dominant paradigm of singular identities. However, there is much to be said about relations of power that occur among transnational youth that I bring to light using a postcolonial approach. I am mindful, however, of Ghassan Hage's exhortation (2009) that it is important to capture power relations, but "what is bad is when you think you have captured *the* relation because the relation is *more* than the power relation." He argues that relations are multilayered and always more than just the economic or political: "there is always an excess" (ibid.). Similarly, David Linger (2005: 11) critiques studies that treat the individual as "*not* unique, *not* psychologically complex, *not* the product of a developmental process, and, it would appear, *not even conscious.*" The individual is more than the mere subject of social construction. An anthropological lens coupled with my emic perspective enables me to critically analyze the power relations that influence transnational youth without losing sight of their individual subjectivities or that they are human beings with emotions.

The ambiguity of the researcher's status as insider and/or outsider featured in the data collection process. I spent two semesters at an international school in Jakarta (and an additional two weeks at a smaller international school). Gaining access to the school and the social circles within was relatively easy because I had attended similar international schools myself. The principal was very supportive of my research because he self-identified as a TCK and could personally relate to the struggles and benefits of a transnational upbringing. His family was friends with David Pollock, the coauthor of the popular book, *Third Culture Kids: Growing Up Among Worlds*. However, my status shifted constantly as I conducted participant observation among a diversity of research participants, due to both my cultural background and (perceived) age.

On my first official day at the international school, the principal encouraged me to attend the casual, weekly, ten-minute teacher meeting and asked me to introduce myself. This was to ensure that the teachers were aware of my presence as a researcher in order to ease my access into classrooms. "I'll be going to classrooms and hanging out with students during recess and other times—basically, I'm 'going native,'" I jokingly said as I made double quotation marks in the air and some of the teachers laughed. I explained that I was researching "people who grow up moving around from country to country, otherwise known as Third Culture Kids." I assured the teachers that I was not researching pedagogy and therefore would not be assessing teaching methods. Afterward, the vice principal showed me the class schedules, and I randomly chose classes to attend and observe. I tended to attend social science and humanities classes because they involved more classroom discussions. This was how my data collection through participant observation began.

Over the course of a year, or two semesters, I "hung out" with students on campus, and sometimes off campus. A typical day entailed going to classes with students, hanging out with them during recess, and attending extracurricular activities. At times I would follow a particular student around for a day with their permission. This gave me insight into their immediate friendship circles, and the social groups and parts of the campus that featured most in their lives. I found that some students hardly crossed paths with students from certain groups, depending on with whom and where they hung out. The main groups among the juniors (eleventh grade, about 16 years old) and seniors (twelfth grade, about 17 years old) were the English-speaking, Indonesian-speaking, Korean-speaking, and Japanese-speaking groups. I also frequented the staff lunchroom, as well as parent gatherings, in order to understand the adult influences in students' lives. During the weekends, I sometimes unintentionally hung out in social circles that included people with a transnational upbringing because my own upbringing meant that I was naturally drawn to them. This resulted in data that emerged from impromptu interviews and discussions about my research in various locations in Jakarta.

My insider status also facilitated access to social groups on campus. When students and teachers spoke with me, there was a sense of mutual intelligibility—that I understood their transnational experiences. However, my specific background and linguistic ability added nuance to this insider status. Some student groups were easier than others to approach because I had a "feel for the game" (Bourdieu 1990: 66). I approached the Korean-speaking group last because I felt they would be easy to approach. I spoke English and Japanese, languages that were dominant internationally and regionally, respectively, which made it easy to gain their interest. Being an adult was an advantage too because Korean students were quite respectful of adults (though some treated me more like a friend after a while).

I gained instant access to the Japanese group as soon as they found out I was a native speaker of Japanese. They acted as though they had found an ally in me who was capable of acting as a "cultural broker" for them between the English- and Japanese-speaking worlds (Geertz 1960: 228; Wolf 1956). Being a cultural broker by virtue of being fluent in both the dominant and minority culture of a given social space is a theme that recurs in this book through the experiences of the participants and my own as a researcher (Irvine 1989: 57). Over the year, the Japanese hangout area became my default resting place, where I would go after I had expended my energy hanging out with other students. Another group I could relate to well was made up almost exclusively of students of Asian descent who were fluent and comfortable in English, but were not as westernized as some of the other Asian students who hung out in the more dominant English-speaking groups.

I was surprised that the Indonesian group was not as easy as the Japanese group to approach. I attribute this to the fact that they did not need me as a cultural broker because they were capable of using their economic capital to gain status in the school social hierarchy. At least one Indonesian-speaking student tried to suss out my family's socioeconomic status in Indonesia to see where I stood on his social grid. It was, however, the dominant English-speaking groups that took more courage on my part to approach, though I was not conscious of this potential difficulty during the first three weeks of fieldwork.

Initially, the students all appeared very young to me. I could not tell who was more or less fashionable, or who seemed more or less popular because they were all "just kids" in my eyes. A majority of the students were of Asian descent. I had lived in Australia for several years and so the North American(ized) accent (or the "international school accent," as some teachers called it) that many of the students spoke with grated against my ears because I was unused to it. But after about three weeks, the accent started to neutralize in my ears, and my eyes also adjusted. Soon, I could distinguish between the students who were more westernized and those who were not, between the popular ones and those who were not, etc. Their fashion styles were different from each other and I wondered how I had not noticed it initially.

It was around this time that I began to feel intimidated by the students who were considered more popular by others. The power relations that I noticed in the field and remembered from my own high school experience were influencing my perception of where I stood with the students. Although I was an adult researcher, I felt like a teenager mired in the social hierarchy of the school. I reminded myself that my eyes were deceptive and that as an adult and researcher I could exempt myself from the power relations at play among the students. I moved at regular intervals between student groups in order to see the campus from different perspectives without locking myself into any particular group. In this way I also prevented the social hierarchies among students from dictating my emotions, which would have affected my confidence in approaching some of the groups. It also ensured that I did not appear partial to any particular group.

Curiously, being a researcher who was culturally fluid also meant that participants sometimes forgot my ethnic or cultural background and divulged their prejudices against certain groups of which I would otherwise be considered a member. At other times, they spoke to me as an outsider even though I saw myself as one of them. My status as an insider or outsider within the school was not fixed. It shifted in relation to different social groups because transnational social spaces are complex.

One of the main activities involved in conducting participant observation among young people is "hanging out." In my case this happened mostly on campus. Some of my colleagues who have also researched schools found this difficult to do, and preferred to work with adults (for example, teachers and parents). Others, including myself, found it easy because we genuinely enjoy talking to young people. In my case, it was partly due to my personality, background, and physical appearance, which enabled me to "pass" as a student. I found it a luxury to spend time in a transnational space where most were bilingual, many trilingual, and some quadrilingual. I enjoyed meeting students who could speak a combination of at least three of the languages I spoke, which was rare outside the international school setting. Hearing students switch accents and languages at will made me realize how much I had missed being in a transnational environment. There was a sense of mutual intelligibility that I had not experienced in a long time. In a way, it felt like "home."

My youthful look made it easy to blend in with the students. I dressed neat and casual—not as neat as the teachers, but not as casual as the students—in order to fit in with both milieus. Teachers and students mistook me for a student (often a senior) on an almost weekly basis. I made sure students were aware that I was a researcher for ethical reasons and convenience—it was easier to gain their attention by telling them I was a researcher who was "writing a book" about them. It made them feel special. On a couple of instances, a ninth-grade student asked if I was in ninth grade. Needless to say, I was stumped. I was already in my thirties. In these rare instances, the student lost all interest in me when I told them that I was an adult. They were simply trying to establish whether I was "one of them." For the most part, however, students seemed to think that being an adult made me "cool" because it meant I was more mature, experienced, and knowledgeable. But I soon discovered, from the topics they broached with me or discussed in my presence, that, for some, "mature" simply meant that I was supposed to be more experienced with sex, drugs, and alcohol. In contrast, when I attended parent gatherings (almost exclusively attended by mothers), I was regularly asked what grade my children were in. I went from being perceived as a teenager to a mother with children of my own within the span of a few minutes. I attribute this to not only my ambiguous physical appearance, but also the constructed nature of social spaces (Lefebvre 1991).

The senior prom dance night drew attention to my peculiar relationship with the field site and participants, particularly as an adult researcher among teenagers. The atmosphere was very different from a regular school day. The air-conditioned gym was unrecognizable in its transformation into a Hollywood-themed ballroom—the floors were carpeted, the walls and ceiling were hidden from view and refurbished with black cloth set up like a tent, the lighting was done up, and a live Indonesian band played on stage. Nothing was left to the imagination.

The students, teaching staff, and I were all dressed in evening gowns and suits. The student-teacher dynamic was different that night.

"Feeling awkward are we?" teased the principal, who stood nearby as I lingered near the entrance unprepared for the new setting. I was unsure with whom I should be standing and talking—students or teachers? It was as though I had gone back to the first day of fieldwork when I had to carve out that elusive comfortable space for the semi-adult-researcher-friend. Teachers were extra vigilant and the rules were strict: no students were allowed in or out of the building between 9:30 PM and midnight. The principal explained that this was to ensure that students could not tell their parents they were coming to the prom and then steal away to nightclubs. The strict rules caused tension in some cases: a few students were locked out because they were late, making the student-teacher relationship more dichotomous than it usually was and my liminal position more precarious. Some of the teachers felt equally uncomfortable in their temporary role as chaperones. I eventually managed to alternate between hanging out with students and teachers, but the night highlighted that social relations, including those between the researcher and participants, are situational and social spaces are socially produced (ibid.).

Just as my own positioning in the field shifted, the recurring themes and patterns from the research show that transnational spaces are produced through social relations that are unequal. Young people experience transnational spaces and global mobility in different ways, which in turn has diverse impacts on being a "Third Culture Kid."

Notes

1. Some parts of this preface were first published as part of a chapter in *Writing Out of Limbo: International Childhoods, Global Nomads and Third Culture Kids* (Bell-Villada and Sichel 2011). Reproduced with permission from Cambridge Scholars Publishing.
2. See Robert Phillipson (1992)
3. For example, I met a Japanese teenager who had lived in Sweden for several years during elementary school who found it difficult to fit in when he returned to Japan and subsequently developed *tōkōkyohi*. In his case, he woke up one morning to find that he was physically unable to walk.
4. I use the terms "Anglophone" and "English-speaking" interchangeably to refer to those who have acquired a natural command of English regardless of their family's linguistic background.

Acknowledgments

This book could not have been written without the international school students, alumni, parents, and teachers who shared their time and stories with me. I thank them for being open, vulnerable, and kind. Though a single book may not do justice to all their experiences, I hope that they can hear their collective voices in these pages in some measure. I have used pseudonyms for both individuals and the school to protect privacy.

I owe much to Lyn Parker for seeing me through the writing of this book and giving generously of her time to reading and critiquing countless drafts. Likewise, I am indebted to Loretta Baldassar for her many strategic advice that advanced the book's intellectual argument beyond what I could imagine. I am grateful also to Fazal Rizvi, Anne-Meike Fechter, Mark Allen Peterson, and the two anonymous reviewers for reading and providing constructive critiques on the original manuscript. Many others read earlier drafts of this book—or at least heard its central arguments—and provided insightful critiques that helped develop those arguments, and to them I owe special thanks: Yukimi Shimoda, Richard Martin, Thijs Schut, Chang Yau Hoon, Reto Hofmann, Martin Forsey, Marco Cuevas-Hewitt, Victoria Burbank, David T. Hill, Richard Davies, Katie Glaskin, and Greg Acciaioli. Many thanks also to the dozens of friends, colleagues, and mentors, many of whom are from the Discipline of Asian Studies and Discipline of Anthropology and Sociology at The University of Western Australia, for their feedback on earlier drafts and their support, especially Suzie Handajani, Margherita Viviani, Wen Wen Zhang, Gabrielle Désilet, Andrew Broertjes, Carol Kaplanian, Jonathan Ciawy Tay, Cathryne Sanders, Vanessa Caparas, Lara McKenzie, Kara Salter, Hariyadi, Asim Aqeel, Emanuela Sala, Gemma Bothe, Mee Mee Zaw, Jocelyn Cleghorn, Maki Meyer, Nicole Beattie, Mitchel Low, Rebecca Rey, Ryan Cox, David Barry, Leah Maund, Irma Riyani, Nicholas Kusanto, Angelika Riyandari, Crystal Abidin, Joshua Esler, Noresma Jahya, Alka Sabharwal, Kieren Golby, Carly Lane, Richard Lyons, Sachiko Sone, and Miho Masel. The support of Claire Molloy, Christie Blaikie, Dave Williams, and Alice Williams was also valuable during the writing of the manuscript.

I am deeply grateful to Ruth E. Van Reken for continually encouraging me to take the project to the next stage as she read the drafts and for believing in its value even when I was losing sight of it. My heartfelt thanks to Brice Royer for bringing Ruth's work to a wider audience (including me) and supporting the broader purpose of works such as this. Thank you also to Ann Cottrell, Richard Downie, Nina Sichel, and Gene H. Bell-Villada for reading portions of the draft and their dedication to the community. And I would not have written a book at all if it was not for Rick Butler who taught me how to write and Nancy Venhola who taught me how interesting the social sciences could be, so many years ago.

Finally, I want to thank my family who were supportive throughout the research and writing of this book. This book exists because my mother and father stepped outside their comfort zones to marry and stay together despite the challenges they faced, and the tears they shed, due to differences in language, culture, and age, among others. My mother's childhood dream was to drink coffee and eat bananas everyday, both of which were considered luxury imports in post-war rural Japan. We like to joke that she got what she asked for in my father, who is from Indonesia, a tropical country that produces both items in abundance. Meanwhile, my father went through four different educational systems in three languages due to historical circumstances, and thought nothing of it. The rich environment they created for my sister and I shaped our lives and this research. Through the luck of the draw and government policies of the time, my sister and I grew up as citizens of different countries, which also meant that we had vastly different schooling experiences—she went to an Indonesian school and I to an international school. This in turn has shaped our lives differently. From where I was standing, I was never aware of any significant cultural differences between her and I because family culture came first, but perhaps the view was different from where she was standing. If so, I apologize for not being more sensitive about it as we were growing up. But my interest in this research and the insights gained would not have come about had I not first seen the profound influence of language, culture, and schooling on us within the microcosm of my childhood family life.

Jakarta, 2017

Introduction
Unpacking "Third Culture Kids"

"Let me get this straight," said the immigration official at Raleigh-Durham airport in North Carolina, reviewing the documents that would allow me onto U.S. soil for the first time. "You have a French passport, which was issued in Indonesia, you were born in Australia, and your J-11 visa for entry into the United States of America was delivered in Venezuela. Is that right?"

Indeed, it was. What made the official even more wary was the fact that I sounded distinctly American, without a trace of a foreign accent. "Your English is amazing, how much time have you spent in the United States?" he asked. "Approximately 18 minutes," I said. "This is my first time."

He was incredulous when I explained that I had acquired an American accent while studying in international schools overseas, but eventually issued me a verbal "Welcome to America." It was to be my fifth country of residence in 17 years, only two years of which were spent in France, my "passport country."

According to a fairly new area of study, I am a "Third Culture Kid"—a TCK—or an Adult Third Culture Kid, to be exact.
—Anne-Sophie Bolon, *New York Times*, 2002

"This is my country, so the *bules* [white folks] shouldn't mess in our country," said Dae Sik while perched precariously on the back of a bench near the school fountain. Dae Sik was an international school student who spoke Indonesian, English, and Korean. He was talking about Indonesia, the place where he grew up. Yet, Dae Sik was technically South Korean: his passport said so; his name said so; and ethnically speaking he was. I decided to press him on this point: "But, aren't you Korean?" I asked. "Of course," he responded, "it's in the blood." As far as Dae Sik was concerned, there was nothing inconsistent about seeing Indonesia as his country, while at the same time identifying himself as Korean.
—From a conversation with an international school student in Indonesia, 2009

When I first went back to high school at thirty-something, I wanted to write a book about people who live in multiple countries as children and grow up into adults addicted to migrating. I wanted to write about people like Anne-Sophie Bolon who are popularly referred to as "Third Culture Kids" or "global nomads." There was growing hype about the richness of their globetrotting lifestyle and open-mindedness on the one hand, and the psychological costs of being repeatedly uprooted during childhood on the other hand. On a theoretical level, I was interested in the role of socioeconomic factors in shaping cosmopolitan identities among young people with internationally mobile childhoods. I wanted to probe the contradiction between the celebrated image of "global citizens" and the economic privilege that makes their mobile lifestyle possible. From a personal angle, I was interested in exploring the voices among this population that had yet to be heard (particularly the voices of those of Asian descent) by documenting the persistence of culture, race, and language in defining social relations even among self-proclaimed cosmopolitan youth.[1]

In carrying out the research, I wanted to immerse myself in the lives of these young people in the manner of classical anthropologists, and the international school was the closest that I could find to a "village" of Third Culture Kids. So in 2009, I went back to high school as an adult. I went to classes and hung out with teenagers for a full year, along with their teachers, parents, and alumni. I observed them, interviewed them, and took notes.

Eight years later, as this book goes to print, a parent of an international school student, upon reading some extracts, exclaimed: "I know which groups of kids you're describing, exactly! It's spot on. Those groups still exist."[2] More importantly, despite the mainstreaming of the term Third Culture Kids among the global elite and the proliferation of international schools in major world cities, there is still a dearth of critical analysis of this phenomenon.

The focus of this ethnographic study is an archetypical international school located in Jakarta, Indonesia, which I dub the "The International School," or TIS. It is a school that caters to both the children of foreign expatriate families, as well as wealthy, upper-class Indonesian families. Inside its imposing gates, there were over sixty nationalities represented in the overall student body and over twenty nationalities in the teaching staff. The typical scene at TIS seemed to defy national imaginaries. As students flood out of the classrooms at the buzz of the recess bells, one can hear a Russian teenager speaking fluent, colloquial Indonesian to a classmate; Indian teenagers speaking English with an American accent, then switching to an Indian accent and back again within a matter of seconds, depending on who they were talking to; and a Taiwanese teenager speaking English, Mandarin, and Indonesian in one sentence. Children of international marriages were part of the norm. It was no wonder that TIS proudly presented itself as an ideal setting for raising "global citizens." But an intimate look at the social lives of its students reveals that crossing cultural boundaries—even among internationally mobile young people—is not a straightforward process.

This book analyzes the processes through which young people learn to engage across difference in social environments that are transitory. The book is as much about young people who experience a high level of international mobility while they are growing up, as it is about the international schools that many of them attend across the globe. It explores the lives of transnational youth who experience mobility by moving across national borders repeatedly before they finish high school or by attending an international school with a transient student body within their birth nation. Unlike the traditional picture of a migrant—even the temporary, serial adult migrant—many transnational youth do not have a life before migration that is then punctuated by a life-changing move to a destination country.[3] They are often born in a foreign country where they have no citizenship or leave their country of citizenship when they are too young to remember and spend most of their lives in a country where they live in transit, where they do not have the legal right to remain permanently, all the while carrying an expectation to eventually repatriate to their country of citizenship.

They live in a host country and, over time, multiple host countries. But for those who attend international schools, they are not expected to integrate into the country where they live as temporary migrants. Instead, they are expected to integrate into, or assume as normal, the transnationality of the so-called third culture of the international school where they socialize with friends who are similarly in transit. Being in transit defines their childhood, life, and identity. When they do "repatriate" to their country of citizenship, they are in fact migrating out of a transnational social setting and into a new country that they may or may not have visited during their summer vacations. Even so, their lives and the choices they make are in many ways shaped by the nationalities inscribed on their passports, which symbolize the transnational reach of national (social and economic) structures.

These young people grow up transnationally, are expected to be international by default, and learn to make meaning out of the national and transnational structures that influence their lives. But they are not homogeneous. Although the cohort I studied shared a degree of economic privilege, they experienced and interpreted their transnational upbringing in different ways depending on their linguistic, cultural, and national backgrounds, as well as their "race" and gender. Transnational youth practice cosmopolitan engagement across difference in a diversity of ways that reflect their ambivalent identities as they manage, internalize, and contend with a web of national and transnational sociocultural hierarchies. At school, some are seen as "international" while others are seen as "ethnocentric" not because the latter is not engaging across difference, but because the way they engage across difference takes a different form. The form of cosmopolitan engagement the youth practice varies according to their backgrounds.

International Schooling

This book is not about international education per se, but the context of the international school and its ideology of being "international" had a strong influence on the social lives of the transnational youth who I met and often befriended. The school celebrated the idea of being international, parents sought it for their children, and the children internalized it.

Being international is an ideology with a global reach that is shaping transnational and national class structures, and the educational landscape that acts as its reproductive engine. If national education had been established to turn colonial and feudal subjects into national citizens (Parker 2003; see also Rizvi 2009), then international education purposes to produce and reproduce "global citizens" in the face of an increasingly transnational economic system. Over the past four to five decades, the international school market has, according to Nicholas Brummitt and Anne Keeling (2013), "changed beyond recognition," especially since 2000. During this period, the estimated number of international schools across the globe burgeoned from over 300 in the late 1960s (Bunnell 2013; 2014; see also Leach 1969) to 2,584 in 2000 and then to 8,257 schools by July 2016, which cater to over 4.3 million students, with Asia being the main region driving this growth (Keeling 2016; Brummitt and Keeling 2013).[4]

However, these figures do not reflect an immutable reality due to the contested definition of international schools. One thing that is clear is that much of the growth is fueled by the insatiable desire for English-medium and Western-style education among the growing middle and upper classes, particularly in developing countries. In Indonesia, the impetus for the growth also came from a change in government policy in 2003 that lifted the restrictions placed on Indonesian nationals from attending international schools and encouraged English-language education. Given the dramatic growth, there has been sustained interest among researchers to map the "changing landscape" of international schools (Bunnell 2014: 16).

One of the most prominent debates in the literature has revolved around the definition of international schools (see ibid.). Much of this discussion is characterized by attempts to analyze international schools based on a dichotomy between those that are market driven (to satisfy clientele demand for schooling) and ideology driven (designed specifically to further "international understanding and cooperation"), even while recognizing that many schools may fall along a spectrum between the two (Hayden and Thompson 2008: 22; see also Hayden 2006; Matthews 1988; Cambridge and Thompson 2004).

The discussion has been mainly generated by the changing clientele of international schools. As international schools became more popular among the local middle and upper classes, often referred to as host-country nationals, growing numbers of international schools were established as for-profit private schools in contrast to forty years ago when they were established mainly as not-for-profit or embassy schools for expatriate children (Brummitt and Keeling 2013). While international schools catered mainly to the children of expatriates, who made up 80 percent of the student body more than thirty years ago, rather than to local children, the trend has been reversed in recent years with local students making up 80 percent of the student demography (ibid.: 40).

Students of host countries are often contrasted with this traditional clientele drawn from children of expatriate families, often referred to as "global nomads" (McCaig 2002) or "Third Culture Kids" (Pollock and Van Reken 2009 [2001]). When researchers of international schools and expatriate children as well as practitioners at international schools refer to these two seemingly distinct categories of students, they often imply that the former is (parochially) "national" while the latter is more "international" in their outlook (e.g., Tamatea 2008).

In fact, it did not take long before I realized that it was difficult to fit the young people I met at TIS into separate boxes set up through a binary framework of "expatriate" and "host nationals" or "international" and "not international" or "Third Culture Kid" and "non–Third Culture Kid." For one thing, peer groups at the international school appeared to be formed irrespective of the length of time that members spent in Indonesia, whether or not they were expatriates or host nationals, or how many times they had migrated.

Similarly, whether or not a student clique was considered diverse did not depend on the actual composition of the groups. For example, teachers and administrators, as well as other students, liked to point out that the "Indonesians" tended not to mix, something that had a bearing on their standing in the eyes of staff, for whom the ideal student is the global citizen. Indonesians added to the school's overall sense of diversity by their presence, but fell short on being international. By contrast, English-speaking groups were generally perceived by staff to be the most "international" because of the perceived mix of nationalities and physical differences represented in those groups. Meanwhile, other students spoke of these groups as westernized and "white." Both the "Indonesian" and "international" groups were heterogeneous. But the labels they attracted—"white," "Indonesian," or "international"—depended on who was calling the shots. The fact that the English-speaking groups shared a sense of familiarity with Western culture became invisible when internationalism was at stake. Whether or not someone was cosmopolitan lay in the eyes of the beholder.

Becoming "international" is not merely about learning to engage across difference, though that is part of it. It is also about reproducing and expanding an economic and political order that goes beyond national boundaries, in which being international defines the cosmopolitan cultural capital that gives transnational elites an edge in the globalizing economy (Igarashi and Saito 2014; Weenink 2008). In addition to being able to engage across difference, being international involves speaking English, preferably like a native speaker, and being westernized, among others (Igarashi and Saito 2014; Peterson 2011). It is about being able to operate in the so-called third culture of a transnational world left behind by a colonial past and modernized by contemporary capitalism. TIS's administrators and teachers propagated the ideology of being international in their marketing material, classrooms, and events, such as United Nations Day, and often spoke privately to me about which of their students they think are or are not "international." Many parents consumed this ideology and went to great lengths to provide educational opportunities that would ensure that their children became international. The children, in turn, shaped their identities around being international.

Narrating an Imagined Community with "Third Culture Kids"

But growing up in the third culture, especially as a serial migrant, has its emotional and social costs. This has spawned both popular and academic literature on "Third Culture Kids" (Useem and Downie 1976) and the related term "global nomads" (McCaig 2002) over the past decade. When I first began the preliminary research for this book in 2008, a Google search for the term "Third Culture Kids" only yielded a handful of entries. Almost a decade on, the term has taken on a life of its own with the internet seemingly churning out new publications on Third Culture Kids everyday, from blog entries to articles on major English-language media outlets such as *CNN, The Guardian,* and *Aljazeera.* The term has become increasingly popular as one of identification among those who grow up with a high degree of international mobility in their childhood and teenage years. The academic literature is also growing, albeit with one caveat: most writers have been unable to integrate the concept of Third Culture Kids into their research in an analytically satisfactory manner. This shortfall is a result of their failure to grasp the idea that despite the academic origins of the term, it works best as an emic or insider concept rather than an analytical concept.

"Third Culture Kids" was coined in the 1970s by the anthropologist/sociologist Ruth Hill Useem (1973; Useem and Downie 1976) to describe American children, including her own, raised in the recently decolonized India of the 1950s and 60s (see Useem 1993). It later became the subject of a seminal book, often dubbed the "TCK bible," entitled *Third Culture Kids: Growing Up Among Worlds* and published initially in 2001 (Pollock and Van Reken 2009 [2001]). The findings are based on a prolific number of surveys and informal interviews, as well as David Pollock's extensive experience of working with internationally mobile children, who found the concept helpful for understanding their own experiences.[5] Pollock's coauthor, Ruth E. Van Reken, is a white American missionary child who grew up in Nigeria in the 1950s and struggled with the same issues outlined in the book well into her adulthood after her repatriation to the United States at age thirteen. Neither Pollock nor Van Reken were academic researchers; instead, they were motivated to research and write about Third Culture Kids due to the psychological issues that they commonly observed among children with an internationally mobile upbringing, regardless of their parents' occupation.

It was not until 2007 that "Third Culture Kids" entered the internet lexicon when a young man of mixed descent set up the first online community for those who, like himself, grew up internationally (see Tanu 2015). Brice Royer, who at the time was in his twenties, is a Canadian citizen and had lived in seven countries by the time he was eighteen years old due to his father's career as a UN peacekeeper.

His mother is Ethiopian and his father is of mixed French-Vietnamese descent. Royer started the online community because he had become physically ill from the stress of repeated moves and not having a sense of belonging. He suffered from chronic pain in his hands and arms such that he was unable to even shower by himself for a few years. But the medical doctors were unable to diagnose his illness, stating that there was nothing physically wrong with him. Instead, Royer's recovery was prompted by his encounter with the concept of Third Culture Kids, through which he came to terms with his mixed identity. Having seen the profound impact that a mere three-word phrase could have on himself, Royer set up the online community TCKid.com in 2007 to reach out to others facing similar issues of belonging that result from serial temporary migration in childhood. Although he is no longer involved in the project, his work brought the concept of Third Culture Kids to the online medium and triggered the exponential growth of its usage.

Others who have had internationally mobile childhoods testify of similarly life-changing experiences. As I mentioned in the preface, I personally benefited deeply from the work of Pollock, Van Reken, and Royer. To take another example, Ellen Mahoney (2014), an American who grew up in Japan, the United States, and Singapore, claims that she suffered from a seven-year depression due to the sense of displacement she experienced upon repatriation until she was introduced to the concept of Third Culture Kids. Two of her childhood friends also struggled after repatriation, one of whom committed suicide and another attempted suicide. These experiences prompted her to design mentoring programs for internationally mobile youth to cushion their experiences of repatriation. I met Mahoney in 2014 at the conference held by Families in Global Transition, an organization founded by Van Reken to further the knowledge of practitioners and researchers of expatriate communities. One of the keynotes delivered at the conference was a one-woman play performed by Elizabeth Liang called "Alien Citizen." Van Reken told me that I should not miss the play, but I was skeptical of what one person on a big stage could achieve. By the end of the play, however, I and about a third of the two hundred or so attendees were left in a sobbing mess. The play recounts Liang's (2017) childhood moves between "Central America, North Africa, the Middle East and New England," and the impact that her mixed white American and Chinese Jamaican heritage had on her. Despite its focus on the theme of migration, Liang says that some of her most loyal fans are white Americans who have never left their birth towns because the themes of isolation, rejection, loss of relationships, and sexism that the play touches upon are universal.

No doubt there are also many who may find no use in the term "Third Culture Kids." Nevertheless, it does not detract from the fact that the concept has played a significant role in the lives of many others. "Third Culture Kids" is better understood as an emotionally powerful insider construct that narrates identity and belonging for people with a transnational upbringing in the same way that "Italy" or "Indonesia" can represent geographical and emotional homelands, though they may be insufficient as analytical concepts.

The basic "profile" of a TCK as defined in the literature is that they grow up outside their "parents' culture," are interculturally competent, feel they are a part of many cultural traditions and yet do not fully belong to a single one, and instead their "sense of belonging is in relationship to others of similar background."[6] Most literature on Third Culture Kids uses approaches in psychology, sociology, and education, which emphasize developmental and socialization processes (e.g., Schaetti 2000; Pollock and Van Reken 2009 [2001]; Hayden and Thompson 1995; Kanan and Baker 2006). The literature that draws on psychological approaches focuses on individual identity development and the trauma of multiple separations caused by the international moves that TCKs make, not out of their own choice, but as a result of their parents' choices. Like studies on minority youth (e.g., Jensen 2008; Phinney 1990; 2008), the concept of Third Culture Kids is used as an alternative model to the dominant developmental model of white males in industrialized Western countries. The research is often conducted by those who self-identify as TCKs or have previously worked with TCKs.

The strength of the TCK literature is its ability to address the impact of mobility and cultural exposure on the psychological development of young people as individuals. The term "Third Culture Kid" can act as a powerful narrative tool to help those with a transnational upbringing locate an emotional homeland—in the absence of a geographic homeland—where they find the language to express their experience of multiple geographic and cultural displacement.

As an insider construct, TCK narrates transnational belonging in three distinct ways. Firstly, it provides a sense of continuity over time amid repeated international moves, weaving together fragmented experiences that occur in distant places with different people. Secondly, it provides a sense of coherence for the fragmented identities of internationally mobile children by articulating a sense of hybridity (Hall 1996; Bhabha 1994). Thirdly, it alludes to a sense of mutual intelligibility shared by those who are affected by the experience of repeated geographical and cultural displacement in childhood. The concept narrates a shared memory of repeated loss of place and relationships with each move and a sense of familiarity with cultural in-between-ness. Abbas El-Zein (2002: 230) writes, "The migrant loses the concise language of familiarity and shared memory, the ability to evoke worlds of associations with a few hints and words." It is this lack of language that the Third Culture Kid narrative fills by naming the mutual intelligibility shared among those who have an internationally mobile childhood, albeit a relatively privileged one.

Continuity Over Time Despite Displacement

The psychologist Erik Erikson (1959; 1968; 2008) claims that adolescence marks a crucial phase in a person's development as they go through a process of establishing who they are within and who they are in relation to others. They begin to internally address the question, "Who am I?" to find a sense of self that remains more or less coherent in the face of change (Schwartz 2001: 7; Schachter 2005: 141). Michael Berzonsky (2005: 129) explains that, "personal identity implies that a specific person continues to be the same person across varying conditions and over time." One way a young person explores this sense of self is through intimacy with another person. According to Erikson (1968: 42), "to a considerable extent adolescent love is an attempt to arrive at a definition of one's identity by projecting one's diffused self-image on another and by seeing it thus reflected and gradually clarified. This is why so much of young love is conversation." It is through interaction with others that a person learns how they are similar and yet different to others. While "intimacy" may be defined differently across contexts, the "feeling of knowing ourselves and being known by others" is a basic human need (Pollock and Van Reken 2009 [2001]: 146). Erikson (1959: 102) states that in adolescence "the young individual must learn to be most himself [*sic*, universal male] where he means most to others—those others, to be sure, who have come to mean most to him."

According to Pollock and Van Reken (2009 [2001]), those with a transnational upbringing may find this process challenging because their transient lifestyle means that their sociocultural context—and with that the people who know them—change frequently. As children, most cannot choose to move or stay. Some move internationally multiple times before they finish high school. Without agency, even economically privileged international mobility is experienced as a form of displacement (Coleman 2011; Schwartz, Côté, and Arnett 2005). Pollock and Van Reken (2009 [2001]) explain, "With one plane ride a TCK's whole world can die." They have to trade in their social network of relationships, crucial to adolescent development, for new ones each time they move. Others may stay in their birth country or only sojourn to one country before repatriating, but they experience mobility indirectly if, for example, they attend an international school that caters for expatriate families and therefore has a high student turnover rate. Even though they stay in one place, those who know them change with each new academic year as their old friends move away and new ones come. Some have reported losing their entire social circle at the turn of a single academic year. In this way, the people who mean the most to them are often geographically scattered. A therapist is noted to have said of her clients who have a transnational upbringing that "few of them had any idea what it meant to be a person" (Pollock and Van Reken 2001: 146). Each time their social circle changes, they need to start their relationships over. While reinventing oneself can be constructive, it can also interfere with the process of coming to know and being known by others. High mobility interrupts the development of a shared history with others.

A highly mobile childhood produces a collection of life experiences that are fragmented by the geographical and social displacement brought about by each move, which affects identity development. Pollock and Van Reken's (2009 [2001]) conceptualization of Third Culture Kids recognizes the significant impact that mobility has on relationships and identity development. They use the concept to identify a set of characteristics that are often, though not always, shared by those who experience a high level of mobility during childhood such as rootlessness, restlessness, and unresolved grief due to loss of relationships. By identifying a set of common characteristics, the concept of Third Culture Kids weaves together the fragmented experiences that occur with different sets of people in disparate places into one continuous life story. It narrates a sense of continuity for individuals in spite of the multiple moves that they or their friends make. The concept of Third Culture Kids narrates an imagined history among people who may not personally know each other (Anderson 1983).

Coherence Despite Cultural Hybridity

The TCK concept also enables a sense of coherence for the fragmented identities of those who grow up in multiple cultural milieus by narrating and thus normalizing cultural mixing. Internationally mobile children frequently negotiate socially constructed boundaries that vary with context as they are growing up, making it challenging for them to develop a singular, static, bounded sense of belonging that can produce a one word answer to the question, "Where are you from?" (Fail, Thompson, and Walker 2004).

Anne-Sophie Bolon, who I quoted at the beginning of this introduction, is a case in point. The immigration officer that she met with was confounded that none of Bolon's answers relating to the multiple categories used to imagine communities matched the other—nationality (French), place of previous residence (Indonesia), place of birth (Australia), current place of residence (Venezuela), language (English), and accent (American). The nation-state remains the dominant point of reference in constructing difference and imagining communities (Anderson 1983). Languages and accents are not merely practical tools of communication for they signify membership to specific sociocultural groups (Bourdieu and Thompson 1991). Bolon's account highlights the disjuncture between the communities imagined by oneself and those imagined by sometimes powerful others. "One man's imagined community," writes Arjun Appadurai (1996: 32), "is another man's political prison." Bolon's imagined community is that of a third culture, which stands in contrast to the imagined national community that the immigration officer had in mind, as symbolized by Bolon's French passport.

Dae Sik's story also defies the notion of singular identities, while highlighting other categories of difference that remain pertinent to cultural imaginings. Dae Sik used the expression "it's in the blood" to refer to a sense of primordial belonging to Korea based on descent and ethnicity. He homogenized and racially constructed the Western students at his school as *"bule"* or white "Other," and thereby positioned himself with the Indonesian "Us" by declaiming a sense of (borrowed) nationalism. Conflicting uses of categories of difference—ethnic, national, and racial—coexist with ease in Dae Sik's expression of his identity as he seamlessly shifted between them, depending on what was being asked of him. It is as Stuart Hall (1993: 362) states, "identity is always an open, complex, unfinished game—always under construction." Identity positions are held temporarily and situationally.

One of the most researched issues on Third Culture Kids is their experience of cultural marginalization upon repatriation to their country of citizenship. Richard Downie (1976) found that American citizens raised overseas who repatriated for college had to set aside their transnational experience in order to fit in because mainstream America would only validate or could only relate to one aspect of their identity—the American part. It is challenging to establish who one is in relation to others when only a fragment of one's self is being validated, while the rest of the self that does not align with the dominant culture is dismissed or ignored.

Nathan's experience of repatriation provides a striking picture of the power of the dominant culture to define another.[7] I interviewed Nathan as part of my research while he was working as an educator at an international school. Both of Nathan's parents are American. His mother is a "blonde-hair, blue-eyed hippie" and his father is a Native American from the "high plains Sappony tribe in North Carolina." But Nathan grew up mostly in France until his family returned for a year to the United States in the early 1980s when he was fourteen. He was fluent in French, but not in English. Nathan said of that particular move:

> So we went back to the States. I went to the public school in Philadelphia and ... the school didn't know what to do with me. I could not read, write, speak English. So they were very confused. Here's this little American kid who has very low levels of comprehension. So they gave me an IQ test. I did *extremely* poorly on it, as you can imagine, because it was in English. And so I was labeled as "educably mentally retarded" [sic] and placed in a Special Education classroom for my eighth-grade year. ... So as a TCK ... as a kid who *really* ... I mean as an educator, I look back and I go, "Oh my goodness, was I ever mislabeled?" I mean I was ESOL [English for Speakers of Other Languages], yes, but I certainly wasn't "educably mentally retarded." (Interview, March 2009)

At the time, Nathan's inability to speak English was interpreted as an intellectual disability that marked him as deviating from the norm. His transnational experiences did not fit in with the mainstream narrative of an imagined, singular "American" community, rendering him mute in the American context.

The need to negotiate various cultural contexts causes some with transnational upbringings to act like "cultural chameleon[s]" (Pollock and Van Reken 2009 [2001]: 99). They learn to pick up the cultural cues, languages, accents, and mannerisms of their surroundings so as to blend in with the dominant culture. By the time I met Nathan, he was fluent in English and sounded distinctly American. He admitted that his accent changes depending on with whom he is speaking to because he will naturally pick up the other person's accent. Those with a transnational upbringing can acquire a diversity of "cultural capital" (Bourdieu 1986: 243). Yet, knowing how to play the game of acting out certain parts of their identity at different times in order to fit in does not necessarily mean that they like playing the game. Some struggle to accept that their identity is multiple, fragmented, and negotiable (Ang 2001; Hall 1996). They feel as though they are putting on different personas. They may also appear to those around them as inauthentic (Pollock and Van Reken 2009 [2001]). Some who feel unable to weave a coherent narrative of their culturally fragmented lives express a sense of loss by taking on what Erikson (2008: 236) calls a "negative identity," where being different *is* their identity.

Pollock and Van Reken's work embeds the notion of hybridity in their description of Third Culture Kids: "The TCK builds relationships to all of the cultures, while not having full ownership in any." Nathan was able to make sense of his experiences of cultural displacement only after he encountered the term "Third Culture Kids" through Pollock (Pollock and Van Reken 2009 [2001]), who later became a family friend. Nathan recounted,

> My parents, after one year, moved to Germany. We moved to an international school, where, for the first time in my life, I was actually with other international kids, TCKs. Everything else, I had been with French kids ... and ... not really understanding who I was as an American. Pretty negative experience when I went back to eighth grade in America....
> Then for the first time in an international school at ninth grade, I realize "Oh, this is who I am."
>
> And Dave Pollock actually came to speak at our school, and it was the first time that I had ... heard this term, "TCK." And that identity switched something in me. Understanding that ... actually helped me. This helped settle some things in me. Was I retarded, was I less than intelligent? Was I going to wrestle with this whole—was I French, was I American, was I German? But all of a sudden being given an identity, and surrounded with kids who had a similar identity, even though all of them had a different story, which is a part of the beauty of being a TCK is that our differences are actually the thing that unites us. (Interview, March 2009)

Nathan was "given an identity" through spending time with others who had shared his transnational experiences and discovering a language through the concept of Third Culture Kids with which to narrate those experiences that did not fit into the French, American, or German narratives of singular, bounded national identities.

According to Kate Walters (2006: 52), the TCK narrative normalizes a person's transnational upbringing, which they may have hitherto considered pathological because their experiences seemed different from and incomprehensible to others. Upon hearing about my own experience of coming across the literature on Third Culture Kids, a man described to me the profound impact that the literature had had on him:

> There was an instant release and lots of things started to make sense ... to hear that I wasn't the only person to be moved on a much deeper level by this understanding helps tremendously.... Boy, it's fantastic not to have to fit into some other culture-box—it's hard not being Black, Trin-

idian, English, Scottish, American, Chinese, or Ghanaian but instead a strange mixture of the above. That's a little hard to deal with.

The weirdest thing is when I find the roles within my above-mentioned mix clashing, which means that depending on my surroundings I am more or less masculine/black, etc., but *never* the norm (emphasis originally in boldface). [I] don't know how much sense that makes, but understanding that I don't fit anywhere is a big relief. (Email correspondence, 19 December 2008)

Due to his mixed background, he felt that in some contexts he was too masculine and too black for those around him, while in other contexts he was not masculine or black enough. He felt a "big relief" in knowing that it is okay or normal, so to speak, to be mixed.

As previous research has shown, coming across the term "Third Culture Kid" is, for many, a life-changing experience (Walters 2006; Pollock and Van Reken 2009 [2001]; Schaetti 2000; Fail 2002). Sherry Ortner (2006: 125), borrowing from Richard Sennett (1998), writes that narratives fulfill the "need for conceptual, cognitive, symbolic tools for reorienting and reconstituting the self" within a postmodern world. Narratives hold together seemingly disjointed events and fragmented pieces of a person's life to give it meaning through a sense of continuity and coherence. Identifying as a TCK provides a sense of coherence amid fragmentation by normalizing experiences of repeated geographic, cultural, and social displacement and ambivalent feelings about belonging. It dissolves the seeming contradiction between coherence and fragmentation by reconstructing fragmentation as hybridity. Jan Pieterse (2001: 229) writes, "Hybridity is an argument against homogeneity, not against coherence." To be sure, I am not suggesting that cultures exist as essential wholes that can be blended like colors. Instead, I am referring to a sense of not fitting neatly into the discourses of or expectations for singular identities whether due to being mixed cultured or having grown up within an expatriate culture (Knörr 2005). As an insider construct, TCK narrates a form of hybridity that at once challenges the notion of singular, bounded identities as it enables a sense of coherence for otherwise fragmented experiences by situating them within the larger sociohistorical context of a globalizing world.

Mutual Intelligibility within the "Third Culture"

The concept of Third Culture Kids further challenges singular and bounded constructions of identity by alluding to a sense of mutual intelligibility that stems from a shared transnational upbringing. A recurring theme on the TCKid forum is the difficulty faced by TCKs in expressing their feelings and sharing their transnational experiences with those who have not had a transnational upbringing. In contrast, TCKs feel they do not have to explain themselves in detail to be understood when speaking to fellow TCKs. A Korean alumnus of TIS said it was "healing" to return to the school for a visit almost two decades after she had graduated and to also meet up with a former teacher. Eun Joo explained, "everything about [the international school] made sense.... I fit in like that piece of puzzle that's been missing for years. ... I didn't have to explain anything to anybody.... Mr. [Salamon] just 'got it.'" Through meeting someone who could understand her, the international school environment helped normalize Eun Joo's experiences. The interaction, as David Morley (2000: 48) writes, "is not dependent on long explanations but can proceed on the taken-for-granted premises of a set of shared assumptions." While Mr. Salamon did not self-identify as a TCK, he was the child of European migrants to the United States and had taught at the international school as an expatriate teacher for over two decades. He was familiar with the transnational experiences of his students.

Although TCKs come from diverse backgrounds, their shared experience of mobility and cultural displacement offers a platform for mutual intelligibility to the extent that their differences become momentarily suspended. As Nathan mentioned earlier, "part of the beauty of being a TCK is that our differences are actually the thing that unites us." The sense of mutual intelligibility among TCKs based on the experience of mobility and cultural hybridity is a constant theme in the literature (Fail 2002; Schaetti 2000; Pollock and Van Reken 2009 [2001]). From the purview of anthropology, Ira Bashkow (2004: 452) notes that individuals of diverse backgrounds can negotiate differences to create "an exaggerated impression of mutual understanding" that enables them to feel as though they are part of the same tribe. Richard Jenkins (1997: 10) similarly contends, "mutual intelligibility of the behaviour of others' is a fundamental prerequisite for any group." It gives the impression that they are members of the same group who are "fundamentally 'playing the same game'" (Barth 1994: 15). At the individual level, their habitus gives them the "feel for the game" (Bourdieu 1990: 66). According to Jenkins (1992: 75), habitus is a "'tendency,' 'propensity' or 'inclination'" toward certain matters, behaviors, and ways of thinking rather than others. At the collective level, habitus facilitates a sense of mutual intelligibility through a shared set of dispositions. Furthermore, if habitus is internalized structures, then it follows that an individual and group of individuals can internalize a multiplicity of structures that affect them differently depending on the context.

The literature that utilizes the concept of Third Culture Kids and takes it for granted often mistakenly assumes that mutual intelligibility signifies the inconsequentiality of differences. In her dissertation on students at an international elementary school, Leah Frederick (1996: 282) goes so far as to write that she "was convinced TCKs were special" in reference to their ability to transcend differences. Helen Fail's (2002) study of TCKs who are nonnative speakers of English corroborates this argument, but none of her interview questions allowed for the participants to discuss the impact that language, ethnicity, or culture had on their transnational experiences. These examples and others assume that transnational social spaces are neutral and that transnational experiences by default produce internationally minded cosmopolitans (see also Fail, Thompson, and Walker 2004; Ferstad 2002; Wurgaft 2006). The literature paradoxically essentializes the "third culture" by assuming that there is only one way to be a Third Culture Kid.

In fact, mutual intelligibility is situational. Those growing up in the "third culture" are diverse and their sense of mutual intelligibility shifts in relation to various factors. Factors such as cultural background, nationality, "race," and class do not become irrelevant; they instead continue to shape the subjectivities of those with a transnational upbringing. While some research suggests that young people may not automatically transcend difference by virtue of their transnational upbringing, these works are still few and far between (Allan 2004; Konno 2005; Sparrow 2000).

The TCK concept challenges bounded, singular definitions of identity based on the nation-state, though in its application it runs the risk of essentializing the "third culture." As an insider term, it narrates continuity over time and coherence by normalizing the experiences of fragmented identity resulting from geographic and cultural displacement. It narrates transnational belonging by acknowledging the sense of mutual intelligibility that arises out of a shared experience of transnational social spaces, which is characterized by mobility and some sense of hybridity. The concept is the response of a group of people, with a set of shared experiences, to a world where mobility and the transnationality of economic, political, and social realms are increasingly becoming the norm for many. Benedict Anderson (1983) argued that nationalism had helped build an imagined community in Indonesia among an otherwise ethnically, religiously, and linguistically diverse set of people through a shared sense of history. But national narratives that once fulfilled a positive use are seen by some as beginning to expire as they look for alternative narratives, and by others as being under assault as they defend it with fervor. In this changing world, the TCK concept has gained traction because it offers a transnational narrative for imagining a community among a growing population with a transnational upbringing that is deeply affected by mobility.

From "Third Culture Kids" to Transnational Youth

As an analytical concept, Third Culture Kids is difficult to use. It tends to be applied prescriptively and is unable to adequately address the diversity and sociocultural inequality that exists among those who participate in transnational social spaces because it was never designed for such use. It was designed to identify the shared traits and experiences of individuals with a transnational upbringing and further developed to allow them to imagine a community vis-à-vis others. It was not designed to understand the political dynamics that occur among them as a social group. Both practitioners and researchers have so far been caught up in trying to determine who is or is not a Third Culture Kid, without realizing that their application of the concept is Eurocentric and not reflexive of the concept's sociohistorical specificity. In contrast, this book shifts the analysis from the individual to the group by using an anthropological approach that is self-reflexive and considers the sociohistorical context of this population.

The TCK concept finds its historical origin in a time of postcolonial turbulence when nationalism was taking hold across the globe in the 1950s and 60s.[8] During this time, Useem, a member of the Department of Sociology and Anthropology at Michigan State University, was conducting research on what she calls the "third culture" that mediated relations between the growing number of American expatriate workers and host-country nationals in India at a time of global economic, political, and cultural transition from colonialism to American-led global capitalism (Useem, Useem, and Donoghue 1963: 169; Useem and Useem 1967). As Useem studied the adults, she noticed that her own children and those of other Americans growing up in India were practicing a culture that was unlike that of young people growing up in the United States for they had been influenced by their experience of growing up overseas. Useem subsequently turned her attention to the children growing up in the educational school setting of the third culture (Useem 1973; Useem and Downie 1976).

Third Culture Kids have therefore been defined as those who spend their formative years outside their parents' home country ("first culture") as "visitors" in one or more host countries ("second culture") to develop a "third culture" or an "interstitial culture" (Useem and Downie 1976; Pollock and Van Reken 2009 [2001]). Given the context in which the term was coined, "Third Culture Kid" relies on binary frameworks, such as "home country" and "host country," and categories that appear mutually exclusive, such as "American" and "Indian." While the concept argues for a postnational or transnational form of identity, these frameworks and categories remain analytically anchored to methodological nationalism, which assumes "the nation/state/society is the natural social and political form of the modern world" and takes the nation-state as the starting point of analyses (Wimmer and Glick Schiller 2002: 302). However, categories derived from methodological nationalism are unsustainable in a field where identities are a messy business—complex, shifting, and overlapping (Hall 1996).

More recently, Gene H. Bell-Villada and Nina Sichel (2011) traced the genealogy of the Third Culture Kid experience back to the colonial era, when European imperial powers sent their people overseas to serve in colonial outposts. In their introduction to a collection of memoirs, essays, and research, Bell-Villada and Sichel (ibid.: 4–5) write, "Many of these voluntary expatriates would in turn have offspring, who grew up as what we might today consider TCKs, and who might feel the same conflicting emotions vis-à-vis their 'mother country' ... colonialism, in a sense, first created Third Culture Kids." This historical lineage has contemporary significance due to the cultural legacies of colonialism.

The conflicting emotions described in the TCK literature are not unique to children of white colonial expatriates or mobile professionals. Scholars have written extensively on the impact of cultural displacement and hybridity on the (formerly) colonized, many of whom were equally mobile whether by choice or otherwise. In fact, the experiences of TCKs of non-Western background reveal a historical continuity with westernized local elites of former colonies and children of migrants in settler countries and former colonial metropolitan centers, but their stories have remained invisible in the TCK literature.

Anthropological studies that have applied a postcolonial analysis to people who live transnationally as adults show that colonial discourses continue to influence the ways in which Western expatriates perceive and interact with host-country nationals (Fechter 2007; Leggett 2010). Even so, Anne-Meike Fechter and Katie Walsh (2010: 1197) acknowledge in their special issue on expatriate communities that such studies have a "somewhat myopic focus on Western expatriates" (e.g., Benson and O'Reilly 2009; Coles and Fechter 2008; Farrer 2010; Fechter 2007; Korpela 2010; Leonard 2010). They recognize that there is a need to study the relations between Western expatriates and other expatriates as well as locals, and the way they perceive each other.

The literature on expatriate and local children in the context of transnational spaces is similar. Much of this educational and psychological literature uses Third Culture Kids as an analytical concept and fails to take the sociohistorical context and sociocultural inequalities within the third culture community into consideration, as previously discussed. There is also an emerging body of anthropological work in this field. Unlike the educational and psychological perspectives, the anthropological perspective enables researchers to interrogate the issue of national and/or transnational class reproduction. Some focus on expatriate children either as returnees (Knörr 2005; Goodman 1990) or in the context of international schools (O'Reilly 2009; Sander 2014; Désilet 2014) and outside the context of international schools (Korpela 2016; Fechter 2016) as they live overseas. Others focus on local children attending international schools (Peterson 2011; Imoto 2011). These studies tend to acknowledge the TCK concept only in passing, as though they were at a loss as to what to make of a concept that is highly popular but analytically flawed. However, none focus on the social dynamics that occur *among* the various seemingly disparate groups—children of Western expatriates, other expatriates, and locals—in politically imbued transnational social or educational spaces. Most studies follow the lives of members of one or two particular nationality groups. Others analyze either expatriate children or local children, but not both because they are treated as belonging to two distinct categories.

In summary, the Anglophone literature on participants of transnational spaces has been unable to integrate the perspectives and experiences of its diverse population under one analytical lens for three reasons. First, it uses the nation-state as its analytical starting point and assumes the mutual exclusivity of the national and transnational, leading to the use of binary frameworks. Second, it uses a Eurocentric perspective that fails to take the sociohistorical context into consideration. Third, the scope of research has been limited by methodologies that overlook the social processes involved in becoming international.

Meanwhile, Mary Hayden (2011) notes that the growing popularity of international education and the internationalization of national education means that national and international education are merging. Children of the local elite, particularly in former colonies, are also attending international schools and national educational spaces are becoming more diverse and transnational (Rizvi 2009). These trends require an approach that is able to integrate seemingly disparate groups under one analytical lens.

Bringing together the diverse range of experiences of mobility and international schools for young people into one theoretical space requires the use of a more encompassing term that avoids the definitional problem of "TCK." In this book I have opted to use the term "transnational youth" to mean simply any young person who is affected by international mobility either directly, by moving from country to country, or indirectly, by growing up in a transnational environment such as the international school where the people around them are highly mobile. This book treats the national and transnational as mutually constitutive in order to analytically integrate the perspectives and experiences of Westerners, locals, and other non-Westerners who inhabit transnational spaces (Smith 2001; Delanty 2009). I define transnational spaces as social spaces wherein multiple national and transnational discourses converge. The national and transnational economic and cultural hierarchies intersect in the transnational spaces of international schools to affect the perceptions and experiences of young people.

Being "International" as an Empirical Phenomenon

One of the main contributions that this book makes to the study of internationally mobile children and international schools, specifically, and migration, more generally, is that it takes the transnational, rather than the national, as its analytical point of departure. This represents an analytical shift from methodological nationalism to methodological cosmopolitanism in the study of a diverse group of people (Beck and Sznaider 2006). This shift enables us to bring a diverse group of transnational youth into one analytical space. To be clear, this book is not offering a newer, better form of cosmopolitanism or an ideal way of engaging across difference. Rather, it suggests that we study the cosmopolitanism of being international not as a moral, philosophical ideal, but as an empirical, sociological phenomenon (Igarashi and Saito 2014; Beck and Sznaider 2006). There is a diverse range of equally valid ways of engaging across difference or forms of cosmopolitanism that may coexist in a finite transnational space, and their relationships to each other need to be understood in order to analyze the institutionalization of global inequality. Methodological cosmopolitanism offers an approach that can reveal the tension that ensues when a diversity of actors, such as Anne-Sophie Bolon and Dae Sik, meet and interact in a transnational social space as equal targets of an international school's globalizing mission.

At The International School (TIS), the ideology of being "international" is promoted as the ideal form of engagement across difference and the only one that is valid, when in fact it is only one form among many. Being international is a form of cosmopolitanism that privileges those who have a certain set of cultural capital, such as being "westernized" and/or being able to speak English fluently. As a result, those students who do not possess the right set of cosmopolitan cultural capital, or enough of it, are seen as failing to become international, even when they are perfectly capable of engaging across difference through other means. While westernized students at TIS were labeled "international" by staff and students, others were labeled as "Indonesian" or "Korean" or "Asian" despite the fact that all students had to engage across difference on a daily basis by virtue of attending an international school with a diverse body of students and staff.

Much has been said of how parents use their economic means to acquire cosmopolitan capital for their children as a way to achieve upward social mobility or reproduce their class status within their national contexts. In his study of local Dutch parents who put their children through internationalized education in the Netherlands, Don Weenink (2008: 1092) argues that cosmopolitanism is a "source of power" and a "form of social and cultural capital." Further afield, cosmopolitan cultural capital is often seen as synonymous with Western cultural capital, sometimes combined with westernized international education. Roger Goodman (1990) argued early on that Japanese returnee children, commonly referred to as *kikokushijo* and often children of corporate elites at the time, used their experience of living overseas as cultural capital to enter good universities upon repatriation. Similarly, Mark Allen Peterson (2011) analyzes the way the Egyptian elite reproduce their eliteness by sending their children to an American international school in Cairo to acquire cosmopolitan capital through the consumption of Western education and other Western goods. My findings confirm that cosmopolitan capital is used to reproduce national class structures.

Less has been said, however, of how cosmopolitanism is institutionalized as cultural capital (Igarashi and Saito 2014) and the way this reproduces transnational class structures in which the sociocultural hierarchies found within transnational social spaces reflect the global economic hierarchy. Like Hiroki Igarashi and Hiro Saito (2014: 223), who wrote on the role of higher education, I use Bourdieu's concept of cultural capital to understand the ways in which an international school produces the "seemingly contradictory nature of cosmopolitanism as cultural capital" that simultaneously operates "as a marker of inclusiveness and as a basis for exclusion." At TIS, those who fell short of being "international" on the school's terms were sometimes labeled as "not really TCKs" by staff and often blamed for self-segregation, when in fact it was the school that failed to recognize the exclusivity inherent in their definition of being international. Scholarly oversight on this matter has been partly due to the methodological approach used and the researcher's background. As I have mentioned before, research conducted outside of the discipline of anthropology has tended to reproduce the moral value that society has attached to the notion of being international in their scholarly work rather than interrogating it against its sociohistorical context.

The ethnographic participant observation method I used allowed me, as a researcher, to immerse myself in the lives of transnational youth and systematically observe the day-to-day social interactions that influence the ways in which they become international. The literature on international schools emphasizes the importance of the "informal aspects such as mixing with students of other cultures both inside and outside school" over the more formal aspects of international education in nurturing intercultural understanding (Hayden and Thompson 1995: 341; see Hill 2007). TIS's advertising material likewise cites "immersion" as the only way to acquire "true internationalism." Despite acknowledging that social processes are crucial to becoming "international," ethnographic research by long-term immersion on these social processes has been rare until very recently, as I have mentioned. My research is part of a body of emerging ethnographic work on internationally mobile children inside and outside international schools that has been more critical of the class dimension of international mobility among children (e.g., Désilet 2014; Fechter 2016; Korpela 2016; Sander 2014).

However, this book is the first to integrate the perspectives of a diversity of social groups that are present in a single transnational social and educational space in order to critically analyze how being "international" is institutionalized. It does so by offering rich data on the insider perspectives of multiple social groups at TIS. Part of the reason I was able to access this data is because I am a native speaker of English, Japanese, and Indonesian, and have advanced fluency in Chinese (Mandarin), as well as the accompanying cultural fluency for these languages. The impact that the researcher's linguistic and cultural fluency has on the field and the data collected should not be underestimated, particularly given that researchers have limited time to conduct intensive fieldwork (see Tanu and Dales 2016). My linguistic and cultural background, coupled with my own transnational upbringing, allowed me to capitalize on the sense of mutual intelligibility that I shared to varying degrees with those I researched in order to build trust—an element that is crucial to ethnographic fieldwork—in a much shorter period of time than it would have otherwise been possible.

The insight I gained through immersive fieldwork led me to conclude that it was more useful to treat all the students at TIS as "transnational youth" who are equally affected by the transnational structures that shape their world, regardless of whether the school sees them as having successfully become international or otherwise. However, as Andreas Wimmer and Nina Glick Schiller (2002: 326) warn, in moving beyond methodological nationalism it is "important to remember the continued potency of nationalism." In promoting the ideology of being "international," TIS in fact inadvertently reinscribes the national among transnational youth at every turn. Ulrich Beck and Natan Sznaider (2006: 8) also write, "Cosmopolitanism and nationalism are not mutually exclusive, neither methodologically nor normatively." Hence, I incorporate the national context of the host society and other countries into the analysis. I also emphasize that I interrogate the school's ideology of being international and the cosmopolitan practices of transnational youth within the context of converging transnational as well as national discourses.

Transnational youth internalize both national and transnational structures as habitus, which in Bourdieu's (1990: 56) words is "embodied history, internalized as a second nature and so forgotten as history." Habitus is the process through which a shared sense of metaphoric place facilitates mutual intelligibility or, in Gillian Bottomley's (1992: 122) words, "a commonsense understanding of the world, and especially of what is 'natural' or even imaginable." Habitus is so natural, like the air we breathe, that we forget it exists. Habitus impacts on the way transnational youth and other actors, such as parents and staff, interact with each other at TIS and the way they engage with the school's ideology of being international.

Importantly, transnational youth share a sense of place or habitus in some ways with each other, but not in all ways, at all times, with all transnational youth. It is analogous to how Italians may share a sense of place in some ways but not in all ways, at all times, with all Italians. Students internalized the Eurocentric sociocultural hierarchies that informed the school's ideology of being international (i.e., the rules of the game) in varying ways that reflected their diverse backgrounds. Consequently, not all students had the cultural capital (i.e., the capacity) to play the game successfully. This created varying responses among them. Some played along, others challenged it, and still others did both.

Yet even when they did challenge the hierarchy, the ways in which they did so were constrained by the Eurocentric transnational structures they had internalized. Bottomley (1992: 123) notes, "Habitus is not determining, but it is a powerful mediating construct that can predefine what is necessary or even imaginable."[9] Despite the school's ideological commitment to nurturing a spirit of engagement with the Other on equal terms, the internalized Eurocentric structures remain powerful in mediating social interactions at TIS. A teacher referred to it as the "hidden curriculum" (Snyder 1970). These structures shaped young people's responses to the school's mission of making them "international."

On the one hand, these responses reproduce the external structures that underpin the Eurocentrism of the ideology of being "international" by encouraging the growth of a transnational capitalist class (Sklair 2001) that is westernized to some degree. On the other hand, they complicate the external structures by diversifying the growing transnational capitalist class to include those who practice cosmopolitan engagement across difference in ways that are labeled, by themselves and others, as being "Asian" or, for example, being "Indonesian." Nevertheless, in both cases, transnational youth draw on a "cosmopolitan style" that signifies their privileged place in a capitalist, postcolonial world based on their "education, experience, and taste," which reflect the Eurocentric ideology of being international (Peterson 2011: 216).

Cosmopolitan Capital

For the purposes of this book, I differentiate between cosmopolitan ideologies, practices, capital, and subjectivities. Cosmopolitan ideologies pertain to attitudes and beliefs about peaceably engaging with the Other; cosmopolitan practices refer to the ways in which one engages with the Other; cosmopolitan capital refers to the cultural capabilities and social networks that enable one to practice cosmopolitanism (Bourdieu 1986; Weenink 2008); and cosmopolitan subjectivities refer to the ways in which people feel or do not feel cosmopolitan. I argue that cosmopolitan ideologies, practices, capital, and subjectivities are embedded within structures of power (Werbner 1999; Hall and Werbner 2008).

Bourdieu's notion of capital has extensive application in this book for analyzing social interactions among actors at the school and the way they engaged with the ideology of being international. Bourdieu (1986: 241) describes four forms of capital, which he also refers to as "accumulated labor": cultural capital, symbolic capital, social capital, and economic capital. Most pertinent to this book is cultural capital in its embodied state in "the form of long-lasting dispositions of the mind and body" as discussed above (ibid.: 243). It encompasses language, accents, and taste for "clothes, types of food, drinks, sports, friends" (Bourdieu 1989: 19) and the way a person carries themselves. It can be transmitted through educational institutions, as well as socialization within the family.

Closely related to cultural capital is symbolic capital, which Jenkins (1992: 85) summarizes as "prestige and honor." Symbolic capital gives recognition to economic and cultural capital as a sense of distinction. If cultural capital is "primarily legitimate knowledge of one kind or another," then symbolic capital produces "common sense" and determines what can be considered legitimate (Bourdieu 1989: 21; Jenkins 1992: 85). At TIS, those with Western capital, including the ability to speak native-sounding English, are constructed as culturally superior and authentically "international" (e.g., chapters 2 and 4).

Social capital refers to "membership in a group" or a "durable network of more or less institutionalized relationships of mutual acquaintance and recognition" (Bourdieu 1986: 248). I will show that social capital and the ability of students to mobilize their social capital (by drawing on their cultural capital) influences their relationship to each other and the staff, and thereby the way they practice cosmopolitanism.

The notion of economic capital is relevant because the experiences of transnational youth are classed. Economic capital marks the collective privilege of those at TIS. However, even among a privileged cohort, some are more privileged than others in different ways. This principle prompted some parents to use the education offered by TIS, an English-medium international school, to convert their own economic capital into (cosmopolitan) cultural capital for their children (chapter 4) by enrolling them in the school. The notion of economic capital is also relevant in that it can be used to challenge others' cultural capital. The ability and disposition of transnational youth to engage with the school's ideology of being international and practice one form of cosmopolitanism over others varies with the capital they possess and habitus through which they operate.

One of the central arguments of this book is that the school's ideology of being "international" is a Eurocentric form of cosmopolitanism, and its Eurocentrism has implications on the social dynamics of the school. This ideology defines difference based on colonial conceptions of "race" and culture, and only recognizes as "international" the cosmopolitan practices that privilege Western cultural capital. The literature on Third Culture Kids and the dominant (Western) culture of transnational educational spaces privilege an elite form of cosmopolitanism, which I refer to as the ideology of being international, that reflects contemporary transnational capitalist structures and the continuity of colonial cultural legacies. Specifically, TIS endorses a notion of being international that is characterized by speaking (native) English, maintaining a certain distance with the local, having Western capital by acting "white" or "Western," and engaging with those who are "racially" different. While the ideology of being international promotes peaceable engagement among transnational actors, it also reproduces transnational and national class structures by privileging Western capital. Meanwhile, the data reveals that there are many different ways of practicing cosmopolitanism that do not reflect the purported ideal. There were young people at TIS who were practicing cosmopolitanism in ways that did not fit the school's ideology of being international. This made them *appear* as though they were refusing to engage across difference.

Cosmopolitanism is practiced in many different forms specific to the sociohistorical context because it is a dialogical process of engagement with the Other. I emphasize Gerard Delanty's (2009: 53) words that "the very notion of cosmopolitanism compels the recognition of multiple kinds of cosmopolitanism." I use cosmopolitanism as a conceptual framework that recognizes that openness to the Other leads to a multiplicity of ways in which social interactions and identifications across difference occur in transnational spaces.

The people I studied experienced global mobility from a position of privilege in relation to the majority of the world's population. They are the children of a population who Leslie Sklair (2001: 10) refers to as the transnational capitalist class: "It is domiciled in and identified with no particular country but, on the contrary, is identified with the global capitalist system." Nevertheless, the people I studied were not always in a position of privilege relative to the dominant culture *within* elite transnational spaces because these spaces are not neutral. Further, because they move countries as dependents of mobile professionals rather than by their own volition, in some ways transnational young people have no say in crossing cultural borders and have to practice cosmopolitanism from a place of relative lack of power. I argue that transnational youth practice both "cosmopolitanism of the above" and cosmopolitanism from a place of relative marginalization in ways that shifts relative to the context (Hall and Werbner 2008: 346).

Crucially, the different ways in which young people experience transnational spaces influence the way they think and feel. Ortner (2006: 107) refers to this as "subjectivity," by which she means, "the ensemble of modes of perception, affect, thought, desire, and fear that animate acting subjects ... as well [as] the cultural and social formations that shape, organize, and provoke those modes of affect, thought, and so on." Cosmopolitan subjectivities are shaped within structures of power. Cosmopolitanism from above enables a sense of being "a citizen of the world." This kind of cosmopolitanism requires one to invoke privilege (Calhoun 2008). It is a Eurocentric form of cosmopolitanism that has historical continuity with the colonial discourse of being at home everywhere in the Empire (chapter 1), as well as one that panders to the cultural requirements of a capitalist modernity (chapter 4). This is the form of cosmopolitanism that characterized TIS's ideology of being international. But in order to practice it, students needed Western capital, which was not available to all in equal measure. Those unable to uphold or embody the school's ideology of internationalism, due to insufficient Western capital, practiced alternative forms of cosmopolitanisms, which were not necessarily recognized as such by their practitioners, let alone by the dominant school culture. These forms of cosmopolitanism were practiced from a place of marginality vis-à-vis the dominant Western culture of the school.

When practiced from a place of marginality, cosmopolitan engagement with the Other produces a sense of ambivalence. Of this ambivalence, Hall (2008: 347) says, "this is inevitably the site of what Du Bois called 'double consciousness,' and of what, somewhat unadvisedly perhaps, I have elsewhere called 'hybridity.'" In contrast to the felt cosmopolitanism of the dominant Western culture, some students at the international school expressed their cosmopolitan tendency or hybridity as a process of becoming "Asian," among other things. Transnational youth situationally shift between multiple practices of cosmopolitanism depending on their positionality (or status in any given social hierarchy), and in turn this shapes their subjectivities in different ways. They practice cosmopolitanism by becoming "Western" and/or by becoming "Asian," "Indonesian," "Korean," and so on. These processes are not mutually exclusive. Cosmopolitanism is an expression of mutual intelligibility among those who traverse existing socially constructed boundaries in the same way that nationalism expressed a sense of mutual intelligibility among those who traversed preexisting nonnational boundaries (Anderson 1983). Cosmopolitan ideologies are prisms through which communities are imagined in an increasingly globalizing world.

Structure of the Book

This book can be divided into two broad sections. The first four chapters interrogate the broad structures that define the ideology of being "international." Much of the discussion focuses on the school, the staff, the parents, and alumni (of TIS and other international schools), though the perspectives of the students are also presented. Chapter 1 sets the scene by introducing The International School (TIS), situating it in Jakarta, Indonesia, as a postcolonial locale, as well as contextualizing it within the global trend toward internationalization of education. It outlines and critiques the symbols and rituals that revolve around the school's ideology of being international, including its annual celebration of United Nations Day. It also maps the various student groups. The rest of the book explores the tensions that arise as the school's ideology of being international intersects with national and transnational cultural hierarchies to produce diverse practices of cosmopolitanism.

As language is a theme that permeates the research, chapter 2 outlines the way colonial and capitalist discourses relating to language, particularly English, shapes the subjectivities of transnational youth. Chapter 3 focuses on the way the school imagines an international community that is expatriate, broadly Western, and distant from the local. Chapter 4 shows that parents and students are driven by global economic and political forces to pursue Western cultural capital that is packaged as cosmopolitan cultural capital. It also explores the discourse of authenticity that mediates the perception that some of these pursuits are more acceptable than others.

From chapter 5 onward, I turn the focus onto the social dynamics that occur among the transnational youth studying at TIS, and their perspectives. Chapter 5 looks at with whom and where students choose to hang out, and the way social status or popularity and spaces are racialized such that students with Western capital seem to have a stronger sense of belonging at the school than the others. It also shows how others challenge the Eurocentric notion of being international. Chapter 6 explores the variety of cosmopolitanisms that are being practiced and the differing labels that they attract. Chapter 7 delves deeper into the processes of gendered racialization that occur in transnational spaces by looking at romantic attractions.

Chapter 8 brings the book together by returning the focus to the Eurocentrism of the school's ideology of being "international" as expressed through United Nations Day. It breaks down the social dynamics surrounding this particular event to show that students compete to become "international," resulting in a hierarchy within a hierarchy that resembles a fractal. Methodologically, this chapter also highlights the insights of those of mixed descent whose ambiguous physical appearance bring social fault lines into relief.

The school's ideology emphasizes visible diversity based on colonial discourses of "race." It looks favorably upon the visible "racial" heterogeneity of the English-speaking student groups by rendering their cultural homogeneity invisible. Similarly, it looks unfavorably upon the racial homogeneity of those who choose to segregate from or challenge the hegemonic cosmopolitan practices, by rendering their cultural heterogeneity invisible. This selective vision results in a Eurocentric cosmopolitan hierarchy, and it is within this framework that students used both acquired and inherited capital to compete to become "international." While TIS endeavored to produce "global citizens," it did not sufficiently recognize that transnational spaces are not neutral and that cultural hierarchies based on global, regional, and national hierarchies continue to impact social relations among transnational youth and the way they practice cosmopolitanism.

In all, the chapters together demonstrate that the ideology of being "international" is institutionalized to act as a vehicle for the reproduction of the transnational capitalist class as well as national elites. In turn, transnational youth employ cosmopolitan practices situationally as social strategies to manage their hybrid identities and navigate transnational spaces.

Ethnographic Writing

While the first four chapters of the book emphasize interview data, the analyses would not have been possible without the understanding gained from daily on-site observations of social interactions, which are described in more detail from chapter 5 onward. The data presented in this book is drawn mainly from participant observation at TIS's high school campus and in Jakarta at large, and in-depth interviews with over 140 students, staff, and parents from the school, as well as alumni of international schools in various countries.[10] I also conducted two weeks of additional participant observation at a smaller international school in Jakarta, which informed the analyses, and maintained contact with international school communities in Jakarta to keep abreast with new developments.

This book uses several ethnographic conventions. Pseudonyms are used for the school and all participants to protect their anonymity. Descriptions about people are left vague in cases where naming the specific national, ethnic, linguistic, or cultural background of the participant (usually a staff member) in combination with their marital status or other information would reveal their identity to those who have been associated with the school. For example, instead of "Chinese Jamaican," I might say, "Asian Caribbean." In one or two cases, I have used two pseudonyms for the same person in different sections when a substantial amount of personal information is divulged. Unless otherwise indicated, conversations that I heard during participant observation are reconstructed from field notes. Finally, I use the term "school administrators" to refer to the principal, vice principals, activities director, academic director, and sports director of TIS.

Notes

1. Sections of this book have previously been published in Tanu (2011; 2014; 2015; 2016) and Tanu and Dales (2016). They are republished in parts here with permission.
2. Email to author, 7 June 2017.
3. See Ossman (2013) for "serial migrants."
4. The early figure varies depending on the definition of "international school" used (see Bunnell 2014 for a discussion). The recent figure is derived from statistics provided by the International School Consultancy (ISC) founded by Nicholas Brummitt, which is used by prominent researchers in the field (see Pearce 2013). ISC defines "international school" as any school that "delivers a curriculum to any combination of pre-school, elementary or secondary students, wholly or partly in English outside an English-speaking country, or if a school in a country where English is one of the official languages, offers an English-medium curriculum other than the country's national curriculum and is international in its orientation." The definition used is simultaneously broad, as it includes English-medium schools without a critical view of its curriculum, and narrow, as it does not include schools that use languages other than English while teaching an international curriculum.

   Furthermore, according to ISC, Asia has 54 percent of the total number of international schools and 60 percent of the total number of students. It should be noted, however, that ISC defines "Asia" to include Western Asia and the Middle East. Of the top fifteen Asian countries/territories ranked by the number of schools, eleven are located in East Asia, South Asia, and Southeast Asia. Indonesia is listed as having 190 English-medium international schools.

5. In addition to David Pollock's work, Ruth E. Van Reken conducted 300 official surveys in 1987, and subsequently gathered qualitative data in the form of thousands of informal interviews through letters, phone calls, and in-person meetings. Van Reken (email to author, 12 January 2017) explains that after awhile the stories "all sounded the same except for the details," which indicates data saturation, to the point where "I could guess, within about five years, their [interviewee's] age depending on what they were telling me about where they were in their journey."

6. From "The 'TCK Profile' seminar material" (1989: 1) as cited in Pollock and Van Reken (2001).

7. Pseudonyms are used for all research participants to protect anonymity.

8. See Tanu (2015) for a more detailed history of the term "Third Culture Kids."

9. See Baldassar (1999) for an example.

10. High school consisted of grades nine to twelve, with student ages ranging from fourteen to eighteen years, though at least one student interviewed was nineteen years old.

CHAPTER I

Being International

"I am a citizen of the world," was a common answer given by international school students to my question, "Where do you consider home," or "What do you say when asked, 'Where are you from?'" This was not surprising, given that many of them would have lived in three or more countries by the time they graduate from high school. Other versions of the answer were, "I am international," "I am a global citizen," or "I am at home everywhere." More often than not, though, these answers were said with a sense of being "ahead of the pack" compared to those who adhered to more localized identities, as though rootlessness was the ultimate way to be. It reflects the way in which the international schools attended by many of those I interviewed idealized the notion of being "international." This is encapsulated in the inclusion of the word "international" in their school names and the terms "global citizen" or "world citizen" on their school websites. Yet it must not be lost on us that international schools are embedded within a globalizing marketplace and transnational class structures.

The website Living in Indonesia: A Site for Expatriates lists sixty-nine "international schools" in Indonesia, though the definition used appears nebulous (Expat Web Site Association 2017). Most of them cater to the children of affluent, jet-setting families from expatriate communities, as well as local, upper classes, and are located in the bustling metropolis of Jakarta, the capital city of Indonesia. Among these schools, "The International School" (TIS), where I conducted this research, prides itself on being a "true" international school. TIS sets itself apart from local schools in many important ways: its original purpose, curricula, student and staff body, architecture, resources, and landscaping. TIS has a diverse student body in terms of nationality and the cultural background of the students and actively promotes the notion of being international. But there are inherent contradictions between TIS's mission to overcome boundaries of nation, race, culture, and class and its practices, which reinscribe these boundaries in constructing idealized ways of being international. TIS's case shows that the notion of being international is, in fact, constructed by and dependent upon colonial and capitalist discourses of national, racial, cultural, and class differences.

This chapter provides an overview of the main field site, TIS, with a focus on the way being international is officially constructed at TIS by the school's administrators, marketing materials, and United Nations Day program. It contextualizes TIS's efforts of promoting the notion of being international within national and global trends toward the internationalization of education. The chapter also maps the most conspicuous social cliques among students as they form the starting point for the analytical discussions in subsequent chapters.

The International School and Jakarta

The International School is a coeducational school that was initially established by foreign foundations to service the children of the United Nations and diplomatic staff stationed in Jakarta.[1] It is currently run as a not-for-profit organization that is overseen by a board of trustees. Until 2003, TIS accepted students of all nationalities except Indonesian nationals due to Indonesian government regulations that prevented its citizens from enrolling in international schools. Indonesian students used to attend the school in its early days but later the government prohibited its citizens from enrolling in international schools to ensure they were educated as Indonesians in Indonesian schools. A school DVD on TIS's history suggests that the government's prohibition at the time was "a major upheaval for everyone because the culture was then removed from us and the school took on a different tone after that."

TIS has survived several sociopolitical upheavals in Indonesia and continues to thrive in their aftermath. The latest occurred on the heel of the Asian financial crisis when riots swept through Jakarta and other major cities and triggered the end of Suharto's 32-year rule in May 1998. Foreign nationals, as well as many Chinese Indonesians who could afford to, fled the country. According to a teacher who was present at the time, TIS was "locked down" as staff and students tried to make their way home and to the airport.[2] Indonesians who were ethnically Chinese were targeted during the riots due to their status as a conspicuous ethnic minority that has historically been used as scapegoats during times of crises. Many of the Chinese Indonesian students who were at TIS during my fieldwork explained that they were enrolled in local elementary schools at the time of the riots. Many spent the few years immediately after the riots living overseas, mainly in Singapore. The following academic year saw TIS's student body reduced by about a quarter because many foreign expatriate workers and their families who had fled Indonesia did not return, or returned but left their families behind in their home countries.

Around this time, changes in patterns of education for the Indonesian middle and upper classes began to reflect the global trend toward the internationalization of education. In the 1990s, the then Indonesian Department of Education and Culture opened opportunities for schools to develop an international standard of education. At the time of research, Ag Kustulasari (2009: 95) listed over sixty "international schools" across Indonesia, thirty-two of which were established in the 1990s.[3] These range from schools that use a national curriculum from overseas (e.g., the Japanese curriculum) to English-medium schools that use internationally recognized curricula (e.g., International Baccalaureate).[4] Private "national plus" schools that claimed to have an "international" dimension to their curricula were also established during this time and grew in number, though this category of schools later disappeared in 2014 as the laws changed (Mayall 2010).[5] At the time, these national plus schools generally offered a national curriculum supplemented by a focus on English and/or Mandarin language development, and/or used English as a medium of instruction in some or all subjects.[6]

The end of Suharto's centralized New Order regime was followed by an era of *reformasi* (reformation) that saw a move toward the decentralization of many aspects of state governance, including education. In 2003 the Ministry of National Education (MONE, previously the Department of Education and Culture) issued a law commonly referred to as the "National Education Policy,"[7] which stated the importance of English-language education for *"pergaulan global"* (global interaction).[8] This has been cited as the impetus for the growth of national plus and international schools (ibid.; Kustulasari 2009). The government also relaxed the restrictions it had placed on Indonesian nationals enrolling in international schools.

From 2003, the number of Indonesian nationals from the local elite and upper-class families who enrolled at TIS rapidly increased. The large number of Indonesian students altered the student demographic and the school's social dynamics. "Indonesia" became more present on campus. At the same time, Indonesian students were of concern to the school as they were perceived as failing to be international and were stereotyped as privileged children who were not committed to achieving academically. These perceptions highlight the tension between the Eurocentric construction of the school's ideology of being international and the students' diverse ways of engaging with this ideology.

The law governing international schools changed again in 2014. The Ministerial Decree 31/2014 on Education that was issued in April redefined the concept of international schools in Indonesia.[9] Currently, the categories of schools allowed to operate in Indonesia are national schools, which offer the national curriculum, embassy schools, which offer foreign curricula and are only accessible to foreign nationals, and *Satuan Pendidikan Kerjasama* (SPK)[10] schools, which offer overseas programs such as the International Baccalaureate and admit both foreign and Indonesian nationals. From December 2014, all schools that wanted to continue enrolling Indonesian nationals were required to apply to become an SPK school by entering into a Cooperation Agreement with a foreign education institution. TIS fell under this category of schools. These schools were also required to stop using the term "international" in their school names and offer mandatory Indonesian language, literature, civics, and religion courses as well as national examinations to Indonesian students. Many international schools changed their names during this time.

However, TIS students did not feel the impact of the legislation in the first year after it came into effect. According to alumni who graduated from TIS in June 2016, the school dynamics had not changed because most of the Indonesian students had managed to avoid attending the new classes, which were being offered as part of the extracurricular program, by obtaining a waiver from the Ministry of Education. By 2017, however, Indonesian students were no longer able to apply for exemptions. Yet, despite changes like these, the school's ideological paradigm and its impact on the core social dynamics on the campus has remained stubbornly consistent over the years as determined from interviews with past and recent alumni, direct observations during fieldwork, and information obtained from those involved with TIS in 2017 when this book went to print.

At the time of fieldwork, TIS had over eight hundred high school students representing fifty or so nationalities, with the majority being from South Korea (approximately 25 percent), Indonesia (approximately 20 percent), the United States (approximately 15 percent), Australia, and Canada. The high number of Korean nationals reflects the rapid growth of Korean communities (both permanent and temporary/expatriate migrants) in Indonesia and elsewhere since the 1990s. The number of students from Anglophone countries had declined around the time of the 1998 riots. Most students, including Indonesians, spend some or all of their time growing up outside their passport country (or countries, for those who have more than one citizenship), and often they live in several countries before completing high school. Most were of Asian descent, though many were also of mixed descent.

The high school administrators and teaching staff represented about twenty nationalities, though they were predominantly from white-dominant Anglophone countries such as the United States, Canada, the United Kingdom, Australia, and New Zealand. The teaching assistants, administrative support staff, and other support staff (e.g., cleaners, gardeners, and security guards) were almost all Indonesian.[11] But they tended to be invisible in the students' social world, except to the Indonesian students, who had an easygoing relationship with many of the security guards.

In Indonesia, TIS was perceived as a Western educational institution, which had implications for its sense of security in a largely Muslim country, especially since the 9/11 terrorist attacks. In 2002, suicide bombers linked to Jemaah Islamiyah bombed two nightclubs in Bali, killing 202 people, most of whom were Westerners. Since then, Indonesia has experienced similar attacks in Jakarta and Bali that often targeted Western interests, though most of the victims were Indonesians.[12] Two of these bombings occurred during my fieldwork, while the most recent bomb attacks occurred at a Starbucks café in the central business district of Jakarta in January 2016 and at a bus terminal in East Jakarta in May 2017. Security checks (though mostly superficial) at entrances have long become a permanent fixture at major hotels, malls, business skyscrapers, and apartment buildings in Jakarta and other major cities.

In November 2003 newspapers reported that international schools were allegedly included in a terrorist target list. This prompted TIS (and other international schools) to upgrade its security, such that the entrance looks imposing both in terms of the physical structure as well as the ten or so guards who secured the entrance. Then, in July 2009 and midway through my fieldwork, two luxury hotels in Jakarta's business district of Mega Kuningan were attacked by suicide bombers. Six of the seven victims were Westerners. The attacks occurred during TIS's two-and-a-half-month "summer" break. In the ensuing months, a bright orange police car[13] was continually parked at the front gates of TIS's high school campus. Both before and after the Mega Kuningan bombings, only cars with permits or those whose registration numbers were listed on the clipboard carried by one of the security guards were allowed through at any time. Other visitors had to enter the campus through pedestrian gates. Those who had a TIS identity card could walk through freely, while others had to register their details and exchange an identity card with a visitor pass—a standard procedure at many elite residential and office buildings—before being allowed through the gates secured by guards.

While the police car and imposing security gates were installed based on real security threats, they were also symbolic markers of the school's separateness from its local environment in terms of class and culture. Located in an affluent neighborhood, TIS is an enclave for the privileged, as are many other international schools in Indonesia. Every weekday morning and afternoon, the narrow street in front of TIS was jammed with traffic created mainly by the chauffeured private cars and the large busses that dropped off and picked up students. Private traffic spilled over onto the public road as the guards supposedly directed traffic, giving priority to the upscale busses contracted by TIS for its students.

Inside the gates lies a well-maintained, green, oasis-like campus that belies the bustle and smog that characterize Jakarta. Some of the school's impressive facilities, such as the multiple gyms, pools, and sports grounds, compared favorably with those of elite universities in developed countries. Every high school classroom was air-conditioned, carpeted, and fitted with electronic boards. Like other international schools, TIS was often featured in local English-language magazines and newspapers catering to Jakarta's expatriate and upper-class population as a celebrated symbol of high-quality education and a "cosmopolitan" lifestyle.

Lianne, an alumnus, remarked of TIS, "It was like a completely independent country or something" that created "an immediate bond" among fellow students and alumni based on a shared experience of the world within the gates. Lianne felt this way even though she had graduated from TIS in the mid-1990s before the sophisticated security structures were installed. In fact, Marie Sander's (2014) study of expatriate children in Shanghai and the highly secured international schools they attend shows that the exclusivity of international schools and their role in creating a sense of belonging among transnational youth is not unique to TIS or Indonesia. At TIS, the sense of being international was enhanced through imagining a community that was seen as separate from the local.

Articulating Internationalism

TIS is a school that offers high-quality education (at a cost), providing its students with opportunities to study at leading universities in the world. Among the class of 2009, 98 percent entered college or university, with 55 percent of them in the United States, followed by Australia, Canada, the United Kingdom, Korea, and Japan. TIS is also a school that proclaims noble, cosmopolitan intentions of educating students so they can serve the world as best they can. The school's sense of connection to the global, its sense of being international, and its celebration of diversity permeated everyday life. The ideology of being international was a driving force for the school. Mission statements, symbols, rituals, and curricula that supported this ideology were present both physically and discursively together with the contradictions inherent in these.

Mission: Educating "Responsible World Citizens"

TIS's 2009 promotional documents reflected its long-time visions. These documents stated that TIS was committed to nurturing "life skills which define our international community and global perspective." Among TIS's many educational goals was that of educating "responsible world citizens" who respect cultural diversity, engage with the host nations, serve the community, are caring, and can speak another language, among many other things. This goal is promoted by many other schools that similarly market themselves as international. The term "responsible world citizens" appeared in several documents, as did terms like "international mindedness" and the notion of educating students regarding "issues of global significance" and "world issues." These emphases are common to international schools (Hayden 2011; Hayden and Thompson 1995). TIS purposed to instill a sense of "pride" in their students regarding their own cultural backgrounds while complementing this with the ability to consider "multiple perspectives." In other words, one of TIS's central aims was to nurture in their students the ability to engage peaceably across difference.

To this end, TIS claimed to offer learning experiences that are "international in their design and highlight the commonalities of the human experience." These learning experiences are gained through the international curriculum as well as immersion in a diverse transnational space. One of TIS's more recent 2013 documents stated, "The school helps you realize that the only way to really become a 'responsible world citizen' is through immersion. Your teachers will offer perspectives from twenty nationalities and your friends, from sixty." The staff member in charge of public relations said she believed that TIS was the "true" international school. More recently, TIS's online promotional materials from 2016 have been stripped of the word "international" and more emphasis has been placed on the fact that its students are being educated while living in Indonesia. Nevertheless, they have maintained the notion of educating students to become people who contribute more to the world.

Accordingly, it was important for the school administrators that students mixed with each other in ways that reflected a sense of internationalism and openness to difference. The school administrators were concerned that some students appeared to self-segregate into groups based on nationality.

Curriculum: The International Baccalaureate Program

TIS uses English as the main language of instruction and draws on international curriculum as well as others from English-speaking countries, offering the International Baccalaureate (IB) diploma in addition to the regular TIS diploma. The IB curriculum in particular is highly sought after by parents because it offers strong academic training and the qualification necessary to apply to world-ranking universities. National as well as international schools are increasingly adopting the IB curriculum as the internationalization of education continues (International Baccalaureate Organization 2013b). The International Baccalaureate Organization was founded in Geneva, Switzerland, in 1968 and its program was initially designed to prepare internationally mobile students for university. The program seeks "to provide students with a truly international education" (International Baccalaureate Organization 2013a). The IB mission statement says that it aims to develop "young people who help to create a better and more peaceful world through intercultural understanding and respect" and "who understand that other people, with their differences, can also be right" (International Baccalaureate Organization 2013c).

Rituals: For Global Citizenship

Early in my fieldwork, I noticed that "global citizenship" was the buzz term floating around campus, particularly among the staff. The East Asia Regional Council of Schools (EARCOS), through whom the Global Citizenship Award handed out at TIS is organized, describes a global citizen as one who is: "a proud representative of his/her nation while respectful of the diversity of other nations, has an open mind, is well informed, aware and empathetic, concerned and caring for others[,] encouraging a sense of community and strongly committed to engagement and action to make the world a better place. Finally, this student is able to interact and communicate effectively with people from all walks of life while having a sense of collective responsibility for all who inhabit the globe" (EARCOS 2010). There were numerous activities at TIS that were designed to raise global citizens. Some of these activities emulated organizations whose aims are to tackle global issues.

The Model United Nations (MUN) club is a classic example. Typically, students learn to debate and deliberate over international issues as mock delegates representing various countries, often countries other than that of their own nationalities. The MUN club activities usually culminate with students traveling overseas to a regional MUN conference with students from other international schools in Southeast Asia.

Another example is the Global Issues Network (GIN) conference held in Beijing in 2008, which was organized by EARCOS. It inspired some of the students who had attended the Beijing conference to host a local conference in Jakarta during my fieldwork. The main aim was to raise awareness about global issues pertaining to the environment and poverty, as well as to inspire young people to become part of the solution and raise funds for the cause. There were students from other schools ranging from international schools to Taiwanese, national plus (of the time), and (Indonesian) state schools. An ethos of *noblesse oblige* underpinned the effort. An invited speaker, orphanage supporter, and alumnus of TIS said, "We come from a very privileged background, so we need to spread the word." His aim was to encourage as many young people as possible to be involved in similar efforts. At the end of the academic year, the student organizer of the local GIN conference was presented with the "Global Citizenship Award."

It seemed ironic, however, that the school whose students possibly used the most amount of energy per capita in the country had organized a conference to raise awareness of environmental issues. As one student discovered in her environmental issues class after having calculated their energy consumption, she would need several planets like Earth to support her lifestyle if everyone was to live like her. My field notes are littered with comments that I made about the cold air-conditioning inside the buildings. Like myself, students often wore sweatshirts, hoodies, or cardigans in the classrooms to keep warm despite the hot tropical climate just outside the doors. While the intentions were noble, the global outlook that was being nurtured at TIS presupposed economic privilege.

Imagined Communities: A Global International School Community

TIS had well-established ties with other major international schools across Southeast Asia. These ties were fostered through regular regional competitions and meetings for the school sports, dance, music, and MUN teams. There was a lot of publicity surrounding these regional meetings. They were usually preceded with pep rallies to support the school teams. Students involved in these activities traveled overseas or hosted students from other international schools in the region when the competitions were held at TIS. Again, being international required a degree of economic privilege that enabled students to participate in regional and international events.

Although TIS's website indicates, at the time of writing, that there may be a move toward establishing stronger links with communities within Indonesia, it is clear that TIS students are socialized into a transnational lifestyle mainly with students from other international schools both in Indonesia and overseas. Some alumni who were living in Indonesia explained that they mostly socialized with graduates of TIS and other international schools. Others explained that they would choose international school graduates as work partners or employees over graduates from other schools because they can trust them more in terms of ability and culture. These preferences indicated a sense of exclusionism and elitism that ran in stark contrast to the school's claim of nurturing students who practice cosmopolitan engagement across difference. TIS enables its students to foster cosmopolitan social capital among others like themselves.

Symbols: Nationalities, Flags, and Obama

It was common practice to foreground the number of nationalities represented in the student body and teaching staff in the school's promotional material. As one former staff member put it, "what we wanted was for people not to be insular, not to feel as if their way of life was the only way. And what a perfect set up for that when you had 55, 60 different nationalities" (from a DVD on TIS's history). The school administrators believed that the diversity of backgrounds represented at the school, as signified by the number of nationalities, promoted openness to difference. It was therefore a selling point that made them feel more than justified in their claim to being an international school.

Students were encouraged to flaunt their nationalities as part of the school's celebration of diversity. Peering through classroom windows, it was difficult not to notice the posters hanging on the walls with pictures of national flags and other national symbols that students had drawn. Many of these posters contained symbols from sometimes two or three or more countries to represent the student's sense of identity. Some of these countries represented the students' nationalities, others the parents' nationalities or ethnicities, and yet others where students had lived. Students typically told me about how mixed or "international" their friendship groups were by counting the number of nationalities they represented. One of the main prisms used to identify difference was nationality. Being international presupposed the national.

The school's celebration of diversity was also apparent in the way Barrack Obama's election was a hot topic on campus. The start of my fieldwork coincided with the 2009 US presidential inauguration. As a biracial child to a Kenyan father and a white American mother, who had spent part of his childhood outside of his passport country in Indonesia, Obama was treated like a poster boy for TIS. In one classroom, the teacher displayed for several months a custom-made pull-up banner of Obama, which he seemed to have personally ordered. During the first weekly meeting for teaching staff that I attended, the principal announced that there would be a live screening of the inauguration ceremony that night at the school. "Today is momentous. A TCK, multiracial president has been elected. It is a great day. It is a historic moment," he declared.

In the ensuing days, Obama was popular among teachers as a subject of class discussions. Mr. Salamon, a social studies teacher, showed a video clip from the inauguration in his class, and discussed how multiracial Obama's family was, drawing attention to the new president's biracial half sister of Indonesian and white American descent and her Asian Canadian husband. The excitement over Obama was a celebration of diversity in its visually apparent, "mixed-race" form, and the way in which it crossed national boundaries. The discourse being promoted was that being international or a TCK presupposed the nation-state and "race."

More Rituals: United Nations Day

Deep inside the campus was a light blue United Nations flag hoisted on a flagpole. Much of the school's ideological commitment to global well-being was expressed through activities relating to international organizations like the United Nations. United Nations Day was the school's most emblematic ritual for expressing this commitment to being international.

The main event in the morning included a colorful procession of flags that represented the nationalities of the high school student population. The flags were carried into the theater by students, most of whom were dressed in the corresponding national costumes or their creative interpretation of such costumes. The flag procession was complemented with performances by the dance teams, choir, band, and string groups.

Another highlight of the morning was the music and dance performances by the Chinese, Indian, Indonesian, Japanese, Korean, and French clubs, which were formed specifically for putting on performances on United Nations Day. The French club was made up primarily of students of different backgrounds who were learning French; the Korean club was made up of Koreans; while the Chinese, Indian, Indonesian, and Japanese groups were mixed. Students spend a whole semester staying back afterschool to practice for these performances. Once the performances were over, everyone filed out of the theater at lunch time for an afternoon of international cuisines as the high school campus was turned into a vibrant marketplace of food stalls, many of which were attended to by the mothers of the students.

Students and staff came dressed in traditional outfits. Most preferred to wear outfits that they felt represented their cultural, ethnic, or national background, while others wore outfits from countries other than their own. One pair of students with whom I chatted wore outfits that represented each other's countries. A male Indian teacher came dressed in a Manchurian outfit complete with the round hat and fake braided queue ponytail attached to it. Others tried to have some fun by wearing costumes that represented their countries in a less conventional manner. Some male Chinese-speaking students came dressed in Hawaiian shirts and boxer shorts, cheekily claiming to be imitating petty Taiwanese gangsters. A few sporty male students who were Western nationals took advantage of the opportunity to flaunt their toned bodies by painting their national flags on their faces and bared chests. It was a lively festival with a kaleidoscopic display of costumes, food, and performances. The school indeed had reason to celebrate diversity. However, as I elaborate later (in chapter 8), the celebration of United Nations Day revealed a performance of diversity that emphasizes visible difference, such as nationality and "race," in forms that can be consumed.

Students: Being "International"

Having immersed myself for one year in TIS's campus life, it was apparent that the school was committed to fostering cosmopolitan outlooks and practices. Extracurricular activities encouraged students to engage with each other and the host country through charity work, such as raising funds and visiting orphanages. I observed classroom discussions that challenged students to consider views different from their own. In one ninth-grade Asian Studies class, the atmosphere became tense as they discussed religion. The teacher showed a documentary about a few Muslim individuals from culturally diverse backgrounds, including a white Texan convert, making the Haj pilgrimage to Mecca. During the discussion, there was a student who was atheist and another who was a committed Christian, and each seemed to feel uncomfortable with the other's view. At one point the atheist student said, "I don't think we need God." Though she added, "I don't want to offend anyone," for good measure, the tension between her and the other student was palpable. The Christian student tried to defend her beliefs, but I could feel that she was offended, as was the atheist student. A third student asked, "How different would the world be without religion?" The atheist student responded, "Religion makes people feel comfortable. If there was no religion then there'd be no chaos." The teacher himself used to be Christian but later decided to leave his faith. He ended the class discussion with, "I have to say this. Whatever religion changes your heart is good. To make you think about justice, equality, etc. It's the heart that is important." Later, some of the more senior students explained that they usually became better able to accept differing views as they matured in age.

One student noted that those who make obviously racist remarks may be ostracized by their peers until they learn to guard their mouths. Sometimes this was done in jest, and at other times not. My observations confirmed this strong stance against prejudice. A male student, Levi, whose mother was Indonesian and father was white American, was known to make racist remarks, particularly against Indonesia. When he did this, his friends "exiled" Levi, partly for fun, by banning him from entering their hangout area for either a few minutes or a whole recess break. Levi continued to engage in friendly conversation with his mates while walking around the periphery of the hangout area but was not allowed inside. On another occasion, Levi conveyed his strong dislike of Indonesia to me directly in such a way that another student, Maya, who was listening to our conversation, explicitly called him out for making racist statements, abruptly stood up, and left the scene to express her disapproval.

Likewise, a poetry reading from a past United Nations Day performance, which I watched on DVD, summarized what I refer to as the school's ideology of being international. The descriptive phrases used in the reading were imbued with notions of being international, global citizenship, and TCK-ness. Thirteen students took turns reading lines such as, "I am a stranger," "I am the mix of colors," "I am the misplaced foreigner," "I am the expatriate," "They thought I only spoke English,"

"I am the diverse sister," "But I won't care. I will not be treated as an outsider," "The wall will slowly crumble," "They will see I'm human too," and "Living in both worlds." The reading culminated with all the students declaring in unison, "(And they will accept), I too, I too, I too am a citizen of the world." The notion of belonging nowhere and everywhere at the same time, of visible diversity, of being third cultured, of being a citizen of the world permeated the discourse of being international at TIS.

Overall, TIS was a model international school in the way it managed diversity among its (economically privileged) students. The school's strategy of nurturing cosmopolitanism through close encounters with the Other in the transnational space of the school appeared effective. However, Daniel, who was the student council president during the first half of my fieldwork, argued to the contrary. While Daniel believed that schools like TIS offered "significant exposure [to] other cultures and other people" and valued this exposure, he also said, "I just don't think it's fool proof. I think there needs to be other elements." Immersion alone is not enough.

School Culture: It's American. It's European. It's Asian. It's International?

TIS's ideology of being international is premised on the assumption that transnational social and educational spaces are neutral when they are not. I asked students, staff, and parents at TIS what they thought was the dominant culture of the school or had the most influence on campus. The responses varied.

"Definitely American, I mean, they've got proms," said a male Japanese student in twelfth grade. British and German students concurred, and cited as proof the pep rallies that were associated with American culture and some courses in the curriculum that were American. A Dutch mother agreed, saying that in the Netherlands schools do not organize big sports events as they do at TIS. However, when I asked an American student the same question, he thought otherwise. In his view, the dominant cultural influence at TIS was British. He mentioned the International Baccalaureate program as evidence because it was modeled after the British university preparatory program. Each seemed to define the dominant culture of the school's transnational educational space by the influences that made it different from what they were used to.

In contrast, Shane, whose father was British and mother was Indonesian, confidently declared that the dominant culture was "Indonesian."

He hung out almost exclusively with the Indonesian-speaking groups, and held a competitive attitude toward the male English-speaking students despite being a British citizen himself. Shane defined the school culture by what *he* wanted it to be so that it would affirm his place in the school.

Meanwhile, a Japanese mother, who was married to an American man, said that the school was *too* Asian, using a slightly disapproving tone that suggested she would have preferred if it were less so. She seemed to feel that the strong Asian presence made the school less "international."

Most were unaware of the influence of their own culture on the school, but highly aware of how the school culture differed from that with which they were familiar or regarded as the norm. As the fieldwork unfolded, it became clear that the school administrators, teaching staff, and some parents felt that although TIS was supposed to be the "true" international school, its mission was compromised by the excessive presence of Korean students, mainly, and Indonesian students. These two student groups were perceived to be ethnocentric and unwilling to become international because they appeared to associate exclusively among themselves, even though this was not always the case. The Japanese groups were similarly perceived as ethnocentric but were less conspicuous due to their smaller size. Many among the school staff assumed that friendship circles were a matter of mere choice, and gave little consideration to the relations of power present in the school and the way these social relations constrain choices for friendship.

Mapping Student Cliques

On my first day at TIS, one of the teachers showed me an article in the school's student magazine entitled, "The great divide." The student article contended that while the school "provides the ideal setting for internationalism," students still practice "self-segregation based on characteristics ranging from nationality and religion, to even sexuality and extra-curricular activities." While some degree of social grouping is expected, the existence of "Korean," "Indonesian," and "Japanese" student hangout areas was a sore point for the school administrators. These groups were particularly apparent in the upper grades, which were the focus of this study. They appeared to be large, entrenched, nationality-based groups that were perceived by teachers and students as ethnocentric and self-segregating. But these groups were not cohesive wholes with indisputable boundaries. They are better described as Indonesian-speaking, Korean-speaking, and Japanese-speaking groups, based on their strong preference for these languages over others, to account for the national and ethnic diversity found in each group.

Meanwhile, there were student groups that represented, for the school, ideal "international" groups. These were the English-speaking groups that were racially (in the colonial sense of the term) diverse, and whose members were often referred to as "everyone" even though they only represented about a third of the student body. The English-speaking groups commonly referred to themselves using labels that described their smaller sub-cliques, such as "white kids," "stoners," "gossip girls," "Dutch boys," and so on. Of these, "white kids" was a rather ambiguous designation because it sometimes referred to the small high-status cliques among the English-speaking groups, and at other times to the English-speaking groups as a whole, depending on who was using the term—an insider or outsider to these groups.

There were many other smaller cliques as well as a lot of interaction between members of the various major groups. In the upper grades, there was a male Indian group and a noticeable mixed-grade Mandarin-speaking group, among others. There were some who regularly floated in and out of two or more groups and were not rooted in any because their network of friends spanned different groups. I refer to these students as "floaters." Some students, such as those who may have been friends when they were younger, were rarely seen together on campus though they may occasionally hang out together off campus. In other words, some had different sets of friends on and off campus. If cliques appeared distinct at TIS, it is because the campus environment reinforces boundaries that are more easily crossed or blurred outside the structured school grounds.

There was concern among the staff about the impact of the larger groups, which dominated the hangout areas, on student social dynamics. According to the school's public relations manager, it was intimidating to walk past some of the larger cliques even as an adult, let alone as a fellow student. She noted that a parent had asked the school administrators to make architectural changes to the hangout areas to reduce the cliquishness. But tearing down the main outdoor hangout areas was not an option during the semester. It was over the summer break that the school made some changes. The two-and-a-half-month "summer" break was based on the northern hemisphere calendar and occurred in the middle of my yearlong fieldwork that lasted from January to December of 2009. The twelfth-grade students that I observed during the first half of my fieldwork graduated in May of 2009.

When those who were previously in eleventh grade returned in early August as twelfth graders for the second half of my fieldwork, they found that the senior hangout area had changed a little. There were ten new sets of wooden picnic tables with large umbrellas installed in the main senior hangout area. The school staff wanted to see if the new arrangement would break the larger groups into smaller cliques. When the new semester began, the public relations manager apologetically said to me that she hoped the new tables did not disrupt my data. As it turned out, it made it easier for me to identify some of the smaller cliques because it caused the English-speaking and Indonesian-speaking groups among the new twelfth graders to hang out in smaller groups at different tables. The locations they chose to sit at reflected their status, as I will discuss in detail later.

Although the larger linguistically defined student groupings were observable in all grades, they were more distinct in the upper grades because cultural socialization plays a greater role in determining in-groups and out-groups as children become older. The school administrators mistakenly assumed that the groups that often use languages other than English to communicate among themselves did so because these groups were formed based on nationality or ethnicity. The administrators perceived these groups as problematic because they presented a less-than-integrated picture of TIS. The concern over the large number of students from particular nationalities led the school administrators to place a cap on the number of students enrolled from each nationality—except those with citizenship to countries represented by the foreign foundations that established the school, all of which were Western. This occurred the year after I had completed the fieldwork, but it was already being discussed while I was there. Although this decision appears reasonable on the surface as a measure to ensure the school has the "right" mix of students, it begs the question: Who gets to decide which sorts of mixes are acceptable and which are not? Who can decide who is or is not being international?

The Gatekeepers

Upon hearing about my research, it was not unusual to have teachers assure me that I had come to the right place because, they said, most of the students were "TCKs." Some added, however, that the Koreans were "not *really* TCKs" because they only hung out with other Koreans. Hanging out with those from the same ethnicity was taken as evidence of their inability to be international or interculturally competent. On another occasion, a teacher remarked over a casual chat that the Koreans tended to be "monocultural." This was despite the fact that almost all the Korean students were bilingual (Korean and English) and some trilingual (e.g., Indonesian), in contrast to the many in the English-speaking groups who were monolingual and had never attempted to hang out with the Koreans. According to this teacher, some stayed very much within the Korean community and did not "assimilate," while others branched out. The use of the word "assimilate" presupposes a one-way process in which there is a normative culture that all students are expected to adopt, as opposed to a mutual, interactive process where members of different cultural groups move toward one another.

The same was said of the students in the Indonesian-speaking groups. In late May, the school held a senior graduation breakfast for the class of 2009. The day before, I had seen florists come and set up flower arrangements at the high school tennis courts using jasmine that hung from a pillar that had decorations woven from young coconut leaves. When I arrived early on the day, large round tables with table cloths had been set up on one side of the courts and nearby was a long table lined up with silver-colored buffet trays.

Although I usually hang out with the students, that day I decided to sit with the teachers at one of the tables at the back. Students trickled in and filled up the seats one by one. The Indonesian students arrived late. By the time some of the Indonesian students leisurely walked in together, the other students had already sat with their usual friends at the tables. There were only two empty tables left. So the Indonesian students chose to sit at the empty table closest to the other students and furthest away from the teachers, where I was also sitting. It seemed like a logical teenage choice. Then, one of the staff members, a guidance counselor from North America, leaned over to another staff employee and myself as he pointed at the table where the Indonesian students had sat. He half whispered to us that the Indonesian students tend to separate themselves from the others. The other teacher agreed. I was puzzled that they had put the blame on the Indonesians who had nowhere else to sit. So I feigned ignorance and said, "Oh, really? And who else does that?" The counselor pointed to another table and said, "See the Japanese boys sitting over there?" He explained that it was the same for Koreans students. But after noticing that some of the Korean girls were sitting with the Japanese girls, he added the caveat that some of them do mingle with non-Koreans. The counselor suggested that the Indonesian students stick together because they come from wealthy families and are therefore from a different socioeconomic class compared to the other students.

Even though the Indonesian students had nowhere else to sit by the time they had arrived, it was the Indonesian students who were blamed for self-segregating, not the English-speaking students who had arrived earlier and who, like the others, had deliberately chosen to sit with their friends, in their own groups. Self-segregation as a practice was mainly associated with the non-English-speaking groups. The onus for integration was placed upon students who are not part of the normative English-speaking group(s). In part, the discourse that celebrates visible diversity based on race and nationality made the English-speaking groups appear more diverse and the Korean-, Japanese-, and Indonesian-speaking groups appear more homogenous than they were. The staff played an important role in deciding who was "international" or a "Third Culture Kid" and who self-segregated.

But not all students were able to be international in the way the school envisioned because to be international they needed Western capital, including fluency in English among other things. There is a productive tension between the transnational identities that the young people at TIS shared and the differences in the way they were able to practice being international. This tension needs to be understood within its sociohistorical context of a global trend toward the internationalization of education.

Internationalization of Education

According to Nadine Dolby and Aliya Rahman (2008), research on international education emerged 125 years ago and evolved with changing historical circumstances. Research had been sparse until the recent turn of the century when interest in international education and the number of international schools proliferated because "the pressure to 'be international' and to 'internationalize' dramatically intensified in all aspects of education" (ibid.: 679). However, research on the role of international schools in shaping cosmopolitan subjectivities is lacking despite growing scholarly recognition of its importance (Dolby and Rahman 2008; Hayden 2011; Hayden and Thompson 1995; Matthews and Sidhu 2005; Mitchell 2003; Rizvi 2009).

International schools are a context for international education. While the origins and definitions of international schools are contested, their growth reflects global developments (Hayden 2011; Hayden, Thomp-

son, and Walker 2002). According to Mary Hayden (2011: 214) the periods following the First and Second World War saw the first growth
spurts: "Schools such as the International School of Geneva and the Yo-
kohama International School, both originating in 1924 (Knight 1999;
Stanworth 1996), were founded largely as a means of catering for the
children of expatriate diplomats and employees of transnational organ-
isations who followed their parents' globally mobile professions around
the world, and for whom education provided locally—perhaps because
of language or a mismatch with university entrance requirements in the
home country—was deemed unsuitable." Decades later, teachers from
the Geneva school designed the International Baccalaureate program
after realizing that the cultural diversity within international schools
required a pedagogical approach that fosters open-mindedness and accommodates the "multiplicity of views" present in the classrooms (Hill
2007: 253; International Baccalaureate Organization 2013a).

Existing research has hitherto made distinctions between national
and international schools by assessing their purposes and outcomes.
National curricula and schools, which in the twentieth century were
used for nation building, were concerned with turning "subjects to
citizens" (Parker 2003; see also Rizvi 2009). National schools are perceived as a site for the cultural reproduction of national class structures. In contrast, international education prepares "young people to
cope with life in an increasingly interdependent world" (Hayden and
Thompson 1995: 328). It arguably turns national citizens into "global
citizens" suited for a globalizing world (Phillips 2002; Resnik 2008).

More recently, Hayden (2011: 215) argues that earlier categoriza-
tions of international schools have been "overtaken by events" and
calls for new research approaches that recognize that national and international education may be merging (see also Hill 2007). Economic
globalization has led to the growth of the transnational capitalist class
(Sklair 2001), and the increased need for national elites and upwardly
mobile classes to acquire cosmopolitan capital (e.g., Peterson 2011).
These groups are converging with greater intensity in educational contexts. The "postcolonial elite" of host countries are increasingly opt-
ing for international education (Hayden 2011: 217). Fazal Rizvi (2009)
notes that national educational spaces are also becoming more diverse
and transnational as the internationalization of education continues.
Hayden (2011: 220) summarizes, "On the one hand, national education systems are introducing international elements.... On the other
hand, international education in the form of international schools has
rapidly emerged as a means of catering not only for the globally mobile
professional classes, but also for the socio-economically advantaged

national elites for whom an English-medium form of education is perceived to bestow further advantage."

In Indonesia, this merging of categories is aptly illustrated in the recent move to bring schools that previously came under the two separate categories of national and international schools under the single SPK category by requiring schools to incorporate both national and international elements of education. International education is a highly sought-after commodity. As providers of international education, both private national schools that incorporate international elements for their mostly local students and international schools that cater mainly to the children of expatriate professionals can cost as much as approximately USD 33,000 per year at the high school level.[14]

Nevertheless, studies of international schools and their students are constrained by a methodological approach that is unable to adequately address these changes because it uses the nation-state as the analytical starting point (Wimmer and Glick Schiller 2002). Methodological nationalism focuses on binaries that contrast international education with national education and international schools with national schools (Hayden and Thompson 1995; Lallo 2008; Wylie 2008). It constructs difference as national difference. Thus the research often implies that international schools are better than national schools because they help students transcend national differences. Students who prefer to mingle with those who speak the same national language are assumed to be unable to overcome national differences and to have failed to become international. Methodological nationalism is unable to conceive of cosmopolitan practices as diverse because its analytical framework is dependent on binaries such as national-international and parochial-cosmopolitan.

Methodological nationalism is further unable to conceive of class structures as transnational. Consequently, it overlooks the role of international schools in reproducing the cosmopolitan capital of the transnational capitalist class. Instead, the literature differentiates between schools that are ideologically driven or market driven (Hayden 2011). Some scholars argue that international education promotes international mindedness, which in turn produces responsible global citizens (Gellar 2002: 178). Failure to do so is not attributed to any flaw in international education, but to the narrow-mindedness of students and parents (Tamatea 2008). This interpretation exempts the ideology of being international from critique. These same assumptions which attribute failure to the individual, were reflected at TIS.

The two-dimensional approach to defining international schools and their clientele is unhelpful. To be sure, some researchers have begun

to problematize the dichotomous approach that prevails in the literature (Bunnell 2014). Hayden (2011), for example, recognizes that the
national and international may be merging in the international school
sector, and calls for an approach that views international schools as
transnational spaces and their students' cultural identities as complex.
Meanwhile, others prefer to avoid interrogating the term "international
school" for political reasons. Tristan Bunnell (2014: 42) notes that one
author expressed concern in 2003 that a prolonged discussion on this
matter could highlight the "hegemonic aspect" of the international
school "as a form of education of the 'globally mobile, mercantile elite.'"
Bunnell (2014) himself contends that such an inquiry is necessary. It is
precisely this "hegemonic aspect" that I address by interrogating the
concepts of "international" and "national" in both the literature and in
practice. These concepts are neither self-evident nor mutually exclusive, as though they belong on opposite ends of a dichotomy.

International schools reproduce social and cultural capital that is increasingly defining both the transnational capitalist class and national
elites. Don Weenink (2008: 1091) refers to this social and cultural capital as "cosmopolitan capital," which he defines as "a propensity to engage in globalizing social arenas" and "bodily and mental predisposi-
tions and competencies (savoir faire) which help to engage confidently
in such arenas." Mark Allen Peterson (2011: 7), in his study of Egyptian upper classes, conceives cosmopolitanism as a "set of practices
(Bourdieu 1977; 1984) through which the Egyptian upper classes and
those with upwardly mobile aspirations construct themselves as transnational elites." Cosmopolitan capital includes Western education, fluency in English, international mobility, global social networks, familiarity with global popular culture, and certain ways of carrying oneself.

Phillip Brown and Hugh Lauder (2009: 144) argue that we need
"a far more nuanced account of education and social class" that considers the "mosaic of global power and privilege that is part nation-
ally based and part transnationally based." The ability to engage with
those who are different, as implied in the notion of being international,
is nurtured within this mosaic of power. As Rizvi (2009: 284) notes,
"identities are forged in histories of differentially constituted relations
of power; that is, knowledges, subjectivities, and social practices, including practices of cultural negotiation, are established within asym-
metrical and often incommensurate cultural spaces, even more so in
transnational spaces." The globalizing marketplace has made class
structures increasingly transnational. Education is internationalizing
to accommodate this change. Our understanding of these changes also
needs a paradigm shift.

Shifting the Paradigm

This book studies the social realities of an international school in Indonesia within these global trends. I use an anthropological approach to empirically test the ideological basis of international schools. I conceptualize TIS as a transnational (social and educational) space located within the national territory of Indonesia and treat the national and transnational as mutually constitutive (Smith 2001). At TIS, diverse national and transnational structures converge within a local setting. National and transnational discourses intersect in nuanced ways to influence the social dynamics on campus. The convergence of a diverse set of young people who are in pursuit of the same cosmopolitan capital produces diverse ways of practicing cosmopolitanism. However, the ideology of being international has yet to recognize that cosmopolitan practices are diverse. This book explores the tension that emerges out of this mismatch by using methodological cosmopolitanism, by which I mean that I use the transnational (rather than the national) as my analytical point of departure. I assume that cosmopolitanism is the norm at TIS, and by doing so I am able to focus on exploring the diverse ways in which people engage in cosmopolitan practices rather than trying to define the ideal form of cosmopolitanism or who would fit into such a category.

Using a postcolonial lens, I problematize the international school as a transnational site of cultural (re)production where colonial and capitalist discourses intersect. This book will make visible the Eurocentrism of the dominant form of cosmopolitanism and denaturalize its universality. I argue that international schools reproduce the transnational capitalist class and national elites by maintaining cultural hierarchies that privilege Western cosmopolitan capital. In the next chapter, I illustrate the overarching importance of language in shaping cosmopolitan subjectivities. English in particular is a powerful form of cultural capital that enables transnational youth to practice cosmopolitanism as defined by TIS's ideology of being international.

Notes

1. Throughout this chapter and the book, information that can identify the school has been deliberately left vague or omitted and only approximate figures have been provided to maintain the school's anonymity.
2. Interview with a teacher, 25 August 2009.
3. Thirty-one of these "international schools" were established prior to the 1998 upheaval. Although the definition of "international schools" is con-

tested, Kustulasari (2009) classifies these thirty-one schools as "international" because they offered international curricula or were founded by foreign foundations.

4. The incredibly diverse range of "international schools" listed indicate both a lack of clarity with regard to the definition of "international schools" and the eagerness with which schools advertise themselves as "international" (Hayden 2011; Hayden and Thompson 1995; Hayden, Thompson, and Walker 2002).

5. Like international schools, many national plus schools were liberal in the way they defined "plus" in the education service they provide.

6. Adding a Chinese (Mandarin)–language component became popular after 2001 when the government ban on Chinese-language material was lifted.

7. The full title is "Law of the Republic of Indonesia Number 20 of the Year 2003 on the National Education System" (*Undang-undang Republik Indonesia nomor 20 tahun 2003 tentang system pendidikan nasional*).

8. Chapter 37, Article 1.

9. The full title is "Regulation of the Ministry of Education and Culture of the Republic of Indonesia Number 31 of the Year 2014" (*Peraturan Menteri Pendidikan dan Kebudayaan Republik Indonesia Nomor 31 Tahun 2014*).

10. It can be translated as "Collaborative Education Unit" (Expat Website Association 2015).

11. Some of the other support staff, such as security guards and cleaners, were contracted from private companies that provide such services.

12. Other attacks included the Marriott Hotel bombing in 2003, the Australian embassy bombing in 2004, and the second Bali bombing in 2005.

13. This was an unusual color for police cars in Indonesia. I presume it was chosen because it serves as a conspicuous sign to convey that TIS is protected by the state apparatus. One alumni claimed that the orange police car was there for a few years. Even now, similar cars are parked, seemingly perpetually, in conspicuous areas in front of foreign embassies in Jakarta.

14. This figure is an approximation of the tuition fee quoted by the International School of Geneva. In Jakarta, tuition fees for international schools range from approximately USD 8,000 to USD 26,000, not including mandatory capital development and enrollment fees, which can add about USD 5,500 to the cost annually per student. All fees quoted are for the academic year 2016–2017.

CHAPTER 2

The Power of English

> When I spoke English, I felt smart!
> —Lianne

English-language ability plays a profound role in shaping cosmopolitan ideologies, practices, and subjectivities. It give access to power and shapes identities (Burck 2005). On the one hand, we speak language—we use it as an instrumental tool, for example, to assert (racialized) identities or to gain competitive advantage in a globalized marketplace. On the other hand, language constructs us as cultural beings. The language we speak and the accent we speak it with tell a story of where we have been and where we are going. Others use that information to place us within their internalized sociocultural hierarchies.

One of the most obvious markers of being "international" at TIS was fluency in English, preferably native fluency, and preferably with the "right" accent. As an English-medium school, the dominance of English was reinforced in many aspects of the school: English language–based curriculum, teaching staff that was predominantly Anglophone, the separation between mainstream classes and classes for those who still needed English-language support, as well as the prominence of the English-language student groups in the psyche of both students and teachers as the most "international" of all student groups. The willingness of parents to pay the high tuition fees to ensure that their children have not only a good command but also a *natural* command of English attest to the economic value of the English language.

The conflation of English-language fluency with being international and the high status with which it is accorded deeply impacts the subjectivities of transnational youth and their relations with others, including family members and each other. Language plays a significant role in defining social relations at TIS. Specifically, this chapter analyzes the way colonial and contemporary capitalist discourses imbue English with power.

Becoming "International" by Speaking English

The role of English as a marker of cosmopolitan cultural capital at TIS was most visible to those who, like Jenny, did not speak it at home. I had met Jenny's mother, Mee Yon, at a Korean parents' meeting a few weeks before interviewing Jenny. Mee Yon was one of the few Korean mothers who were able to converse in English and she was the one who introduced me to Jenny. At home, Jenny spoke Korean. However, she was able to speak English like a native speaker because she had attended TIS since the second grade. Jenny at the time hung out mostly with the eleventh-grade English-speaking groups that consisted of students of varying nationalities and ethnic backgrounds, including most of the students from English-speaking countries.

That evening, I visited the high-rise condominium where Jenny and Mee Yon were living. It was located in a prime Jakarta suburb. Mee Yon had invited me to join them for dinner at their home. It was just the two of them and, as was customary among middle- and upper-class residents of Indonesia, probably a maid living in the large two-story unit of the condominium. Jenny's father had repatriated earlier to Korea for work and her brother was studying at an Ivy League university in the United States. Jenny and Mee Yon had stayed behind in Jakarta so that Jenny, who was in eleventh grade at the time, could finish high school at TIS. I was there to interview Jenny and had not anticipated that the dinner would be a lavish assortment of sushi and Korean delicacies. Only three interviews out of one hundred and forty were conducted over a meal—the other two were with Mee Yon alone and a friend of mine who had graduated from the same international school as me in Singapore. I ate as much as I could that evening to be polite, but there was clearly enough for twice the number of people present. After dinner, the pair led me to the study with a plate of fruits, where I interviewed Jenny.

Among other things, I asked Jenny about her friendships. Over the years, Jenny had hung out with Korean-speaking and English-speaking groups at different times. In describing her changing friendship circles, Jenny said, "In high school, the Koreans divided more. So I hung out with this one Korean group who were really, like, 'international,' sort of." She made air quotes as she said the word "international." I asked her what made this Korean group international and she responded, "They spoke English." It is likely that they had more in common than simply their language preference, but what is pertinent is that Jenny automatically associated speaking English with being international. It is this association that contributes to the way using other languages, such as Indonesian and Korean, as the primary mode of communication is associated with being simply Indonesian or Korean, but *not* being international.

Jenny seemed a little shy on the evening I interviewed her in her relaxed house clothes and without makeup. But when I saw her a few days later on campus, she seemed more confident and almost like a different person. She wore dark eyeliner, which was typical of some of the girls in the more popular English-speaking and Indonesian-speaking groups.

Jenny was not the only one who associated speaking English with being international. Mina, a Japanese student in her senior year, felt that speaking English made her *"kokusaiteki,"* which is the Japanese term for being international. I met Mina in the first two weeks of being at TIS in an upper-level IB class for second-language speakers of English. It was a class of sixteen students consisting mainly of Japanese, Koreans, and Indonesians, most of whom were ethnically Chinese, as well as an Italian and a German. Although the students were enrolled as second-language speakers of English, at least half the class sounded like native speakers and spoke with a North American accent. A few in fact had a better command of English than they did their native tongues because they had done most of their schooling in English. The Indonesian students in the class often mixed English and Indonesian when speaking to each other. In contrast, among the Japanese and Korean students there seemed to be a strict unspoken rule against mixing their languages with English—a rule I felt compelled to obey when speaking to Mina and her three male Japanese classmates.

When the class broke into small groups, the teacher, Rick Lindsay, gave me permission to walk around the room and talk to the students. When I approached the four Japanese students sitting together, I struck up a conversation in Japanese because it felt unnatural to speak to them in any other language. At the beginning of class I had introduced myself in English, so when the four found out for the first time that I spoke native-sounding Japanese, they were intrigued. Mostly, they asked me about my cultural background and research. In turn, I found out that one of them was known by his English name, "John," because he was born in the United States and another, Koichi, had spent most of his life in Indonesia and was fluent in Indonesian. All four were eager to talk to me as though they saw in me a "cultural broker"—an adult with whom they could relate to even though I also seemed to be part of the dominant English-speaking culture, which was inaccessible to them, by virtue of my native command of English (Geertz 1960: 228; Wolf 1956). In fact, when I bumped into Mina later on in the day as she made her way between classes, she said, almost pleadingly, "Are you free in the last period? Because I need to talk to you."

I met up with Mina for a chat during the last period at the Japanese hangout area in front of the library. It turned out that Mina had much to say on what it means to be "international" and her pent-up frustration with her Japanese schoolmates who, in her view, only socialized with each other. Mina had lived in Jakarta twice. The first time was from the ages of one to eight. When she was in the third grade, her family repatriated to Japan. They later returned to Jakarta when she was about to start eleventh grade. Both times she attended TIS. According to Mina, her parents enrolled her at TIS instead of the Jakarta Japanese School, where most Japanese expatriate children in Indonesia study, because they wanted her to be international. Mina explained, "For starters, both my parents say that they wanted me to be *kokusaiteki*. And my name is 'Mina' because 'Mina' is something that's easy for foreigners to pronounce, right? That's why I got the name 'Mina.'" She followed this explanation with an elaborate account of her relationship with the English language.

> So I attended TIS and ... the Japanese kids who I knew, like when there was a social gathering for all the families at Dad's company, the Japanese kids—the ones who were my age—all went to the Japanese school. And I never felt down at all about this, for being different from the others. In fact, it made me happy. I was fascinated in the sense that, "Oh, so I can speak English," or "I have a different world from these people"—fascinated as in like ... I've always liked the feeling of having something that others don't.

Speaking English and attending an international school gave Mina a sense of distinction that set her apart from others (Bourdieu 1984).

This sense of distinction remained even when she returned to Japan for several years. When she told her classmates in Japan that she was a *kikokushijo*, or returnee student (see Goodman 1990), she said, "They would say to me, 'Can you read the English writing on this mug out loud?' I was in third grade and I'd say, 'Blah, blah, blah, blah' in English, and they would all be like, 'Wooooowwwwwwww!' So then I was really happy 'cause I thought, 'Cool, I'm different. Yeah, I'm different because I speak English.'" Fluency in English accorded Mina privileged status within the Japanese community both while she was in Indonesia and back in Japan.

So upon hearing that her father was going to be restationed in Indonesia, she begged her parents to send her back to TIS where she had memories of a school with a lot of "freedom," especially in terms of students mingling freely with others of diverse backgrounds. But when Mina returned to Jakarta and to TIS at the start of eleventh grade, she was deeply disappointed. Far from how she had remembered it to be in elementary school, Mina found that the high school students at TIS hung out in their language groups instead of mingling with others.

She was critical of all the cliques on campus, but the first on her hit list were her Japanese classmates, some of whom were in Mr. Lindsay's English class with her earlier that day. "They're basically building walls around themselves," Mina complained. Mina perceived them as not being international despite the fact that, for example, Koichi was trilingual with fluency in Japanese, Indonesian, and English, regularly hung out with his Indonesian classmates, and had dated a Korean girl in the past. Meanwhile, her other classmate John had chosen to not hang out with those from the English-speaking groups due to a difference in values. He could not relate to what he saw as their casual dating culture.

In contrast, Mina saw herself as more "international" than her Japanese classmates because even though she did not join the main English-speaking groups, she went out of her way to make friends with those who were not Japanese. I regularly saw her hanging out during recess with friends from the Netherlands, Iran, the United States, Mongolia, and India. Mina constructed herself as more international and therefore better than her Japanese peers, and her use of English with her friends contributed to her sense of being international.

"English is the Power Language"

English gives the speaker status in various contexts, and children internalize this at a young age. Rick Lindsay, Mina's English teacher from North America, saw the impact that English had on his children from both his previous and current marriages to Indonesian women.

> RICK: English is the power language. I know from my background as a teacher, it's the power language. Even within families, children quite early sense which is the power language, and they go to the power language.... There's research that backs me up on this, and I know from my own children as well—English has power.

> DT: Even though they've been at a local [Indonesian] school the whole time?

RICK: Yeah, and their mother's an Indonesian speaker and so on. That's why now—I've got with my new wife, we've got a daughter, two years old—we're trying to do everything we can to get her to speak good Indonesian, but English is the power language.... It's perceived as the dominant language ... by everybody. So that even on television, you know ... watching Indonesian television, I do all the time, even a gossip program—the celebrities break into English. The people being interviewed on the news will use English and they appear, I think, somehow to the general population as wiser or more educated or more trendy, whatever. Whatever they're gonna call it, it's perceived as a good thing. So to use formal correct Indonesian is almost laughed at now. But to use English, oooh, that's good, impressive. And kids pick up on that. They don't realize it, but they gravitate towards the language that has the power. So in the bilingual family I think it's hard to get the children to speak the weaker language.

Despite raising his children with his Indonesian wife in Indonesia, Rick finds that it requires much effort to encourage them to speak the local language that they hear everyday. It is counterintuitive for his children to speak "the weaker language" because cultural hierarchies are intimately tied to language.

The Coloniality and Globality of English

Indeed, the predominance of English and its effect on sociocultural hierarchies across the globe have historical roots, as Norma Field (1996) attests: "the primacy of English is inseparable from the history of the British Empire and postwar American global domination." English-language teaching was central to the British colonial project (Pennycook 1998), including the cultivation of native populations that were "British in taste." Homi Bhabha (1984: 126) writes that "mimicry" of the colonizer's language by the colonized "emerges as one of the most elusive and effective strategies of colonial power and knowledge." It was effective because mimicry was never perfect, rendering the colonial subject forever inadequate—"*almost the same, but not quite*" (Bhabha 1984, emphasis in original). Speaking the colonizer's language and being educated in their ways came to signify a sense of social distinction that colonial subjects continually desired and pursued, thus consolidating the colonizer's dominant position (Bourdieu 1986: 243). Discursive relations between the language of the colonizer and colonized, whereby the former is constructed as superior to the latter, endure to the present day, though they have shifted to accommodate the hegemony of English as the most powerful of all colonial languages. Colonial discourses on culture, language, and "race" linger as they continue to shape the subjectivities of transnational young people and reproduce sociocultural hierarchies.

In Indonesia, it was fluency in Dutch that signified elite status during colonial times. In Java, the traditional *priyayi* nobility and others drew on their exposure to Dutch education, particularly their mastery of the languages spoken by those in power during colonial times, to reconstruct themselves as modern elites (Gerke 2000). According to Selo Soemardjan (1962: 129), "The rise of the intelligentsia to the upper class was recognised by other classes, which tried to acquire the external symbols of this new class by wearing Western-style dress and walking around with a dispatch case in one hand and a fountain pen showing in the upper pocket of the jacket. But by far the most distinguishing symbol of the new upper class was the use of foreign languages, namely Dutch or English." The linguistic markers of distinction remain relevant today. The legacy of Dutch colonialism on local subjectivities is present in the data collected for this research, albeit subtly. Participants who identified as Indonesian in one way or another would commonly mention—without me asking—that one of their grandparents or great grandparents was of European (usually Dutch, sometimes German or Portuguese) descent, or that one or more of their grandparents speak Dutch because they had been educated in Dutch-medium schools.[1] These references to a European connection imply a sense of distinction, that they were different from and superior to the general population in Indonesia.

Two Indonesian university students, Dina and her close friend Camellia, perceived a clear hierarchy of languages among the colonial (Dutch), national (Indonesian), and regional (Javanese) languages in the way they were used in their homes. Although they were not TIS graduates, I interviewed them because they had spent some time overseas before they graduated from high school. While Camellia had only spent one year as a high school exchange student in Italy, Dina had an extensive internationally mobile upbringing, growing up in Indonesia, France, Norway, and Chile because her father was a diplomat. Both Dina's and Camellia's grandparents were Dutch educated and their parents and relatives grew up speaking Dutch.

Neither understood more than a few words of Dutch themselves but they had such similar experiences and perceptions of the way sociocultural hierarchies affected language use among their family members that they kept finishing each others' sentences when I interviewed them together. Dina and Camellia believed that the elders in their families speak Dutch for two reasons: "when they have secrets," such as when they talk about financial matters, and as a mark of distinction.

> DINA: Arrogance. Arrogance. ... They have this attitude when they talk in Dutch. Different when they talk in, it's different, I sense it when they're talking in Indonesian or in English, and then suddenly they switched [sic] to Dutch, it's different. It's the attitude.
>
> CAMELIA: Yeah me too.
>
> DINA: The attitude is, it's like they feel like more "aristocratical" [sic].
>
> CAMELIA: Yeah because ...
>
> DINA: They got the um attitude [puts her chin up in the air].
>
> CAMELIA: No, no, because like this [puts on a facial expression of conceit that outdoes Dina's].
>
> DINA: They have the attitude for being, "We are more important." I think it's because of the colonial stuff, because they always consider that.
>
> CAMELIA: It's true.
>
> DINA: Because only the Dutch educated are considered more, like, well known, educated and, like, hail the Dutch.
>
> CAMELIA: My grandmother, she only speaks Javanese with the, how do you say it ...
>
> DINA: Maids.
>
> CAMELIA: My housemaids or house servants. And they speak Dutch with her family, with her siblings, or with my mom, or with ... or with some important people. But not with the grandchildren and not with other people.
>
> DINA: So you see there are languages that separate us.
>
> CAMELIA: Just make them, like, they are exclusive or something.
>
> DINA: Yes. Dutch is for the exclusive part, Indonesian is like for us, for the kids, and then the dialect is like for the maids. (Interview, 13 November 2009)

Language is tied to class and status. The former colonizer's language had the highest status as the language used with the elders in the family and "important people." By speaking Dutch, the speaker is able to draw on the cultural capital that they inherited through their historical connections to the Dutch-educated elites of colonial times. The national language occupies the middle status, while "dialects" (regional languages) are perceived as low status and associated with lower-class workers. While Dina's reference to Javanese as a "dialect" is partly due to limitations in her English skills, it also suggests the tendency to see regional languages as inferior and not even worthy of being called a language.

In more recent times, the shift from a colonial to a capitalist economic order dominated by the United States saw (American) English replace Dutch as the main nonindigenous language that marks status and privilege. "If the coloniality of the English language is undeniable," B. Kumaravadivelu (2006: 13) observes, "so is its globality," as seen in the dominance of English in scholastic, linguistic, cultural, and economic realms. So dominant is the English language that Robert Phillipson (1992: 2), known for his book *Linguistic Imperialism*, declares, "whereas once Britannia ruled the waves, now it is English which rules them." This has implications for the study of transnational youth and the way language influences their perceptions. A sense of distinction can be derived from having fluency in English, attending English-medium schools such as international schools, and/or having partial European descent (including, e.g., white American). Fluency in English is associated with elite education and having access to the wealth and opportunities found in the international market (Imam 2005), and thereby with cosmopolitan cultural capital.

English as a marker of privilege is often desired at the expense of the national language. Some Indonesian parents and grandparents take pride in their children's inability to speak fluent Indonesian despite being raised in Indonesia. One couple in Jakarta explained that their eldest elementary school–aged grandchild sometimes gets the word order wrong when speaking Indonesian. "When she speaks Indonesian, she has a *bule* [white people][2] accent," added the grandfather with a chuckle. Far from being concerned by this, he seemed to delight in it. Syeda Rumnaz Imam (2005: 478) writes of a similar situation in Bangladesh where the English educated are illiterate in the national language and "tend to look down on" those educated in the national language.

As educational institutions, English-medium international schools like TIS are in a position to shape perceptions in ways that reflect "cultural constructions of colonialism" due to the symbolic meaning of power and privilege vested in the English language (Pennycook 1998: 19). Bill Ashcroft (2001: 39) writes that, for the "colonized child," being educated in the colonizer's language was a process of "hegemony, ideology, interpellation and language" coming together in a "powerful instance of subject formation." While international-school students today are not being colonized, being educated in a language seen as superior to their own still has a similarly powerful influence. Inter-

national schools interpellate or give identity to young people by promoting ways of being "international" that privilege Western cultural
capital, such as the English language.

"When I Spoke English I Felt Smart!"

Lianne, an alumna of TIS, was surprised to find herself speaking at
great length about her relationship with the English language as she
shared her story with me. It was then that she realized that English
had a significant influence on her life due to its symbolic power (interview, 25 July 2009). Lianne speaks English with what sounds to most
like an American accent. According to her passport, however, she is
Singaporean. Her father is Singaporean and her mother is Indonesian.
Lianne grew up in Indonesia, but completed most of her schooling at
TIS. While she now speaks English with native fluency and considers
it her strongest language, it was not always so. When she first attended
TIS in kindergarten, she spoke Indonesian more than English and was
placed in an ESOL class.

We sat at Lianne's kitchen counter as I interviewed her. The morning
sun, or at least the rays that made it through the smog, shone through
the glass windows of the fully air-conditioned Jakarta condominium.
Ten minutes into the interview I asked her what it had been like to
learn English as a second language when she first started attending
TIS. She said, "It was fun, you know, because I loved languages and
I still do. And I think it was fun because I was becoming smarter."
Lianne straightened her back on her kitchen stool, held her head up,
and pointed her nose into the air—all to illustrate, in a playful manner,
the uppity attitude she used to have with regard to her ability to speak
English. "When I spoke English I felt smart!" Lianne laughed. She then
explained why it made her feel smart as she talked about her relationship with her mother. True to her attractive, charismatic nature, she
was expressive and spoke animatedly throughout by manipulating the
intonation, volume, and speed of her speech. "'Cause my mom spoke
to me in Bahasa [Indonesian].[3] My mom speaks great English. She
speaks very well, she's able to communicate, but she prefers to speak
in her native tongue. So that later on I find out, when I'm eighteen or
whatever ... she didn't want me to lose my native tongue. That's why
she kept talking to me in Bahasa. But, you know, the more I learned
English, the more I was able to talk *back* to her in English. And it made
me feel *smart*. So it was fun." Lianne spat out the word "smart" with
gusto and accompanied her speech with lots of facial and hand ges-

tures to emphasize her spoken words. When I noted this, she laughed and explained,

> Yeah, that's ... that's another thing. I remember coming home from school, and I picked up *facial* and *hand gestures* [again, she says the italicized words with gusto]. And, and my mom was like, "Huuuhhh?" I don't think that Indonesians speak with their face ... or they speak with their hands. ... I think it's mostly through words. And so that was another one that I completely, you know, was oblivious to until my mom was like [Lianne changes her voice to sound like a theatrical version of a frustrated mother], "Stop raising your, your hands, they're everywhere!" She would tell me to stop [slows down her speech and softens her voice almost to a whisper]. But I would never because, like I told you, it made me *feel smart* [picks up speed again and rapidly rattles off the italicized words], so much more *clever* than my mom. [Laughs.]

So symbolically powerful is the English language that even as a child Lianne was able to use it to challenge her mother's authority (see Burck 2005). The more her English improved, the more Lianne was able to "talk *back*" to her mother. While Lianne's mother had a good command of English, she did not have native fluency and found herself on the less powerful end of the native-nonnative dichotomy compared to her own daughter. Lianne had gained a natural, native command of English, including the embodied language of gestures, through her educational environment.

TIS molded Lianne's embodied sense of place or habitus such that even as a child she intuitively understood the symbolic power embedded in the English language (Bourdieu and Thompson 1991). Lianne had also acquired a "feel for the game" that is largely dependent on what Bourdieu (1990: 66, 69–70) refers to as "bodily *hexis*," or cultural capital in its embodied form. Bodily hexis encompasses the way a person moves, sits, speaks (e.g., accents), and so on. It tells a story of where we have been and where we are going. A shared bodily hexis contributes to a sense of mutual intelligibility. Bodies express history, as Jenkins (1992: 75) writes, through "the manner and style in which actors 'carry themselves': stance, gait, gesture, etc." Bodily hexis is like the "jizz" of a bird—a term used by birdwatchers to describe "the overall impression or appearance of a bird garnered from such features as shape, posture, flying style or other habitual movements, size and colouration combined with voice, habitat and location" (Birdlife Australia 2013: 3).[4] The origin of the term is unclear (McDonald 1996). Some attribute it to World War II fighter pilots who trained to instantly identify an enemy aircraft by its "GISS" (General Impression, Shape, and Size)—by its features and the way it sat in the air. Others believe the term originated from a corrupted pronunciation of the word "gestalt." It is said that Sean Dooley, an avid birdwatcher, described giss as "the indefinable quality of a particular species, the 'vibe' it gives off'" (Birdlife Australia 2013: 3). Lianne had a giss that betrayed the Western influences she was exposed to at TIS.

Lianne's account of her relationship with English also demonstrates that the postcolonial context of Indonesia magnifies the symbolic power of the English language. The vast economic inequality between the majority of Indonesians and those in the expatriate community reinforces the value of cultural capital associated with the ability to speak English, which is conflated with high status. I asked Lianne how she felt about Indonesians who do not speak English very well, and she was forthcoming about it: "If now, no, I don't care. Before, oh my god, when I was a little kid I would've been a snob about it. Yeah, I would've been a complete snob about it because it means I'm much more superior. Oh, come on you know, there are some things that's like, passed on to you because of [these international schools]." Lianne was soliciting my agreement because she knew I had similarly attended international schools. I laughed with empathy as Lianne continued,

> You should know this. It's like some stool. All of a sudden you're on like a pedestal.... There was a feeling of superiority, definitely, because of the affiliation, because of the command of language, because of people you hang out with, because of the extracurricular activities that were bountiful, the subject we studied, like, come on [again, she solicited my agreement and I nodded].... You know that it was much more advanced, if not interesting, than the local schools. And so, back then ... if the person I was communicating with is not up to my standard, like, forget it. Complete snob.

The inequality between the international and local school environments amplified the sense of cultural superiority associated with speaking English. It was like being placed on a "pedestal."

But the feeling of superiority started to wear off as Lianne grew up. Her negative views toward Indonesia were challenged when she was in tenth or eleventh grade:

> All of a sudden you're going out and you're meeting people from the German school, the French school.... And then for me it was also church because I got my first communion, I had to take lessons with a whole bunch of Indonesians who actually were very cool people [she laughs], you know. It changed. It was humbling because I realized, "Oh there was a world outside of TIS that could have been equally as interesting and equally as awesome."

This girl Mira, she opened up my eyes. She went to school in Oklahoma, I think, and she's Indonesian, and just interacting with her helped me to understand that it was okay—there's a whole different world. And of course by then you were studying world economics, and world studies or whatever it is ... and, "Oh, the world is beyond" [laughs], you know. ... And I had a girlfriend whose boyfriend was, like, a rich Indonesian boy and ... when we hung out with him, it's like, "Aaah [puts on a surprised look], ohhh, okay." Yeah, like, oh my god, there's a whole different world of interesting and awesome and privilege and ... yeah, and money.

Lianne also explained that the "very cool" Indonesians spoke English. Meeting Indonesians who were financially privileged and had Western cultural capital, such as speaking English and going to school in Oklahoma, was "humbling" for Lianne because it disrupted the construction of "Indonesian" as inferior. Even then, however, being "cool" was still associated with financial privilege and exposure to the West.

There were differing attitudes toward speaking Indonesian among those at TIS who were not Indonesian by nationality. There was a wide range of abilities among students who had spent most of their lives growing up in Indonesia. Some, like Rajesh, an Indian national, Stephan, a French national, and Vlad, a Russian national, had native fluency in Indonesian. Rajesh's American friend Tom, however, only had a mediocre command of the language. When I met him, Tom was in eleventh grade and taking private lessons to improve his Indonesian. Tom started taking lessons after realizing that he would soon be returning to the United States for college and had very little to show for the years that he had spent in Indonesia, which accounted for most of his life. There were also many students who could hardly string a sentence together in Indonesian. At the extreme end was Darren, who was of mixed Indian and Australian background. Darren said that if he got into a taxi in Jakarta and the driver could not speak English, he would get out. He said that when he came to Indonesia at about age six, he had as much interest in Indonesian as he did "in a cockroach." These sorts of negative expressions were rarely used, and it is hard to tell why Darren opted to use such strong language. Nevertheless, it did reflect Rajesh's belief that his classmates' inability to speak Indonesian had much to do with their lack of interest in Indonesia. The lack of interest was precipitated by Indonesia's perceived status as an economically and culturally inferior country.

Cultural hierarchies have a profound impact on the perceptions held by transnational youth of themselves and others. Many internalize the structural hierarchies and learn to distance themselves from the inferior, such as Indonesia, and align themselves with the superior, such as the West.

Switching Accents

Accents are also markers of privilege and belonging. Within English, there are distinctions between acceptable and not-so-acceptable accents that are indexed according to a global linguistic order led by the United States and Britain.[5] These distinctions produce varying responses among those who engage with the Anglophone world. At TIS, South Asian students were particularly adept at switching between accents. When the bell rang at lunch break on a typical day, male South Asian students in their senior year (predominantly Indian, with one Pakistani) dashed out of their classrooms speaking with a general "American" accent. One by one, they found each other as they started walking toward the cafeteria, and eventually merged into one group somewhere down the hallway, by which time they were speaking with a distinct South Asian accent. Their practice of switching accents illustrates the complex ways in which "hegemony, ideology, interpellation and language" come together to shape cosmopolitan subjectivities (Ashcroft 2001: 39).

Speaking in a not-so-acceptable accent has negative implications. Akshat was the sole Indian male in his grade who could speak English only with an Indian accent. According to his friend Devraj, people "don't take him seriously." Devraj noted that an Australian teacher had once praised Akshat for speaking English well when in fact it is common for the educated in India to speak English well, but their Indian accent leads people to assume otherwise.

Not being fluent in English or being perceived as not fluent in English due to one's accent can lead to feelings of insecurity. Marco, a student from the Philippines, explained that there is a term in Tagalog that, translated literally, means "nose bleed." It refers to how those who do not speak English well feel intimidated when faced with a native speaker of English: "That's the Filipino term—if you're Filipino and you can't speak English properly.... We call it *nose bleed* if you can't say anything perfect in English.... Sometimes they even say, 'Don't English me, I'm panic.' [We laugh.] You're confused, intimidated and lost for words, I guess, in one single word" (interview, 14 December 2009). While the term can be applied to other languages, Marco said, "the term is usually used more for non-English speaking Filipinos" because it is assumed with English that "you're supposed to know it ... that's why you feel nose bleed for English."

The politics of accents reveals the tension between the state of being "fascinated and lured by power and the Western way of life" and the desire to resist assimilation (Krishnaswamy and Burde 2004 [1998]: 57). Mandeep, whose family was originally from India but had taken up Singaporean citizenship, claimed that he used to have a "proper" Indian accent when he was younger. But he learned to put on an American accent when he moved to the Philippines, where he enrolled in an international school. Mandeep insisted that he did so because he was being "stupid" and that he quit speaking with an American accent once he realized this. When I met him, Mandeep spoke with a hybrid accent that seemed like a softened version of an American accent mixed with an Indian inflection, which became slightly stronger when I heard him speak to his mother on the phone. When I pointed this out, he indicated that he was unaware that his accent had changed. He was unable to switch completely between the two accents at will the way most of his friends could, but he would subconsciously adjust the strength of each accent depending on with whom he was speaking.

According to Devraj, Indian students switched accents because in India they get teased and laughed at if they speak with an American accent. "It means that you've lost yourself," he explained. Devraj had strong opinions about this. It appeared that for Devraj, mimicry without the ability to retain bicultural/bilingual skills is to give oneself over to the lure of the dominant culture while remaining incomplete subjects who were "almost the same, but not white" (Bhabha 1984: 130). Switching accents enables the speaker to access the privileges that English entails, while simultaneously resisting its power to define their identity. Indians, observes N. Krishnaswamy and Archana Burde (2004 [1998]: 155), "have always compartmentalized life and created space in the form of pigeon-holes" as an everyday act of subversion "to keep their feet firmly on the ground" in the face of various colonizing influences.

Devraj spoke to me with an American accent as we casually sat in the library with his friends and said, "I speak to you like this. I switch." He implied that he switched to the American accent for my sake because I was an outsider. The switch comes naturally to them, Devraj explained: "You don't think about it. It's, like, when you switch from one language to another, do you think about it?" He was referring to my ability to switch between English, Japanese, and Indonesian at will. "No," he answered for me, "well, it's the same." Devraj was didactic. When I chatted with Devraj and his friends, they spoke to me, a non–South Asian, with an American accent. They then switched to a South Asian accent within a split second as they turned to address one of their mates—even to utter just one word—and switched again to an American accent as they turned back to me. They also did this in large group settings, such as during the school's Indian club meeting. As the president of the club, Devraj code-switched[6] between accents while speaking from behind a podium depending on which group in the audience he was addressing, the South Asians or non–South Asians.

Indian students at TIS reclaimed the power to mark the boundaries between insiders (South Asian) and outsiders (non–South Asian) by being selective of whether they spoke using an Indian (insider) accent or an American (outsider) accent. They acted as gatekeepers for who was or was not an insider by using accents as their symbolic power.

Linguistic and Cultural Boundaries within the Family

In contrast, rather than compartmentalize her use of language to create boundaries within herself, as the South Asian boys did, Lianne created boundaries between herself and her mother. I asked Lianne how her mother had responded when she started talking back and feeling "more clever" than her mother. As an adult in her thirties, Lianne described her relationship with her mother with a deeper understanding of the cultural challenges that her mother may have faced: "At the time, I wasn't aware of my mother's reaction, or how she may feel. But later on in life, after my dad passed away and I settled in Indonesia, I realized that it was a challenge for her because she really wanted to teach me the values her parents taught her. She wanted me to grow up Indonesian." Lianne's father was a *peranakan* Chinese[7] who had received his education in English during the British colonial rule of Singapore. Lianne was educated at TIS because her father wanted to take advantage of his company's policy of paying the high tuition fees for the children of their expatriate employees. "He wanted to take every advantage of that for his children, and I think he won that education battle with my mom. So, I think, during those days, it was repressed for her. She didn't have much influence in our lives in terms of education or culture or whatever.... But it wasn't really until I settled down [in Indonesia as an adult] and had this job and my dad passed away did she really open up about how she felt—her lack of influence." Although Lianne grew up in Indonesia, she did not "grow up Indonesian" in the way her mother had wished. The cultural influence of the international school environment overshadowed that of her mother and host country. I asked Lianne how it made her feel to hear her mother's views and she responded, "As an adult? Oh, I still rebelled ... this is me thinking, you let dad make the decision, live with it, you know. This is who I am. Deal with it." Tensions may arise when unequal gender relations intersect with linguistic and cultural hierarchies within a marriage. As a wife whose first language (Indonesian) was considered internationally less important than her husband's first language (English), Lianne's mother's desires for her children became subordinate to those of her husband.

Because her father was "not fully Asian," as Lianne described in reference to his British education, it helped her mother "warm up to what her kids would be." But still her mother was caught off guard at Lianne's wedding that year, at which I was present, when Lianne and her groom trotted into the outdoor reception area, barefoot, in an upbeat dance. In her mother's view, it was unbecoming of an Indonesian:

> I don't think that she expected us to be so off the charts because we were still growing up in Indonesia, she was still talking to us in Bahasa, we still went to visit her family. But it just didn't stick because all we knew was what TIS taught us, and what TIS taught us was very American, very westernized. The friends that we made were always the oil kids. I had a lot of friends from Mobile Oil, Schlum ... Schlumberger, you know, all these big oil companies. And ... those guys are pretty much Texan, right? [Laughs at her own exaggeration.]

> So I think it was a losing battle for her. She still tries to get her way, but her kids, we don't ... I don't want to, you know, conform. This is who I am and it's very different, but I love it because it's me. And she has to accept it.

The school environment silenced the influence of Lianne's mother and Indonesia through the absences: the absence of Indonesia in the curriculum in a meaningful way, and the absence of Indonesians among the teaching staff and student body. Lianne had attended TIS at a time when Indonesian nationals were barred by the Indonesian government from attending international schools.

Lianne believes a cultural hierarchy was in operation at TIS, which students internalized. It was, in order from the top, "Western," with "American" followed by "European," and then "Eastern," which includes "half-Indonesians," followed by "Koreans or the Japanese." The curriculum, she argued, shaped the hierarchy because it privileged American knowledge:

> I think because our teachers are mostly Americans, a lot of our study material was based out of the States. I learned what a penny was ... before I learned about the rupiah![8] And social studies was always about American history before world history.

> And then I go to university and it's like, you know, I go to Melbourne ...
> it's like, ooh, colonization, hmm, how come I didn't study that at school?
> Duh, we were being colonized at that school! [Laughs.] I honestly think
> that it was just the system. It was the operating system of the school: the
> workbook, the teachers, and then most of the kids were of course Amer-
> ican kids. It's the oil kids, Mobile Oil, Castrol, right? Whatever, whatever.

Lianne's westernized cultural makeup attests to the power of educational institutions and their hidden curricula to shape student identities and perceptions, and reproduce culture (Levinson and Holland
1996). In the Bourdieusian process of cultural reproduction, Ortner
(2006: 109) explains, "the subject internalizes the structures of the external world, both culturally defined and objectively real" to form a
habitus, which is "a system of dispositions that incline actors to act,
think, and feel in ways consistent with the limits of structure." Lianne
had internalized the structures present at TIS to the extent that it became part of her identity.

The environment outside the school reinforced the privileged status
of the culture reproduced by the school. Lianne elaborates,

> I was not unaware of the opportunity or the privilege it was to attend
> TIS ... because when I go home and when I hang out with my mom's
> friends' kids, you know, they went to this normal SD,[9] and at that time
> no one spoke English. There weren't many language schools, so it was an
> advantage to be able to be speaking ... and going to school where, "Hey,
> my third boyfriend is [the child of] the second whatever in charge of the
> Australian embassy." It's like a privilege to be surrounded by people who
> are from different designations or whatever it is.

Lianne acquired social capital at TIS from the connections she established with classmates of "different designations." The environments
outside and inside TIS worked together to reinforce the distinction
associated with the school's dominant culture, giving further credence
to the school's authority to reproduce said culture among its students.

Lianne now speaks Indonesian fluently, especially since she began
to use it for work, and is married to an Indonesian man. The sense of
superiority she once held has passed, and she has a reflective understanding of the conflicting dynamics that were at work in her parents'
desire for quality education for their offspring. But there remains a certain degree of cultural gap to be reckoned with. On the one hand, as a
child, she chose to draw from the privileges associated with English. On
the other hand, she was socialized into a westernized school culture—a
process that she had little control over. The language she speaks, the
way she carries herself, her understanding of the world—all betray the

influences of her westernized educational background. She still enjoys socializing with other TIS graduates, some of whom she met after she had returned to Indonesia as an adult, due to the sense of connection she feels with them as a result of their shared international schooling. International moves may have featured in her childhood only in an indirect way as someone who stayed at an international school and watched her friends come and go. Still, the experience of being educated at an international school meant that she had to straddle multiple cultural worlds—home culture and school culture—while growing up.

Further, cosmopolitan cultural capital is often not produced in a single generation; rather it is, as in Lianne's case, derived from several generations of transnational engagement. Lianne claims that her Singaporean father is not "fully Asian" because he had been "brought up British" in a "British education system in Singapore" and "his English is very British" (interview, 25 July 2009). This influenced the choices he made for his daughters' names and education: he attempted to balance the cultural influences of the colonizer and colonized. He had an English name, John, but Lianne said that for his daughters "he wanted to have a Chinese name that was acceptable"—in other words, Anglicized. Hence, her name is "Lianne," which sounds like the Chinese name "Li-an."[10] For her education, he chose an international school due to its English-language instruction and reputation as a provider of high-quality education.

The colonial imprint on the previous generation is not unique to her father's life. Lianne's mother's family and cultural background can also be traced back to Indonesia's colonial past. Her mother is "from Manado, but she's very much Dutch" due to both her Dutch education and mixed indigenous, Dutch, and German heritage.[11] "My great, great grandfather is an Indonesian Dutch hero," claims Lianne, "so he was, like, a warrior in World War One, I guess, and he's honored in some Dutch museums. And so they [the family] are very proud of that inheritance." While Lianne described her mother's background as a matter of fact, it was common for other interviewees from former colonies to make references to their colonial links, either through descent or education, as a sign of distinction. Western cultural capital, which can be translated into cosmopolitan cultural capital, is inherited through the generations (Bourdieu 1986). Not only did her parents' inherited British and Dutch cultural capital give Lianne access to the cultural capital reproduced at TIS, it also facilitated her ability to acquire and internalize it. Hereditary cultural capital has significant implications for the variable propensity of students to internalize the school's ideology of being "international."

English and "Expat" is High Status

I will provide two more examples of the impact that English and its symbolic power has on cosmopolitan subjectivities. Afra's story sheds light on the importance of having a "natural" command of English. Afra was an Algerian national who had studied at international schools in several countries (though not Indonesia). He spoke eight languages, including English, which he spoke with a distinct American accent when I interviewed him via Skype (2 March 2009). He said of English, "I wanted to keep up, you know, maintain my English 'cause wherever you go in non-English speaking countries, speaking in English is, like, a big plus." Later Afra elaborated, "I think English, especially American English, is the language of the privileged." He explained that others perceive him in a better light when he is able to demonstrate his (native) fluency in English.

The use of English as a status marker was further driven home when I hung out with Olivia during her visit to Jakarta from another city in Indonesia. Olivia self-identified as a Third Culture Kid due to her transnational upbringing. Her parents are Chinese Indonesians, but she left Indonesia in her early teens and lived in Singapore, Canada, and China before returning to Indonesia as an adult. She was fluent in English, but I also knew that she was a native speaker of Indonesian. Because I was used to code-switching with anyone who was fluent in two or more of the languages I spoke, I repeatedly tried to use both Indonesian and English when speaking to her. However, she spoke nothing but English back to me. Olivia had her reasons, which I recorded in my field notes (3 April 2009):

> By the end of the day I gave up with Olivia and spoke in full English to her. But I actually found it a bit tiring speaking nothing but English with someone who is also a native speaker of Indonesian. After the interview she told me that she had learned during her TESOL (Teaching English to Speakers of Other Languages) program that code-switching is something you do to go downward to meet the other person at their lower level. When I mentioned that I do it to make an emotional connection ... she said that speaking Indonesian doesn't do that for her.

Olivia refused to follow my suit to switch to Indonesian because she thought it would relegate her to a lower status than me. While I could relate to her concerns, it also became clear to me that Olivia was unaware that there are other reasons for code-switching. Some people, like the South Asian boys at TIS and myself, use code-switching to establish insider status with another.

As we were exploring the mall earlier that day, I had noticed that Olivia at first spoke to the shop attendants in English and switched to Indonesian only when it became clear that the other party could not understand English. Olivia later commented that she was humbled by how I had used Indonesian to speak with the shop attendants. This puzzled me, as it seemed perfectly normal to me that I would, as someone who was partly Indonesian and fluent in Indonesian, speak in Indonesian to fellow Indonesians in Indonesia. Olivia explained that she feels the need to speak English to everyone when she visits Jakarta even though she does not do that in her hometown, a much smaller and more modest city than Jakarta. She used English as a marker of privilege to establish her status as superior to those of the shop attendants who were of a lower socioeconomic background. Olivia's actions were partly driven by the pressure to prove herself capable in English in other situations, such as at her workplace, where many of her colleagues, with whom her clients would compare her, were expatriate workers from Anglophone countries. Olivia's credibility in her place of employment was dependent on her ability to speak English. It was also due to the power of the discursive constructions of English and English speakers as superior. Colonial and postcolonial discourses surrounding English are, Alastair Pennycook (1998: 217) remarks, "powerful indeed, and replayed in many contexts." My use of Indonesian in public spaces appeared to Olivia as an act that required humility because I had to relinquish access to the sense of privilege that comes with using English.

Having links with the "expat" community in Jakarta (i.e., social capital) also gives access to cultural capital. Olivia was surprised when I explained that despite attending international schools, I did not share a sense of affinity with the Western "expat" communities. I had internalized the structures myself and did not feel sufficiently equipped with the necessary cultural know-how (capital) to participate in these communities (at least that is how I felt at the time when I was younger than I am now). In her view, I had no reason to feel intimidated on account of the cultural hierarchy that I had internalized since, as one who was "half an expat," I was perceived as being of higher status than her. "Half an expat" was a reference to my mother, who, being Japanese, elevated my position through the links I had with the Japanese expatriate community in Indonesia and with Japan itself, a country that is more economically advanced than Indonesia. Bill Ashcroft (2001: 51) suggests, "The colonized subject may also be the colonizing subject depending on his or her location in the rhizome." In this fashion, my perceived status shifted depending on who served as the point of reference, Olivia or myself.

More than a year later, Olivia went through an emotionally involved process to reckon with the power of these discourses and decolonize herself, so to speak, from the structures that she had internalized. I went through a similar process while conducting this research. In this way, global economic structures intersect with the legacy of colonial discourses to inform the cultural hierarchies that are then internalized to form habitus, which may later require a lot of undoing.

"Natural" English

Parents invested much time and money to enrol their children at TIS early, to expose them to an English-speaking environment, including teachers and classmates who were native speakers of English. Some parents desired not just communicative fluency in English for their children, but native fluency. Still others wanted to ensure that fluency in English did not compromise their children's fluency in the parents' native language. Parents wanted their children to acquire the linguistic and cultural capital necessary to participate successfully in the global system without losing the cultural capital required to operate in their own national system.

Jenny's mother, Mee Yon, was one such parent. Mee Yon, who I mentioned at the beginning of this chapter, had studied at a Korean university majoring in English literature, and had a good command of English, though she had a distinct Korean accent. I interviewed her over lunch at a popular sushi restaurant in a posh Jakarta mall. Mee Yon was dressed well, as always, with her earrings, necklace, and hair in perfect order.

Mee Yon had used different strategies with her two children to equip them with the appropriate language skills. Both children had gone to Korean schools before enrolling at TIS. Sam, the eldest, was moved to TIS in grade seven, while his younger sister Jenny was moved at a younger age, in grade two. Mee Yon explained why she changed strategies with her second child:

> When I came here [Jakarta], I put him [Sam] at a Korean school to let him get Korean language and Chinese character. Chinese character is the basic language for the Korean and for Japanese. So I had to wait until he gets all language skills, and then move him to TIS. While he was at Korean school I send him to English academy and his English skill was very high already. So he took a test, and school asked him to join the mainstream, not the ESOL. So … he could get a kind of advanced courses, and that's why he could get a Ivy League university.

But my little one, she join the TIS [*sic*] at the second grade. 'Cause I felt that my son has still Korean accent, and in terms of natural English, he doesn't feel comfortable. So academic English is very high. He took an MBA. In English exam, he got top one percent. So his English is almost perfect, but still he doesn't feel like using it like a native. So I put my little one in second grade and spend lots of money now for a long time because I'm owner payer.

"I'm owner payer" means that she and her husband paid for their children's tuition fees out of their own pockets. For many parents, this represented a considerable financial sacrifice and investment compared to situations where one spouse was employed by a company that paid their children's tuition fees as part of an "expat package." Despite the cost, Mee Yon decided to send Jenny to TIS from as early as the second grade to ensure that Jenny acquired "natural English."

As academically successful as her son was, it did not diminish the perceived importance of the ability to speak "natural" English. Equally important to Mee Yon was her children's retention of Korean. A Chinese Indonesian mother echoed Mee Yon's sentiment about English. She had enrolled her children at a young age at TIS because she wanted them to have a natural command of English such that they would not have to think about what they were saying. The native-nonnative dichotomy and concern over parental language retention influences the choice of schools, which in turn influences the ways in which identities and perceptions are shaped.

Telling a Story

As cultural capital, the language a person speaks, and the accent with which they speak it, tells a story of where they have come from and where they can go in a world structured by sociocultural hierarchies. Language ability (or lack thereof) and accents are instrumental in positioning oneself vis-à-vis others. English in particular can narrate social belonging as well as act as symbolic power. In some cases, like that of the South Asian students, it is possible to reclaim the power to draw boundaries of belonging through the selective use of accents.

The dominance of English at TIS can be traced to colonial times and its link with contemporary capitalist discourses, as can its impact on the identities and perceptions of those educated at a school like TIS. English is constructed as an "international" language and is a marker of cosmopolitan cultural capital. Subsequent chapters will show that fluency in English affected students' ability to participate in the form of cosmopolitanism promoted by the school's ideology of being "international," with implications for social relations at TIS. The currency of English as cosmopolitan cultural capital is evidence that cosmopolitan practices are embedded within national and transnational structures and their sociohistorical context. But language is not the only tool available for marking boundaries between the cosmopolitan and the other.

Notes

1. Apart from the Dutch, usually only the local elite and upper classes attended Dutch-medium schools prior to the Japanese invasion of 1942 (Mysbergh 1957).
2. *"Bule"* literally means "faded" in Indonesian but is used as slang for "white people." It can be used with a derogatory inflection, but it more often carries a positive connotation relating to white privilege.
3. "Bahasa" is short for "Bahasa Indonesia," which means "the Indonesian language." Foreigners (and sometimes Indonesians when speaking in English) often refer to the Indonesian national language as "Bahasa Indonesia," or simply "Bahasa." The latter results in grammatically incorrect usages, such as "I speak Bahasa," which literally translates to "I speak language." In this book I will use "Indonesian" to refer to the national language as the preferred translation of the Indonesian term "Bahasa Indonesia," unless it is a direct quote.
4. The spelling "giss" will be used in the rest of the book to avoid confusion with the commonly used slang. See also the *Historical Dictionary of American Slang* (Spears 1994) for the origins of the related words *jazz, jasm, jism, jizz,* or *giss.*
5. Blommaert (2010) writes of the commodification of language that sells accents together with the ideological package they carry.
6. Alternating between two or more languages or varieties of language in speech.
7. The term *"peranakan"* refers to descendants of the Chinese who settled in the Malay Peninsula and what is now Indonesia and intermarried with the indigenous population.
8. Indonesian currency.
9. An acronym for *"sekolah dasar,"* which means "elementary school" in Indonesian.
10. As with all other names in this book, "Lianne" and "Li-an" are both pseudonyms and they have been chosen for their convenience in reflecting the original meaning of the conversation with the interviewee.
11. Manado is a major city on Sulawesi island. It is also one of the wealthiest and most-Christianized places in Indonesia, with a long history of European colonization (by the Portuguese, Spanish, and then Dutch) and a tradition of good education.

CHAPTER 3

Living in "Disneyland"

The Sudan was the backdrop to our story; it provided the
terrain of difference that marked us as cosmopolitan. But we
didn't *have* to be there, and the Sudan wasn't really about us.
—Craig Calhoun (2008: 113)

The ideology or notion of being international draws a distinction between privileged migrants and host country nationals by framing the
local setting as a mere backdrop to mark the former as cosmopolitan
or "international" and the latter as parochial (Calhoun 2008). At TIS,
the notion of being "international" endorses a form of cosmopolitanism that draws on Orientalist discourses through which it constructs
the local as an exotic, dangerous Other (Said 1985 [1978]). It purges
the local from transnational enclaves, except in superficial forms, for
it needs the local, but at a safe distance, as a backdrop. Craig Calhoun
(2008: 106) refers to this form of cosmopolitanism as "felt cosmopolitanism," whereby one feels cosmopolitan through frequent traveling
or living in exotic places. At TIS, this form of cosmopolitanism inadvertently privileges being "Western" and "white" through a hidden
curriculum (Snyder 1970) that is given substance by the school's pay
scale, which symbolizes broader economic structures. The hidden curriculum permeates the students' social lives on campus.

Imagining the West and the Rest

TIS is both an educational institution and a transnational space, but
one that is physically situated within the Indonesian nation-state. The
security-obsessed architecture of the gated campus symbolizes that it
is a community marked by its separateness from the local environment. It reflects Anne-Meike Fechter's (2007: vii) research on expa-

triate communities in Jakarta, which she argues was an "expatriate bubble" characterized by the "pervasive importance of boundaries." Likewise, as a school that caters to the expatriate population, TIS is a transnational bubble.

It is, however, analytically useful to remember that "trans*national*" presupposes the "nation-state" in much the same way that "anti-*racism*" presupposes "race" (Smith 2001). The transnational bubble does not make the Indonesian nation-state disappear. Rather, its existence is dependent on the availability of Indonesia to serve as a "backdrop" to throw the cosmopolitanism of the transnational bubble into relief. In his work on corporate expatriates in Jakarta, William Leggett (2005: 272) argues, "Through the colonial imagination a union is forged between Western populations and a divide created between East and West as transnational economic processes become situated within a genealogy of empire."

At TIS, the Indonesian postcolonial backdrop is pertinent to constructing the students, staff, and parents as raced, classed, gendered cosmopolitans. Those who practice "cosmopolitanism of the above" draw on colonial and capitalist discourses to fashion themselves as cosmopolitan in contrast to the local Other (Hall and Werbner 2008: 346). However, the educational function of TIS and the presence of the local Indonesian Other (as well as other expatriate children who do not have Western cultural capital) as students who are equal targets of TIS's project of producing "global citizens" complicate the divide.

TIS's diverse student body makes it difficult to determine who is an expatriate and who is a local. The main types of students at TIS consist of foreign nationals, who consider Indonesia as a temporary place of residence; foreign nationals, who have spent most of their lives in Indonesia but still consider it as a temporary place of residence because they expect to repatriate eventually; "local" Indonesians, many of whom used to live overseas; Korean nationals, who may or may not remain in Indonesia but are part of the growing Korean population that is increasingly becoming a permanent fixture in Indonesia; and children of mixed marriages, namely between expatriate men, mostly Western, and Indonesian women. Despite the analytical difficulty in labeling these groups as expatriate or local, visiting speakers and TIS's staff members who identified as Western engaged in constructing a union among "Western populations" and a divide between "East and West" through a colonial imagination that was supported by the global economic structure. To be sure, this practice was not limited to TIS, as some of the following examples will show. It was common also in other transnational spaces.

The Making of "Disneyland"

> It follows then that repatriation, in comparison, would be
> like visiting a small-town museum when you have just
> seen the wonders of Disneyland.
> —Andrea Martins (2008), cofounder of former ExpatWomen.com

The visiting "expat expert" flashed these words from Andrea Martins during a PowerPoint presentation. I sat up. At the time, I was in the grand, well-maintained, air-conditioned auditorium of TIS. The quote piqued my interest. It was a metaphor to illustrate the reverse culture shock that privileged, temporary migrants (in this case, "expatriate" professionals, or "expats" for short, and their nuclear families) experience upon returning to their country of citizenship at the end of their overseas assignment. The expert was in town to give talks to parents and teachers at TIS about the children of these migrants, who she referred to in her talks as Third Culture Kids. The reference to the host countries of temporary migrants as "Disneyland" was telling of the dominant ideology of being international commonly found in expatriate communities, and not only international schools.

The "Wonders of Disneyland"

According to the flyers that advertised her talks, the expert, who I shall call Vera, had lived around the world with her husband and children as a "diplomatic spouse." The quote she used in the talk describes the repatriated "expat" as someone who feels as though the most interesting part of his or her life is over. Expatriate life, particularly outside the former colonial metropolitan centers, is represented as going away from home to visit Disneyland where presumably ordinary people are transformed into princesses and princes residing in luxurious houses and condominiums—the modern-day equivalent of castles—with pools, maids, drivers, and gardeners, traveling to exotic places, with lives that are sometimes punctuated by the adventures of narrowly escaping local social and political crises. Kathleen A. F. Jordan (1981: 154) writes that the experience of transnational youth repatriating to the United States for college involves "a loss of privilege in terms of life-style, a loss of specialness ... a loss of mobility ... [and] a forfeiture of the fantasies allowed by overseas life and exotic experiences." When I asked about their living arrangements in Jakarta, one TIS student said, "They're pretty much all the same. You know, like these fancy dream houses that you probably would never get anywhere else." While many feel ambivalent about it, the expat life enables middle-class people from the global North to live out a romanticized image of colonial luxury from a bygone era as cosmopolitans of a modern-day transnational capitalist class.

"Disneyland" evokes an Orientalist discourse that constructs host countries as exotic, fantastical, adventurous playgrounds (Said 1985 [1978]; Lacroix 2004). Transnational life is viewed through a contemporary reincarnation of the colonial gaze that places host country localities in the peripheries of the former colonial metropolitan centers—spatially removed and temporally displaced (Leggett 2005). The "wonders of Disneyland" in the exotic Orient come to life when juxtaposed against the "small-town museum" of the developed West. Although the Orient is not merely "a creation with no corresponding reality," Edward Said (1985 [1978]: 5) posits that the discourse is about the "relationship of power, of domination, of varying degrees of a complex hegemony" between the Occident and the Orient. It may seem ordinary and mundane, but the "small-town" represents the norm. It remains positionally superior because the wonder of Disneyland come to life only in so far as it enriches the life of the temporary participant-spectator who will visit and taste of it, but never become part of it (Hage 1998).

The "small-town museum" is also assumed to be the "home" of those who were in the audience for the expert's talk. Despite the diverse backgrounds of the parents in the auditorium, the talk constructed "home" and "away" using a binary framework of "the West" and "the Rest" (Said 1985 [1978]). Some days after the talk, I interviewed Claudia, who felt that the expat expert was speaking only for a select group of temporary migrants. Claudia, whose children attended TIS, was married to a North American, but was herself from Central America.[1] According to Claudia, the talk seemed very "American" and the speaker had exoticized life outside "the West" (interview, 15 May 2009): "She was speaking from a perspective that life is *this* way: we have our kids and we don't have household help, and we don't have poverty that we see, staring at us right outside the door, and we don't have exotic foods. … [But] for Indonesians, some of the Western food can be exotic, if you look at it the other way. It was sort of the perspective that everything is exotic."

By using North America as a point of reference, the speaker had constructed North America as the norm and the host countries (she seemed to have in mind developing countries like Indonesia) as different, exotic Others. In Claudia's view, the speaker was only representing one perspective of the expatriate experience: "It would be nice to see … if someone like Vera Trewin could step beyond her own little world, her own little perception. 'Cause she's just really giving advice to Northern hemisphere people.... I mean ... there's a lot of things that she said that's [sic] very valuable that I totally endorse.... But ... if somehow, if she could put herself in somebody else's shoes, you know, like a Japanese person. Or if there's someone that is actually a little more diverse ... could probably do a better, a more inclusive job."

Claudia used examples to explain that not all the families of TIS students fit the Western "expat" paradigm that Vera had in mind. While Vera assumed in her talk that the norm is for fathers to travel to work from home, Claudia points out that in some societies it is commonplace for fathers to be away from home for long periods of time. Or while TIS assumed that it was commonplace for parents to volunteer at school, many parents of European and Asian backgrounds find this concept foreign to what they are used to. "So ... there might be some things there [in Vera's talk] that's [sic] not very useful to other people.... The majority probably wouldn't mean anything to a Korean family.... It's not something that helps them, you know. That's my guess." Claudia took issue with the way the speaker had assumed the global North to be "home" for all temporary migrants and perceived as the norm vis-à-vis the global South. Although it was presented as universal, in reality Vera's talk represented a limited perspective. It was addressed to those who felt socially distant from the host country and could therefore treat it as a backdrop to their experience of being "international."

This distance from the host country was made clearer during a chat over a drink with Vera and three mothers who helped organize the talks. The three mothers were active volunteers at TIS, and all had at least one child in high school. Nora was a Dutch woman who took me under her wing whenever I attended parent coffee mornings, was supportive of my research, and had been the one who invited me to join them for drinks that day. Having lived outside of the Netherlands since she married her husband over two decades ago, Nora said that she found herself crying as she read and was able to relate to some of the Third Culture Kid literature about changing culturally through living overseas. Then there was Truc, a Vietnamese woman married to an American man. When Vera asked where she was from, Truc replied, "Boston." The rest of us laughed and teased her for being stereotypically American by assuming that everyone knows the names of American cities. The third mother was a Canadian of South Asian background who was married to a German man.

We wanted to go to a café for drinks between Vera's talks, but the nearest place we could get to was a pub in a hotel near TIS. It was within walking distance from TIS, but we took a taxi because it was drizzling. Vera sat in the passenger seat while the four of us squeezed into the back seat. Upon reaching the entrance gate to the hotel, the security guards conducted their routine check. As I mentioned before, it had become standard procedure to do security checks on all incoming vehicles at major malls, hotels, high-end condominiums, and business skyscrapers since the 2002 Bali bombings. But for the most part, such security checks were lax and superficial, rendering them occasionally irritating because they seemed pointless. That afternoon, one of the guards opened the back door where Truc was sitting. He had opened the taxi door by about twenty centimeters, with his hand still on the outside handle of the door, and was about to peer inside the car when Truc abruptly shouted, "If you open it more I'll fall!" and pulled the door shut. She said it in fast-paced English without expecting the guard to understand. The rest of the party in the car laughed and laughed at Truc's reaction. Vera commented, "Oh, you obviously know how to handle them, eh." She said this in reference to Truc's longstanding experience of living in Indonesia.

While the security check seemed like a pointless nuisance, Vera's use of the phrase "handle them" to describe Truc's treatment of the guards symbolizes Truc's more powerful class position since only those in subordinate positions such as children and animals are "handled"—never equals. Treating lower-class Indonesians poorly or rudely is not unique to foreigners, and common also among middle- and upper-class Indonesians. But it was in moments like these that class (as patrons of an upper-class hotel) intersected with Western cultural capital (using English). The distinction between "them" (the locals) and "us" (expatriates) was made possible by socioeconomic inequalities.

The Exotic Other

The Orientalist discourse also romanticizes the Other and exists beyond TIS in the broader international school circles (Said 1985 [1978]). This was made apparent at a regional conference for schools using the International Baccalaureate program held in Singapore in March 2010. While TIS representatives were not present, many other international schools in the region were well represented. One of the plenary speakers at the conference was "articulate to the nth degree," according to my field notes. The slide show that formed the backdrop to his speech was filled with richly colored photographs of various peoples from nonurban areas whom he had studied as an anthropologist at an Ivy League university. In my field notes (25 March 2010) I wrote,

The essence of his message was that there is very deep wisdom that is carried by all these seemingly primitive cultures. He shared that wisdom with us. Mesmerized us with it. How the fishermen of the Pacific islands can calculate the distances while at sea by looking at the ripples in the waters. He also spoke of the Inuit who knew the glaciers were melting just by looking at them, while it takes scientists lots of calculations to say the same things. By the end of it, we were convinced that these seemingly primitive cultures were indeed full of wisdom that we had to heed. *They* knew how to live with nature, *we* didn't. When he finished, we were fully mesmerized, and gave him a standing ovation. It was a dense kind of clap that filled the room. It went on for a while.

It appeared as though the speaker was promoting cosmopolitan engagement with those who are different by encouraging the audience to value the wisdom produced by the Other.

But in a private conversation with my colleague and I, another speaker from the conference, who was also from North America, expressed her discomfort with the speech. She asked us, "Were there any white people in the slide show?" There were not. My colleague and I then realized that the absence of white people in the slide show reinforced the perception of the Other as "primitive," and that there was a divide between the West and the rest (Said 1985 [1978]). According to Ghassan Hage (1998), the exotic, romanticized Other is valued insofar as they enrich the cosmopolitanism of the dominant culture. The power to ascribe value to the Other rested with the observer who *feels* cosmopolitan through the act of ascribing that value.

"I Miss the Riots"

Like the parents, those who self-identified as "TCKs" participate in the Orientalist discourse. Afra, an Algerian national who had grown up in several countries (though not Indonesia), noticed that some TCKs speak of developing countries as though their poor economic conditions or sociopolitical unrest were like adventure rides. He was living in Korea at the time of our interview via Skype (2 March 2009). I first came across Afra through the TCKid.com forums, where he posted comments that expressed his frustration at the way others wrote about the conditions in developing countries. When I interviewed him later he said (with a distinct American accent),

I can relate to the people saying they have unresolved grief or feel like they had a hard time moving from one country to another. I've experienced that too.

But I can't relate to people telling me, "I lived in Africa and everything was anarchic and disorganized and ... I had no sanitation or no running water," or whatever. I mean that's something I've been through in Algeria, not having water running in the sink. And that's a horrible thing to go to. That means you can't take your shower like other people do in the US, and that was no fun for me. Let me tell you, I had very long hair at that time, and it was horrible to wash with a ... with a basket instead of running water. So that's not something fun to go through. ...

I feel almost offended by people who say, "I miss walking barefoot." ... Anything that's a sign from an undeveloped country, you know, like, "I miss the riots," or ... the war ... not the war, people don't say "I miss war." But they say, "I miss the riots 'cause thanks to the riots I couldn't go to school." There have been riots in Algeria when I was there and we couldn't go to school. But we had that tear gas in our balcony and that wasn't fun, you know. So I can't relate to that. ...

People say it was good times not to have running water, or to have an earthquake somewhere. I don't think that's something you should miss.

Even if "I miss the riots" was said with knowing humor, Afra sounded frustrated with the way developing countries are perceived by transnational youth who have the privilege to leave those countries in tough times—a privilege that was not always available to Afra as an Algerian national. While the lack of modern facilities and outbreaks of social upheavals represent one-off incidents (whether they are considered traumatic or adventurous) for some, for Afra they remain a reality from which he cannot completely separate himself as long as his only passport is from a developing country. Maintaining a distance from the host country requires cultural capital that not all transnational youth are able to access.

An Unfamiliar, Dangerous Other

At TIS, social distance from the host nation-state was maintained by forging a sense of community among Western expatriates and constructing the host country as an unfamiliar, dangerous place that was different from the West. In advising parents on how to protect their children from social ills, the school administrators at TIS normalized state-society relations as they are in the global North, particularly in Western countries.

At a general meeting with parents, the principal, vice principal, and several other school administrators spoke on various aspects of the school that they thought were relevant to the parents. The meeting was held during the day in the small auditorium, which, like the large one, was carpeted and air-conditioned. The meeting was attended by parents, almost all mothers, of diverse backgrounds, though the majority were from various Western countries. Korean, Indonesian, and Japanese parents, whose children form the majority of the student body, were conspicuously absent. The few mothers of Asian descent who attended such meetings were often married to men from Western countries, such as the United States, the United Kingdom, Australia, or western European countries.

That day, the advice that one of the administrators gave to the parents about underage drinking was of particular interest. A couple of weeks earlier, the vice principal had alerted parents about a private party that had been organized mainly for ninth graders (about fourteen years old). The school had found out that alcohol would be served at the party and expressed their concern in the email. At the meeting, the administrator called for "expat" parents to be vigilant of their children's behavior with regard to alcohol, which was commonsense advice. Yet, in doing so he invoked a sense of community among "expat" parents against the backdrop of an unfamiliar host country where underage drinking is not regulated:

> The next thing I just want to talk about is the partnership between you and the school in relation to your kids. You may have heard about an email I sent out to you a couple of weeks ago, alerting about an organized party that included alcohol. ... That's the sort of thing that we really value.

> The challenge for us as mostly expat parents is that we're in a society that doesn't have the same situation as home. Even though it's a ... Muslim country, if I'm a Westerner here in Jakarta—and I've noticed with my own kids—my 13-, 14-year-old boy could walk into a bar and be served a drink. No ID needed, no questions asked. You can go to a supermarket and buy vodka mixed cans. My daughter did this. She won't mind me telling you this, she's ashamed of it. She and her friends in eighth grade: straight after school, "Let's just have fun," off to Hero [a local supermarket chain], box of mixed ... [laughs], got *totally* drunk and sick, came home feeling horrible, "I'm never gonna do that again." But me, I had *no* control over that. I had no idea they could just walk into a supermarket and buy this. ...

> So what we're trying to do is go beyond just our own little resources and try and work together on this.

The administrator had assumed that the role the state plays in his home country, Australia, to protect children from exposure to the dangers of substance abuse in public spaces was universal. The absence of law enforcement with regard to underage drinking is seen as being out of the ordinary, even by local standards. He presumed that a Muslim country should have strong enforceable sanctions against alcohol consumption. As a visible minority in Indonesia, the white administrator interpreted his daughter and her friend's experience at Hero, a local supermarket chain, through a racial lens. He attributed their easy access to alcohol to being "a Westerner here in Jakarta." In reality, easy access to alcohol by minors is not particular to Westerners. Indonesian children can also buy alcohol without any form of identification. The practice of showing identification when purchasing goods is barely known. That said, Indonesia banned the sale of alcohol at convenience stores in 2015 to curb underage drinking, but this rule does not apply to other stores, such as larger supermarkets, or in tourism zones such as Bali. At any rate, there was a disjuncture between the school's expectations regarding the role of the state in child protection and the local reality that applies irrespective of the values held by parents, school administrators, and Indonesian society at large.

The world outside the school gates is seen as the unfamiliar, dangerous space of the Other, over which the "international" (Western) community has "no control" and from which children need protection. Generalizing terms such as "Muslim" and "Western" are used to reinforce the difference between the school community and the host country. While the administrator recognized that not all parents are "expats," he conflated the "mostly expat parents" with "us" and "we" who he assumed had a similar cultural background and shared his understanding of "home." Although the parents who were present that day were mostly of European descent, they do not reflect the parents of the general student body, a majority of whom are of Asian descent. He called for a "partnership" between parents and the school so they could go beyond their "little resource[s]" to gain back control in an unfamiliar setting. This was the "challenge" that he felt the school and wider (expatriate) community faced—creating the familiar within an unfamiliar space.

The sense of "challenge," of having to contend with a foreign environment, accentuates the sense of cosmopolitanism felt by the school community (Calhoun 2008). Indonesians and non-Western expatriates, who were largely not present at the meeting, were not necessarily included in the "we" and "us" that represented the Western, expatriate school community, which was conflated with the transnational through a distinction from the local. When the local becomes too familiar, as it does for foreigners who have lived in Indonesia for longer, speak fluent Indonesian, or are married to Indonesians, their ascribed identity shifts from being cosmopolitan to "gone local" (Fechter 2007: 100).

Center of Student Life

Whether or not a student was deemed as "international" was also measured by their level of engagement with school activities. As an alumnus said in a video detailing TIS's history, "School was in many ways the center of activity for the expat community, and especially for the kids who went to school. We'd spend hours here." Marie Sander (2014: 130) found that the situation was similar in Shanghai where international schools served as "community hubs" for expatriate community building among both the students and their parents. At TIS, the normative model for engagement with the school appeared to be based on the assumption that expatriate families arrive with little or no ties to the local community and locates the international school as the central hub of student life in the foreign city. It is within this enclave-like campus that students are expected to find a community servicing most of their needs in addition to that of education, whether it be sports, music, or the occasional family activities. However, students come from diverse backgrounds. Consequently, they have diverse sets of ties and access to various communities in Jakarta. Some students are involved in and contribute to communities outside the school, but these are largely invisible to the school, thus making these students seem as though they do not belong to the school's international community.

Take for example Anaya, who was seventeen and in her last year of high school. Anaya was critical of the school staff for assuming that TIS was her only source of community life. Anaya was born in Spain and had Spanish citizenship through her mother, while her father was an Indonesian national. But Anaya's parents were both of Indian descent and Anaya had lived in Indonesia for most of her life. She had only lived in her country of citizenship, Spain, for one year—the year after the 1998 riots, when she moved to Spain due to the unstable sociopolitical situation in Indonesia. Anaya had moved to TIS from the Indian international school in Jakarta and spoke English, her first language, with an Americanized accent typical of international school students.

Due to her family's cultural background and long-term stay in Indonesia, Anaya was involved in the Indian Indonesian community outside the school that left her having to balance competing demands on her time. "It's just really, really difficult, honestly … trying to balance school with my outside of school life.… School demands so much, and the community ... not even academically, but time, you know. They don't realize that you have a life outside school" (interview, 27 April 2009). According to Anaya, the school places expectations on her time in the name of "school spirit." Whether it was to come and watch the school team compete in a sports game with other (international) schools, or to fulfill her role as stage manager for the school theater team, she sometimes felt that they required "ridiculous amounts of time" and did not take into account the fact that she had commitments outside the school. Anaya cited the school's normalization of the expatriate community as a reason for assuming that the school is the center of student life: "Because it's an international school ... so they feel like, you have nothing else to do outside of school. Yeah, because everyone's an expat, they don't have their family, their extended family, here." Although Anaya's family had a transnational résumé, her family's long-term engagement with the host country diverged from the traditional "expat" pattern of living a temporary life in the host country and having few ties outside the expatriate community. In contrast, her transnational engagement was a mixture of the patterns commonly thought to be followed by expats, diasporas, and other more permanent migrants. Anaya was a student leader for preteens and teenagers at a Hindu temple and fulfilled duties toward her extended family and friends from the local Indian community, such as visiting her grandmother at the hospital or attending weddings of family friends that occur over several days. Anaya was involved in multiple communities. Her more local engagement diminished her availability to contribute to the school's "international" community.

Anaya's complaints, though exaggerated in an adolescent kind of way, were valid, but nuanced. I told Anaya that her experiences sounded similar to those of Indonesian students. Indonesian students were involved in activities in local communities (e.g., taking martial arts lessons not offered at TIS) and were therefore often perceived by TIS as apathetic because their contributions to community life were invisible to the school. Anaya immediately backtracked on her complaints, saying that students should still contribute to school life. It appeared that she either did not want me to defend the actions of the Indonesian students who were negatively perceived by the school or she did not want herself to be placed in the same category as them.

Anaya had previously been critical of her ethnic Indian friends who, like her, had grown up in Indonesia and had moved from the Indian international school to TIS, but who had not integrated into the dominant English-speaking groups at school as she had. She felt that they could have had they tried harder. I hardly saw her hang out with them. Instead, I often saw Anaya hanging out in the mainstream English-speaking groups during recess. She placed a distance between herself and the more local Indonesian-speaking students, including the Indian Indonesians, while simultaneously justifying her inability to participate in school life as much as her "expat" peers.

At times Anaya was also defensive about being negatively perceived by the Indian community for being influenced by the more liberal culture at TIS. When she mentioned this, I was spending time with her and another of her ethnic Indian friends who also usually hung out in the English-speaking groups. They described how they think the Indian community sees them: "They think we party and go clubbing all the time and show our cleavage, but it's not true. We don't" (reconstructed from field notes). While they were explaining this to me, I noticed the irony of the fact that they were both showing cleavage in spaghetti strap dresses and low V-neck tops. Then, when I asked how often she went clubbing, Anaya hesitated for a moment before answering twice a month. They then explained that it is the "older people" who "make a fuss about it" because they feel as though they are unable to afford TIS's expensive tuition fee for their own children. Showing cleavage or going clubbing may not be inherently wrong (though the latter is illegal as a minor), but the defensive and inconsistent explanations are subtly revealing of Anaya and her friend's desire to identify with the dominant, Western culture of the school. In a sense, Anaya and her friend were defending themselves from accusations that they were losing themselves to the more liberal, westernized culture at TIS. Rather than attributing these accusations in part to the fact that they did subscribe to these lifestyles and fashions, they instead attributed them solely to the envy that others felt toward them for having climbed the sociocultural ladder, so to speak. By doing so, they were in effect asserting a sense of superiority not because they wanted to be superior, but because others saw them that way.

Korean students were similarly involved in activities that took place off campus, and their heavy involvement in these activities was perceived as lying outside school norms. At another parent-teacher meeting specifically for Korean parents, the principal and other school administrators expressed the school's frustration over the Korean students' inability to conform to the school culture. The school was concerned that Korean students were sleep deprived and falling asleep during classes because they were taking too many Korean-language-based supplementary classes outside of TIS, which were designed to ensure that they were competitive in their bid to enter Korean universities. While the concern for the students' well being was reasonable, the school administrators verbalized this concern in a way that constructed the Korean students as being outside a perceived norm, and therefore not belonging to the school. At the meeting, one of the administrators said to the parents, "Perhaps, this is not the right school for you," despite the fact that there were few alternatives available to Korean parents for preparing their children for Korean universities.

The dominant lifestyle and culture of the school, as represented by the mostly Western teachers who were temporary migrants to Indonesia, defined the norm for involvement in school life in a way that assumed that students had few local ties and few transnational commitments outside the West (such as preparing for university entrance requirements in Korea). In this case, those who considered the school as a "home away from home" were afforded a greater sense of belonging to the international community of the school while others were seen to be coming short of becoming international.

Institutionalizing Distance from the Local

The discursive construction of distance between the school's expatriate community and the host society is propped up by an economic structure, a feature common to social hierarchies (Bourdieu 1986: 252). The pay scale at TIS rewards employees who are able to demonstrate distance from the host country. There are three main tiers to the pay scale for the teaching staff. The highest paid tier consists of foreigners hired overseas and this made up a majority of the teachers and administrators (hereafter, "overseas-hire foreign staff"). They are paid a base salary that is supplemented by what is popularly referred to as the "expat package" (Leggett 2003; Fechter 2007). At TIS, the package at the time paid for rent, utilities, gasoline, comprehensive medical insurance, and return airfare for the employee and dependents to visit their home country once a year.[2] The middle tier consists of foreign nationals hired locally as teachers and support staff (hereafter, "local-hire foreign staff"). They usually receive the base salary without the package, though their salary was supplemented with medical insurance for the employee only. The lowest tier consists of the Indonesian nationals hired mostly as teachers for the Indonesian program and support administrative staff (hereafter, "local staff"). This pay scale is certainly not unique to TIS. It reflects the inequalities that also characterize local and global socioeconomic structures. The three-tiered pay scale had an impact on the lifestyles available to each group. On the surface this had little bearing on the social interactions between staff at the school on a day-to-day basis, but the instances where the pay scale did influence interactions shaped the subjectivities of various actors.

Local-hire foreign staff seemed most aware and vocal about the impact of the three-tiered pay scale. Rick, a North American, gave a detailed description of the instances when the pay scale intrudes upon social interactions with his colleagues who were overseas hired:

> I could say that it's partly my fault, but it's not entirely my fault.... My personality is such that, I'm quite happy on my own and I don't sort of easily form friendships with other colleagues. I mean on campus yes, but weekends I'm pretty much on my own with my family doing family-related things. So I don't build up my way to sort of build, you know, relationships with my colleagues out of work. That part is my fault. But having said that, it is true that when you're on a different social economic scale, it does influence your choices of activities.

> It really hits home when you, every year ... it's gotten better rather than worse, but the first few years I was here, there was that ... the worst periods were the end of the year and the beginning of the year. Because the last week of June, everybody's talking about the wonderful plans they have for the summer. And what was I doing? I was staying here, right? Whereas they were going off to ... "Oh we're gonna go trekking in," you know, "in Nepal and then we're gonna fly to Europe for a couple of weeks," or ... and I'm staying in Jakarta. Might get a week in Bali, might go to Jogjakarta, might do something local, but otherwise, not anything very wonderfully exciting or something like that, or unique or different.

> And then the week when the class starts in August, well everybody's followed up about their stories, "What did you do?" "Where did you go?" And there's always sort of that deflating moment when somebody says, "Oh what did you do this summer?" And, "Oh I just stayed here," [in a deflating tone], "Oh." There's always that awkward pause, you know, "Ooh, okay" [puts on an awkward, disappointed look]. 'Cause you don't have a great story.... You don't have a great sort of experience that somehow matches or even supersedes their experience. It's all very, "Ooh, okay" [puts on a disappointed look again]. So, "Well, it was nice talking to you. Bye." They don't say it that directly, but sometimes at these parties, the first week back or something, there's a party at somebody's house, it's always that awkward moment. And so, that influences things. Also, people making choices to suddenly jet off to Bali for a weekend or something like that ... just for an ordinary weekend or a long weekend. I can't afford to do that.

An Indonesian teacher recounted similar experiences. Instead of creating social conviviality, opportunities to share positive experiences turn into moments when socioeconomic fault lines are highlighted and reinforced.

Rick described situations in which his limited economic capability relative to his overseas-hire colleagues meant that he could not involve his family in socializing with them, thus creating an unequal relationship.

RICK: So as I said, you get into these situations where ... well this is very personal, but I don't mind.... Our department used to have these big deals when somebody left, at the time it was back in around 2000 or so, and they chose for us to go to Darmawangsa [a luxury hotel in a high-end neighborhood by the same name]. Have you ever eaten in The Darmawangsa? It's very, very expensive.

And so the deal was, it's the end of year thing, the person's leaving, so it's a farewell party for this person. So that person and his or her spouse are invited, and we pay all expenses for them too. So we have a nice sit-down meal. You're waited on by the waiters, and so on at The Darmawangsa. But it ends up being about a million [rupiah; approximately USD 125][3] per person. And this is 2000. It's probably about a million half, two million [rupiah; approximately USD 150, USD 200][4] now if you went back and tried to do it.

So if I was to bring my wife to join this outing, that would be two million for one meal for the two of us. So what I would do is I'd go alone so I only have to pay for myself, right? But everybody else would have their spouses there, something like that, and because they're all ... you know, what's another, you know, what's another million here or there, because they don't have to pay for their house, they don't have to pay for their ... you know?

It just ... when you've got a limited, much more limited budget, you make choices based on that budget. So I found that it does interfere with socializing.

DT: With your colleagues?

RICK: Yeah, yeah. Or they're going scuba diving, or they're going doing this, doing that. Well, I really have to weigh the costs, the benefits of this. Well, that's interesting, but I would prefer to save the money for my kids, children's college education, you know [laughs]. Or, if we have to move house or we have to fix our car. That's our priority.

Due to his limited financial capability, Rick needed to compartmentalize parts of his life out of his colleagues' view, in this case his spouse, in order to maintain his social ties to them.

Such social ties were also maintained by reciprocal gift giving, and the inability to reciprocate due to limited economic capital created an unequal relationship. Rick explained:

It does make you a little bit more lonely, I suppose. Because there would have been, I think, a little more natural engagement with the other colleagues, or on the weekend, and so on. That would've sort of, would've been easier to forge friendships 'cause you're sort of living on a more of similar level. You know, "You wanna come to our house and use our pool this weekend while we hang around the barbeques?" Or "Do you wanna just come over?" ... If you're the one who always have to say, "Well gee, can I come," you always sort of feel beholden to others, or a sense that you are. Yeah, you have to be sort of invited, you can't offer the ... extend the same kind of offer to them. Right? I can't say, come [over] and use our pool, 'cause I don't have a pool, right? That sort of thing. Whereas I'd have to wait for you to invite me. You see what I mean? It's different, it's different.

Rick lacked the economic capital that he could convert into social capital to facilitate a "natural engagement" with his overseas-hire colleagues.

Rick explained that he tended to gravitate toward other foreigners in similar situations, as well as host country nationals.

DT: Do you feel as though you can relate more or get along with certain groups of people?

RICK: Yes, definitely yes. Indonesians, Indonesians.

DT: Indonesians?

RICK: Yeah, Indonesians. Yeah, and people who are the local-hires—especially if they're men, and their wives are Indonesians or their wives don't have much salary, so they're in a similar economic bracket, if you like, to me. Because then, we get each other, we understand each other—"Let's do *this* activity," 'cause we know it doesn't ... it's within our budgets and we agree to do that, right?

Social circles are often predetermined by the individual's economic capital, rather than purely a factor of personalities (Ortner 2002; 2003). While he could relate to his overseas-hire colleagues on a professional level, Rick's lower economic status created for him a greater sense of affinity with other local-hire foreigners and Indonesians who were in a similar economic situation.

Spouses also influence one's access to social circles. Rick's first wife was an Indonesian who grew up in several countries and was fluent in English. But at the time I interviewed him, Rick was married to his second wife who was also Indonesian and of whom he said:

My current wife doesn't speak really good English. She can, but she's very shy to use English among a large group of people. So it makes it hard for me to bring her to events that are very busy, you know, *rame* [or *ramai*, meaning "lively" or "crowded"] ... unless I know that she'll go there and see people she knows already.

And it's very interesting when we do go, because I do take her to some things and she'll sort of be quiet and then suddenly she'll see another Indonesian woman, and it's like, boy, she goes over immediately and then will spend the rest of the evening talking to that woman in Indonesian. So she's much more comfortable socializing in Indonesian. So it does limit again, 'cause I don't want to just, you know, completely separate from her when we're at parties, so I end up sort of joining her for a while. But it does ... it's just different, it's a different interaction. We don't interact as a couple so easily with couples here at TIS who are both expats.

Social interactions in transnational spaces are racialized, gendered, and classed. The transnational space that the couple had to navigate is a westernized transnational space that placed Rick, a North American man, in a better position to navigate it than his Indonesian wife. Fechter (2007: 113) depicts a similar scene from a German expatriate gathering in Indonesia, and says of the Indonesian wives of expatriate men: "Clutching their handbags, some of them seemed rather uncomfortable, clinging to their partner while maneuvering their way through the crowd." Similarly, Rick's wife lacked the Western cultural capital, including linguistic capital, to feel comfortable in transnational spaces, let alone seamlessly engage with his colleagues. On his own, he was accepted, but as soon as Rick associated with his wife during these social gatherings, it limited his capacity to participate in a transnational setting (Stoler 1995). According to Bourdieu (1986: 249), social capital "exerts a multiplier effect on the capital [an agent] possesses in his own right." Rick's connection with his wife exerted a negative multiplier effect on him. The nonneutrality of the transnational space made it appear as though the (Western) cosmopolitan man was brought down by his local, parochial (Indonesian) wife.

Economic structures, like the pay scale, provide scaffolding for social boundaries. Individually, awkward moments during office small talk after a holiday season or at social gatherings seem insignificant. Collectively, they remind actors who lack capital that the socially constructed boundaries that appear to blur amid celebrations of internationalism still exist. Students at TIS are by no means immune to the effects of these discourses. The discourses shape the way young people experience and interpret transnational educational spaces.

Hidden Curriculum: "It's Our Daily Experience Here"

Spoken and unspoken social constructions forge cosmopolitan subjectivities, and at times the latter were more salient. They permeated the hidden curriculum—the unintended lessons—that often ran contrary to the educational mission that was premised upon the notion of being "international." The significant socioeconomic distance between the international school students and teachers, on the one hand, and the majority of host country nationals outside the school, on the other, gave credence to a latent cultural hierarchy that placed foreigners at the top and Indonesians at the bottom. Students internalized this hidden curriculum.

Nick, another local-hire foreign staff member married to an Indonesian woman, believed in TIS's good intentions. But he was concerned about the powerful effects of the hidden curriculum on his children who attended TIS.

> I just don't want them to look down on their mother because they go to school in this environment. I think there's institutionalized racism at this school. And I think it's hard to escape that. I can see that that is part of the culture that my daughters are growing up in and that concerns me. Because of Indonesians being very clearly second-hand [*sic*; i.e., second-rate] citizens ... I still don't think we've broken through in terms of classified staff,[5] and even the Indonesian teachers I don't think are treated with the same level of respect as other teachers are.... They're not paid the same. I'm not saying that that's why they're not respected as much, but it's symptomatic.... I don't know what percentage it would be but for certainly the vast majority of our students, they see Indonesians in subservient positions—primarily drivers, nannies, maids, gardeners, secretaries, electricians, and what have you. How many Indonesians do they see in positions of power? They don't, right?

> And this is that whole idea of the hidden curriculum. It's what we say we teach, which I believe we believe in and we're trying to do, but by the very make up of the institution, we are teaching this hidden agenda.... It's not like anybody's setting out to try to teach it, but it's being taught because it's our daily experience here. This is the dark underbelly. ... There's no other school I wanna send my children to, I do really believe in the school and I really believe that it's an incredible education that we're offering ... and the multiculturalism and all of those aspects that are powerful and good. But, there is this dark underbelly that isn't being addressed there. I think it poisons the system to some degree.

While I cannot ascertain whether students were aware of the pay structure (it is likely that they were), the fact that the Indonesian staff was in positions lower than the foreign staff was self-evident. When the social structure is pegged to an economic structure, it becomes "part of the culture" and "daily experience" of actors at TIS—it shapes their attitudes, interactions, and subjectivities. Its influence is, as Nick said, "hard to escape."

The hidden curriculum is seen in the lack of interest in Indonesia and the Indonesian language on both personal and institutional levels. Though interviewed separately, Rick echoed Nick's concerns about TIS's relationship with the host country:

> I think we're in a neocolonial situation here. It's, I think, disgusting in some ways. The lack of knowledge of Indonesia is, I think, deplorable. It's shameful, and that's been fairly consistent ... the lack of knowledge of the language even though they [i.e., past school managers, principals, etc.] had spent many, many, many years here. I mean the principals, out of the high school principals ... maybe Hal [the principal at the time] is the most likely to have acquired some Indonesian and he's the one who's been here the least amount of time. Because he has some other linguistic background, I think. He's only in his third year now, but I think he's planning on, in fact, I know he's starting to take Indonesian lessons, and he'll probably acquire sort of a pretty good practical knowledge of the language.

> Whereas, I don't wanna mention names, but others that have been here much longer—ten we're talking about, or sometimes even twenty years plus—speak practically no Indonesian. I find that shameful. I mean, if I was in the Czech Republic or if I was in Chile or whatever, I would acquire at least a kind of functioning use of the language where you could sort of go out and shop in the language a little bit, you know? You may never get to a fluency of a level of conversation but at least be able to get by. And I don't think they feel the need to do that here and they certainly don't go out of their way to learn it.

My own observations of teachers and students confirmed that while many learn to speak the language, there were also many who had lived in Indonesia for more than a decade or two and were barely able to ask a simple question, such as, to the bus driver while on a school field trip, "Where are we going?"

Rick argued that the lack of interest in learning the language of the host country on the part of TIS's decision makers contributed to the institutionalization of racism. Their attitudes were reflected in the way the Indonesian studies program was perceived. Rick related,

> The school's treatment of [the] Indonesian program, again that I found shameful. I think it is not given the proper attention.... There's a very clear situation happened last year that was ... it was really abysmal what

they did to cover the program for the students. They had a teacher leaving because of pregnancy. ... The person they hired [as replacement] was through me, but against my recommendation because she herself didn't really feel she was the right person. I wasn't saying, "Oh I don't like her, we should get another teacher." She herself felt that it wasn't the best position for her, but they gave it to her because they hadn't gone out to look for somebody else.

They hadn't done the legwork, they hadn't put in the time and that's simply because it was perceived as unimportant. Had it been a Science class or a Math class or English class, they would've gone overseas, they would've spent money, they would've done something. But this was considered as just Indonesian, I'm sure. Maybe they didn't say it overtly, but it was there—it's just Indonesian, just a stopgap measure, it doesn't matter, as long as nobody complains.

So I think the administration doesn't give enough respect to the Indonesian-studies program, it's the same with the way they treat the language—it's only, you know, it's only Indonesian. It's the same people making the decisions that don't learn the language.

The lack of interest in the Indonesian-studies program reflects Edward Said's (1994: 41) words, "One can see in the story, I think, the power to give or withhold attention, a power utterly essential to interpretation and to politics." The school administrators could afford to pay scant attention to the language and knowledge of the host country both as individuals and as decisions makers of an educational institution because they and the school formed part of the privileged transnational capitalist class. "Indonesia," the local, occupied an inferior position not only in terms of the staff pay scale, but also in the "international" curriculum.

The "power to give or withhold attention" in relation to the study of Indonesian language at TIS also appeared in the story that Jesse told. Jesse was an alumnus who had been at TIS for two years, and had gone on to major in Indonesian studies at a university in Australia. During his university course, he went on a language-exchange program to Yogyakarta and Malang, and became fluent in Indonesian. Jesse then visited TIS to see his former teachers. When he started speaking Indonesian to his former Indonesian teacher, she cried. According to Jesse, she was touched because none of her other students had taken the study of Indonesian seriously. Jesse described the Indonesian program at TIS as a "joke." While there are other international schools, even within Indonesia, which put more effort into teaching the language of the host country to their students, negative attitudes toward developing countries and their language pervade the hidden curriculum.

Neither the lack of interest in the local language, nor the lesser significance attached to the Indonesian studies program was accidental. Colonial discourses on cultural hierarchies continue to construct what Alastair Pennycook (1998: 19) refers to as "European/Western images of the Self and Other" and notions of "Superiority and Inferiority." These discourses are supported by contemporary capitalist economic hierarchies. Pennycook (ibid.: 23) writes that "colonialism should not be seen as a forgotten era in the past but rather as the context in which current ideas were framed" (see also Phillipson 1992). I am by no means suggesting that there is a colonial agenda in operation at TIS, but rather that the discursive forces set in motion during the colonial era continue to provide context for present-day perceptions of cultural hierarchies that are structurally embedded in institutions like TIS due to the present-day economic structures. Discourses are not immutable, but they are remarkably resilient over time (Said 1985 [1978]).

Internalizing Hierarchies

The discourses embedded in TIS's structural makeup do not work in isolation. They are powerful because they form the social fabric both inside and outside the campus gates. Colonial and capitalist discourses intersect to reinforce racialized, classed, and gendered social structures, which transnational youth then internalize. Nick and Rick were intimately aware of the impact that these discourses had on young people through observation of their own children.

Nick candidly shared his observations of his daughter's desire to identify as white, like her father, instead of Indonesian, like her mother:

> And Lara [older daughter] for example, doesn't really like going to Ika's [wife] village. Because, I mean … it's weird 'cause Lara's actually a little bit of a racist. She really, she really … kinda looks down on Indonesians, you know? … I remember when I went to dinner and it was just the family and me and the girls and so on. And I made some sort of a self-deprecating joke about being the only *bule* and Lara's like, "No, I'm a *bule*." I'm like, "No honey, you're *campur* [mixed]. You're a mix." "No, no, no, I'm a *bule*," you know? And really, we explained this and, no, she's a *bule*. That's the way she sees herself.

Fechter (2007: 80) posits that even "using *bule* in such a casual, self-deprecating manner represents a power move: through re-appropriating the term, expatriates limit the unwanted connotations that Indonesians' usage of the term might have, thus linguistically regaining a dominant position." Lara recognized, even at seven years old, that she could elevate herself positionally by identifying with her white father. Superiority was marked as white, male, urban, and rich like her father, in contrast to Indonesian, female, and poor villager like her mother.

According to Nick, Lara's behavior is "totally different" when he does not accompany his wife and children to his wife's village. Lara "mixes in" with the Indonesian kids. "But if I go," Nick said, "she stays with me, and we stay, you know, more separate." Lara stays physically close to her father to indicate that she identifies with her father's whiteness. Physical distance reinforces social boundaries that are constructed through embodied racial markers.

Nick could relate to his daughter. As a child of European migrants growing up in North America, he had not wanted to identify with his parents' heritage in his desire to assimilate into the dominant culture, though he later grew out of this as an adult. Nick felt that Lara's attitudes may be a factor of age, and that studies show that many second-generation migrant children grow out of this phase as they mature. But it still concerned him: "How that's gonna play out over time, it's hard to say."

Transnational youth internalize the discourses that work in the social worlds that they live in, both on and off campus, even while they negotiate their positions within these discourses as well as resist and coproduce them.

Straddling Boundaries

In a school ethnography of a private Chinese Christian school in Indonesia, Chang-Yau Hoon (2013) shows that the socioeconomic privilege and the ethnic as well as religious homogeneity of the students meant that the school reproduced class, ethnic, and religious fault lines despite the multicultural rhetoric. Similarly, the hierarchies internalized by the students at TIS reveal that the school's internationalism is not as straightforward as it seems. At the same time that the school promotes internationalism, it also reproduces racial and class hierarchies that then intersect to construct being "international" as "white," privileged, and not Indonesian. To feel "international," one needs to maintain a distance from the local by constructing it as a fantastical, unfamiliar Other—a distance that is institutionalized by the pay scale. Social boundaries between those considered international and local are racialized, classed, and gendered.

Those who occupy a liminal space are acutely aware of the processes of boundary making, rendering them methodologically interesting subjects. Ann Stoler (1992: 550), in writing about colonial concerns about the "métissage," argues that they "straddled and disrupted cleanly marked social divides" and their "diverse membership exposed the arbitrary logic by which the categories of control were made." The local-hire foreign teachers and their children, who are able to shift in and out of both the transnational and Indonesian contexts, feel the effects of the boundaries precisely because their own positional ambiguity requires them to constantly negotiate these boundaries. Attempts to maintain the boundaries even as they were blurred created dissonance among different parties at TIS, which the subsequent chapters explore.

Notes

1. I have provided the names of regions rather than countries for participants whose nationalities are not commonly represented in the TIS population. This is to help preserve their anonymity.
2. From TIS's internal human resource document of 2009/2010. The difference in value between overseas-hired and locally-hired foreign staff came to more than USD 20,000 for a staff with a dependent spouse and two dependent children.
3. Based on the May 2000 exchange rate.
4. Based on the August 2009 exchange rate.
5. Administrative support staff.

CHAPTER 4

Chasing Cosmopolitan Capital

> For the international cosmopolitan class, equipped with
> the best passports that money can buy, and a *habitus*
> that allows them to feel at home in most international
> cities, the world is their turf.
> —Ghassan Hage (2005: 470)

TIS's mission is to educate students to become international. However, TIS's efforts to promote being "international" are frustrated by the national and transnational socioeconomic hierarchies in which cosmopolitan practices are embedded. Students had different starting points in their pursuit of cosmopolitan capital and the ability to practice being international due to their varying family backgrounds. This was because being international requires Western cultural capital that is packaged as cosmopolitan cultural capital, thus giving an advantage to those who were already westernized to begin with. This chapter explores the tension between the school's expectations of its students and the differing ways in which students and parents engage with the school's ideology of being international.

Parents value cosmopolitan capital and chose to enroll their children at TIS to enable their children to acquire this capital. However, both students and their parents who are not westernized, especially those who do not speak English, experience a sense of dissonance when they navigate through TIS's transnational educational space. They are constructed as "Other" by the school, in contrast to the Western "us." Consequently, the varying access that students have to (Western) cosmopolitan capital then mediates the authenticity of their claim to belong at TIS.

On-Campus Gatherings for Parents

The fact that a great number of students feel uncomfortable in the Western setting of TIS remained hidden because most students spoke English to some degree or another. Also, their youth meant that they were expected to be malleable and equally capable of acquiring cosmopolitan capital regardless of their cultural background. In contrast, parent gatherings made apparent the ease with which those who had Western cultural capital navigate the transnational social space of the international school, and the difficulty for those who did not.

I attended parent gatherings that ranged from monthly coffee mornings organized by parents around discussion topics that may interest them to major meetings between parent groups and the high school administrators, college information sessions, and open house nights. Generally, expatriate families of international school children relocated based on the father's employment, which meant that mothers rarely had official employment. This meant that both fathers and mothers attended meetings that took place in the evenings, but those who attended the daytime meetings were almost exclusively mothers. Many of the mothers who attended parent gatherings were highly educated women, including former Fulbright scholars, medical doctors, engineers, and so on. Some had given up their professional careers to become "trailing spouses" for the sake of their husbands' careers (Coles and Fechter 2008). A couple of mothers I interviewed commented that they missed the intellectual stimulation that came with the interview, revealing their predicament. Apart from this, it is significant that the mothers who actually attended the regular parent coffee mornings or the main meetings with school administrators had good command of English.

When I walked into the monthly parent coffee mornings for the first time, I immediately noticed the visible and audible contrast between the parent group and the larger student body. The parent group was made up of roughly twenty women who were predominantly white, representing only a handful of all parents. The few Asian mothers who were present were usually either married to a Western man (often Anglophone) or fluent in English because they had been educated in an Anglophone country. While the English-speaking students, for the most part, had an American or Americanized accent, many of the mothers spoke with a distinct nonnative-speaker accent. This pattern, particularly the fact that the attendees were predominantly white, was repeated at various other parent gatherings.

It was the same at the international school I visited in Singapore in March 2010. I spent a day with Ruth E. Van Reken (2009 [2001]) as she gave several talks about Third Culture Kids to students at an international school, followed by an evening talk for parents. The audience for the daytime talks was made up mostly of students of Asian descent, while the audience for the evening talk was mostly parents (both fathers and mothers) of European descent. The only visible non-white group present at the evening talk in Singapore was the group of self-identified adult Third Culture Kids with whom I was sitting.

At both schools, the demographic contrast between the parents and students was stark. While there may have been multiple reasons why Asian parents generally did not attend the gatherings, one reason is the cultural, including linguistic, dissonance between the school and Asian parents. The transnational space of these international schools provided a more comfortable space for those with Western cultural capital.

The currency of Western cultural capital at TIS was obvious when non-English-speaking parents were faced with the prospect of navigating the transnational social space. At TIS's open house night, parents unfamiliar with the dominant culture of the school looked uncomfortable. All parents were invited to attend an opening ceremony for the night, before visiting their children's different classes by following a contracted version of their children's daily schedules. Each "class" lasted for about ten minutes, during which the teachers briefly spoke about the class. The parents were then given an opportunity to ask questions.

I introduced myself to some of the Japanese parents before the opening ceremony started as we all gathered in the foyer of the main theater for nibbles and drinks. One Japanese mother confessed that she was intimidated by the cultural gap between the school staff and herself. Her poor English was a sore point for her. Her shy and submissive mannerisms corroborated her confession. Even her nail polish looked distinctly Japanese in style. When I asked her whether or not I could follow her around that evening for my research, not only did she give me permission, she seemed grateful I had asked. Even though she was with her husband who was competent in English, my presence meant that she would have someone who was female and fluent, not only linguistically like her husband but also culturally, in navigating both English-speaking and Japanese-speaking spaces. I became the cultural buffer that shielded her from the unfamiliar Anglophone setting. For the remainder of the evening she clung to me, metaphorically speaking. Given the level of discomfort some parents felt in relation to the dominant school culture, it was not surprising that they did not attend many of the parent gatherings.

Korean Parents' Meeting: Miraculous Encounters

The same cultural dissonance was apparent at the annual meeting held between Korean parents and the school administrators. In October 2009, the principal, vice principal, activities officer, academic counselor, and sports officer, who were mostly men, met with Korean parents, who were mostly women, in the school's small theater. Roughly seventy Korean mothers attended that daytime meeting. A volunteer interpreter was present at all times, attesting to the linguistic handicap that Korean parents faced in an Anglophone environment. The five staff members took turns speaking in English, while the mothers asked questions in Korean. The interpreter stood next to the speakers as she interpreted both ways between English and Korean. She interpreted consecutively—the speaker would speak for a little while and then let her interpret before speaking again. Some mothers laughed or whispered comments to each other before the interpreter conveyed the principal's message from English into Korean; these comments were at times humorous, and indicated that these mothers understood English. However, many also responded in an identical manner only after they had heard the interpreter's version in Korean, indicating that there were many among them who did not actually understand English. There was a linguistic gap between the staff who represented the school's dominant culture and the Korean mothers who represented a large proportion of the parent body.

After the meeting, I spoke to the interpreter, So Young, to ask whether I could interview her. She clarified that she was a parent of a child enrolled in elementary school at TIS, not the high school cohort that I was studying. There were high school parents who were fluent in English and capable of interpreting, but they had solicited her help to ensure that all the high school parents could sit and listen to the staff speak. I then asked So Young whether there was someone among the high school parents who spoke English, as I wanted to interview them and I could not speak Korean. She suggested that I approach Mee Yon. So Young, the interpreter, pointed toward the center of the theater where some of the mothers had congregated. "The one wearing the tiger print," she said. I looked and thought I had spotted the person she was pointing at, so I thanked her and off I went, trotting down the stairs with an out-to-accomplish-a-mission strut. I had no time to waste in finding contacts among the Korean parents that day, as I had another interview appointment to rush to soon after.

By the time I walked across the theater to talk to the lady in the tiger print, the school staff had left and I was the sole non-Korean person in the room apart from the Indonesian cleaners who were standing—invisibly—on the sidelines waiting to clean up the theater. While walking hurriedly across a theater full of Korean women, I became painfully aware that my body language, the way I carried myself and moved across space, was out of sync with theirs. The Korean parents seemed to move their bodies independently but in harmony with each other, like a symphonic concert of "miraculous encounter[s]" that occur when one's embodied language matches the general cultural flow (Bourdieu 1990: 66). The Korean bodies by then were huddled in conversation in small groups scattered across the theater. Some were standing and others sitting, most of them chatting away in Korean. Some groups seemed serious and others jovial, but all were in sync with the dominant cultural music that was inaudible to me. Abbas El-Zein writes that migrants "survive by growing new body parts" (2002: 239). In this sense, I did not have the cultural "limbs" (Wise 2010: 935) nor the time to acquire what Malinowski (1922: 8) refers to as "the feeling" for etiquette or atmosphere in the room.

Once at the center of the theater, I sat down on the chair closest to the "tiger print" mother. I arched over to speak to her, as there was another person sitting between us. But the second I opened my mouth and uttered some English words, a look of horror came over her as though she had seen, well, a roaring tiger. I immediately stopped explaining my research and stupidly used English to ask the question, "Do you speak English?" She shook her head, shifted in her seat, and leaned back away from me as much as the available space behind her would allow. She pulled so far back that her chin dug into her neck. I instantly recognized her reaction. She was terrified of English and the proposition that she engage with it.

I had the wrong person. As I looked around, the Korean parents quickly accommodated my awkward presence. I heard someone speaking in Korean to another as though explaining what I wanted. Though I could not speak Korean, I gathered this much from context and the few English or Korean words that I knew and picked up. Soon, someone directed me to another person who had a tiger print top underneath her cardigan, which explained why I did not notice her earlier. She was still in conversation with someone else, but nodded to me to indicate that she knew that I needed to talk to her. This was Mee Yon, who I have mentioned in previous chapters and was fluent in English. Although I had possibly been rude to the Korean parents with my abruptness and awkwardness due to my lack of Korean cultural capital, they did not seem offended. I experienced the power of speaking fluent English. I had the power to intimidate some of them, regardless of my intentions, by doing nothing more than speaking a few words in English. I had the privilege of having my cultural ignorance forgiven and my wishes instantly accommodated without having to ask.

Western cultural capital was accorded privilege even in a space dominated by Koreans. It is an example of how embodied capital influences the level of comfort and privilege we feel in navigating social spaces. In this instance, I felt the foreignness of my body in a space where "Koreanness" dominated, despite the fact that I look physically indistinguishable from Koreans (and was often mistaken for a Korean during my stay in Jakarta). But even then, I could exercise some power by virtue of my Western cultural capital. It follows that in the reverse case, many of these mothers and others like them who did not speak English would have experienced a sense of powerless dissonance while navigating the transnational space of TIS where "Westernness" predominated. When this cultural dissonance is overlooked, it creates the illusion that those with Western cultural capital are collectively more "international" than others because they fit in. Those with Western cultural capital are able to appear more authentically "international" than those without.

Ideal Cosmopolitanism Meets Pragmatic Cosmopolitanism

Language was an issue for the Korean parents, and the interpreter's presence was essential for the meeting. Given the large number of Korean students enrolled, a separate meeting for Korean parents made practical sense for keeping them informed of their children's schooling. But the school administrators thought otherwise because the lack of Western cultural capital, especially English-language fluency, was conflated with not having cosmopolitan cultural capital. At the meeting described above, one of the school administrators said to the Korean parents: "What is happening in here—the fact that there is a separate meeting for Korean parents—symbolizes what is happening out there." The administrator pointed in the general direction of the high school area of the campus. He later reiterated the symbolic link between the two while expressing his concern with the Korean students' tendency to self-segregate. It was constructed as a matter of choice, and that choice, it was implied, was the result of Korean ethnocentrism. The existence of a separate meeting for the large number of Korean parents was perceived not as a language issue but as a refusal to participate in the internationalism the school was trying to promote. The administrator called on the Korean parents to instill more "international" values, which are congruent with the school's values, in their children. The onus to integrate into the school's so-called international culture was placed on the Koreans.

The principal and the vice principal further expressed concern that Korean parents were overly demanding of their children in terms of academic achievement. The mothers in the audience laughed a little at this as though acknowledging that it was true. The principal listed the external pressures placed on Korean students, such as private tutoring, music lessons, and having to attend Korean schools in addition to their regular schooling at TIS. The school believed that students were not getting enough sleep as a result, leading them to sleep in class and cut classes. One of the administrators went as far as to suggest that if parents were sending students to two schools—TIS and the Korean afterschool tutoring classes—then parents might need to reassess their children's schooling needs. "Perhaps this is not the right school for you," he said. The reasons underlying parental school choice seemed at odds with TIS's purported goals of educating global citizens. Their children's failure to become international in the way the school conceived it made their desire for cosmopolitan cultural capital for their children inauthentic and their presence problematic.

The failure of Korean students to integrate with the English-speaking students and the Korean parents' efforts to ensure their children retained Korean cultural capital were seen as a failure to be international. Parents from non-Western backgrounds who sought to produce cosmopolitan cultural capital in their children were perceived as undedicated to the school's ideology of being international. Parent gatherings amplified the sense that Westernness predominated the school culture, which provided the benchmark for measuring the authenticity of being international.

"We Can't All Expect to Live the Same Way"

The school's perception that some students did not fulfill their expectations for an ideal student was affected by the way student contribution to the school community was measured in ways that privileged Western cultural capital. Cultural dominance is not "automatic," but it is, as Stuart Hall (1996: 424) puts it, "actively constructed and positively maintained." Students with Western cultural capital are affirmed in myriad subtle, unintentional ways. The dominant culture exercises symbolic power through the type of sports they offer, the recognition of certain types of extracurricular activities over others, and through the modeling of the culture practiced by the staff (Bottomley 1992; Bourdieu and Thompson 1991).

Measuring Student Involvement

Students with Western embodied or cultural capital (white or western-ized) were relatively well represented in sports-related activities, while Asian students dominated music-related activities. When a slide show of pictures taken during various school events over the semester was presented during a general assembly that involved all high school students, there was a heavy emphasis on sports activities, and less emphasis on music activities. This was partly because the person in charge of posting photographs of extracurricular activities at the time was Dr. Davies, who was sports oriented. He was well liked by students from a diversity of cultural backgrounds, but seemed to have an especially good rapport with the westernized male students who often hung out in his classroom playing mini-basketball. Dr. Davies's preference for sports over other activities inadvertently affirmed the involvement of westernized students over that of Asian students in school activities and regional competitions. I regularly saw Asian students perform in the evenings and on weekends, sometimes just to play or sing one song as entertainment for school events that they were not participating in themselves. These activities were not as spectacular or visible as sports activities, and therefore Asian students were at times perceived by others—and themselves—as apathetic.

Internalizing Negative Perceptions

Many Korean students were academically oriented, gave impressive performances on United Nations Day, and were actively involved in music activities, such as the school band and strings group. Despite this, Dong Gun, a Korean student who was fluent in English, believed the Korean students had a bad reputation among the teaching staff because they were perceived as focusing solely on academic pursuits at the expense of other pursuits. Dong Gun said: "I mean, who's gonna like a group of students who study only? Who don't do much extracurricular activities … don't really, like, have any benefit for the school … contribute to the school, I guess? Who always travel together in their same culture everyday. Never speak English, they speak Korean. Even if teachers just say, 'You have to speak in English.' They always speak Korean. Who would like them, right?" Dong Gun said this with a mixture of frustration over his fellow Korean students, who he felt only hung out with other Koreans and did not contribute much to the school, as well as over the teaching staff for not being accepting of the Korean students:

> But, you know, it's not their [Korean students'] fault, really. It's just the culture that's like that. ... You have to accept it. But there's a huge racism thing, I guess. Teachers are not really fond of them because they're not like everyone else. I think I can say the same thing for Indos because they basically do the same thing, except for the studying part. [We both laugh because the Indonesian students were reputed to party more than study.] But basically we're the same, that's why I think we got along. The Indo, me and the other Indo, we got along together because, you know, we're the same, we're similar but we just go different paths. They [teachers] have to understand that Asians, especially Indos and Koreans, compared to Westerners are different. We think differently. We can't all expect to live the same way even if we're in the same place, same society, right?

Dong Gun's calling the teacher attitudes toward Korean students a "huge racism thing" may appear strong, but it expressed the sense of frustration and resignation that many of the Korean students felt about the way they were negatively perceived at the school.

Despite this, Dong Gun accepted as legitimate the perception that Korean students did not contribute to the school. It had not registered in his mind that Korean students were heavily represented in extracurricular activities relating to music. Dong Gun submitted to the symbolic power to which he was subject (Bourdieu and Thompson 1991). Cultural hegemony requires, as Hall (1996) argues, the consent of those who are dominated. Student involvement in the school community was measured in such a way that the contributions made by those with Western cultural capital were more visible than the contributions made by those without.

Upward Social Mobility

About a month before interviewing Dong Gun, I had observed him and two or three of his male Korean friends at a loss for words in the face of their teacher's inability to comprehend their perspective on Korea's mandatory military service for men. They were having a casual chat in between classes when the topic came up. Short of facing imprisonment, avoiding the twenty-plus months of mandatory military service was rarely a viable option for young Korean men. But Mr. Bailey, their teacher, could not seem to understand the complexity of the situation. "Well, can't you live so that you don't have to go back to Korea? I mean, in this day and age of globalization," he suggested. Dong Gun tried a few times to say, "It's out of a sense of ... a sense of ... ," but he could not find the word "duty." The other boys then tried to explain how they would lose their citizenship. I piped in, "You'll be stateless." They then explained how their parents would have to sign a paper saying that *they* would serve in some sort of public service if their sons did not serve in the army. Whether it was about military service or other issues, it was sometimes difficult for teachers to grasp that the conditions for participating in the processes of globalization were different for TIS graduates depending on their background and nationality.

Dong Gun explained to me that teachers generally did not understand the Korean socioeconomic context that drove Korean students in a seemingly single-minded pursuit of academic achievement: "[It's] the only way we can, in our Korean society, we can go out of our social class, like move on to a higher social class, to go to a better college, to seek better education. It's the only way. That's the only way to live a better life than your parents did. Otherwise you're just a nobody, you're just a nobody. But once you make that jump, you become this really special person, and that's the only way you can do it. That's why they study for hours, even after school." According to Dong Gun, there was a clash between what TIS thought was good for the students and what he claims is the reality that Korean students face upon repatriation to Korea. This clash, I believe, in part led the school administrators to suggest that the Korean parents reconsider whether or not TIS was the right school for their children. In the next section, I provide some context to this difference in opinion, which reveals the dissonance that occurs when national and transnational class structures converge at an international school.

School Choices in National and Transnational Contexts

Both the school and the parents believed that TIS offered something of transnational value that was worth reproducing in the students. They diverged, however, in the meaning they attached to that something. TIS was a popular school with more applications for enrolment than the available student intake. A woman working in the office that handled the school's accounts said she was impressed by the Korean parents' persistence in trying to enroll their children at TIS. She recounted a story of how one such parent came to the office with a bag of cash pleading for them to let her child enroll. The woman had to repeatedly explain to the parent that cash payments were not accepted for tuition fees and that student acceptance at the school was not determined by the form or the amount of payment. This incident symbolizes the strong desire of Korean (and other) parents without Western cultural capital to convert their economic capital into (Western) cosmopolitan capital by paying for their children's international education. Their pursuit of cosmopolitan capital is a "generational project" (Peterson 2011: 33). TIS offered an environment for reproducing cultural capital in their children that these parents could not provide at home.

As an international school, TIS played an important role in fulfilling both national and transnational expectations of their students. In the eyes of Koreans and Japanese, for example, TIS offered high-quality education and an internationally recognized university-preparation program. Students, without fail, spoke highly of TIS's pedagogical approach, which emphasized critical thinking. There is a Korean high school in Jakarta, but parents believed that TIS offered better-quality education. There is also a Japanese school in Jakarta established by the Japanese government, but it only provides compulsory schooling, which ends at grade nine. Japanese families commonly followed one of the following paths when their children reached the end of the ninth grade: the breadwinner (usually the father) would ask their employer to relocate them back to Japan with their whole families, or to Singapore, where there was a locally established private Japanese high school; if the employer did not agree to the transfer, then the mother and children returned to Japan or relocated to Singapore while the father remained in Indonesia—or they enrolled their children at an international school in Jakarta. Choices like these were made depending on circumstance and financial capabilities. International education also provides students with the opportunity to compete for places in world-class universities in Anglophone countries. Its high educational quality, internationally recognized programs, and location (i.e., families could remain together in Jakarta) made TIS an attractive and prestigious school choice.

Moreover, international schools enable some to gain a competitive edge in national education systems in their passport country. For Koreans, the pathway to employment is dictated by a highly competitive educational system. The prestige of the university they attend affects their future employment opportunities. Koreans living overseas are given opportunities by higher-education institutions in Korea to circumvent some of the competition through the special university entrance requirements set up for overseas returnee students. These requirements vary—for example, depending on whether they have been overseas for three, six, or nine years—to accommodate the students' lack of exposure to the Korean curriculum and acknowledge the potential contributions they can make to the university from their international experience. Japan follows a similar, though less regimented, system. Schools and universities have designed separate entrance requirements for *kikokushijo*, or returnee children, to take their international experience into account. Roger Goodman (1990) argues that the special consideration given to *kikokushijos* reproduce class structures by enabling children of professionals who were sent overseas by multinational corporations and government agencies to enter prestigious universities upon repatriation.

Returnee students need to maintain some knowledge of what is taught in their own national curriculum. Korean students utilize off-campus Korean tutorial schools for this purpose. Though they grow up transnationally, young people need to remain competitive in their passport country where they are likely to return to in the future for university and work. The social and economic structures of students' countries of citizenship have a transnational reach.

Managing Cultural Identity

Parents were often faced with the need to balance their efforts to expose their children to cosmopolitan cultural capital with a desire for their children to maintain fluency in the culture of the parents' or passport country. This was partly to help maintain their children's sense of identification with the parents' country and partly for pragmatic reasons: to help them acculturate into the workforce in their country of citizenship in the future.

Parents played a significant role in shaping their children's identity through school choice and influencing their children's cultural orientation while they study at these schools, whether toward the school culture or home culture (assuming both parents are from the same country). For example, Dae Hyun said, "My mom told me to be international, so I avoided the Koreans and hung out with the others. But then she started worrying that I was not Korean enough. So she told me to go hang out with the Koreans. So I did." At the time of my fieldwork, Dae Hyun hung out mostly with an English-speaking group made up of Asian students of various nationalities.

Mina

Mina's story illustrates how employment considerations are intertwined with cultural orientation. When her father was due to be reposted in Jakarta, he initially intended to take up the posting on his own as a *tanshin funin*[1] while the rest of the family stayed behind in Japan so Mina could complete her high school education there. But Mina asked to come along because she wanted to re-experience the international environment of TIS that she had once experienced during her father's first posting in Jakarta about a decade earlier. In convincing her parents, she promised to later attend university in Japan, where she would have a greater chance of being accepted by "a good university" as she would be eligible to apply as a *kikokushijo*. A good university, her parents believed, would shape her into a *"rippa na ningen,"* which can be translated as a "worthy" or "respectable" person.

According to Mina, her parents did not want her to attend university in, for example, the United States. She explained: "They said that for one thing it will cost too much money. Plus, they believe that if I'm gonna work in a Japanese firm, then I would definitely have a better chance of getting hired by going to a good Japanese university than an unknown university in the United States." This statement contains two assumptions regarding the successful use of cultural capital. First, her parents seemed to believe that her language fluency and educational background would present different opportunities in university applications. Mina's capital may work as a competitive advantage relative to that of other Japanese applicants in Japan, lending her opportunities to be accepted in a "good Japanese university"; or it may prove a disadvantage if she has to compete with Americans and other English speakers in the United States, where she would find herself in an "unknown university." Cultural capital can mediate university choices. Second, they assume that the successful use of cultural capital in university choice will translate into cultural capital in the job market in Japan or "a better chance of getting hired." Being successful in the job market in the future is linked to the acquisition of the right balance of (Western) cosmopolitan cultural capital and national Japanese cultural capital.

Mina argued that being grounded in a singular identity is important even in the midst of her pursuit of "internationalism" to avoid being *"chuuto-hanpa,"* or "half-baked": "My younger sister often mixes in English [when speaking Japanese], but I tell her to stick to speaking Japanese at home. And that's because ... I don't think it's good to mix English and Japanese. Because, if you're *chuuto-hanpa* ... so if you're *chuuto-hanpa* in both languages then—and Kubota *sensei* [Mina's Japanese teacher] thinks like this too—you need to have one foundation. If you don't have a definitive foundation, then it'll make life difficult in various ways. For example, if you're *chuuto-hanpa* in both, then you might end up not reading or not being able to speak in either language." The use of the label "half-baked" pathologizes bi- or multi-lingualism and hybridity. Nevertheless, cultural fluency that accommodates singular notions of identity and conforms to the dominant culture of national contexts remains salient in mapping out career and life trajectories.

Yae

Similarly, Yae's parents insisted that she attend a university in Japan, her country of citizenship, to ensure her enculturation there. They argued that it would determine her future success. At the time of our interview, Yae had graduated from TIS the previous year and was visiting from Japan where she was an undergraduate student. She was one of the few Japanese who had no qualms mixing her languages while speaking to her friends. Yae had initially wanted to study in the United States for university, but her parents were against it because she had neither a clear idea of what she wanted to study nor the desire to live there indefinitely. Yae explained:

> They told me, "Do you know what will be most frightening for you in the future? Your passport says that you are Japanese, but not having a Japanese identity, losing it, do you know how frightening that is? There are a lot of people like that in this world. People like that won't succeed. How can they, when they don't know their own identity? You're gonna end up like that too. Besides, even if you go, you won't learn anything in America right now when you're so *chuuto-hanpa*. So if you want to go to America, you should first learn *jyōshiki* [common sense] in Japan, you need to build something up first as a Japanese, then study abroad in America for graduate studies or the like…. There's no point going to America with such a *chuuto-hanpa* sense of determination when you're not even planning to live there indefinitely."

Her parents equated cultural hybridity with "losing" her "Japanese identity," which is something to be feared because in their eyes it offered no future. These fears about cultural hybrids are not new. They existed in colonial discourses of European-indigenous "mixed bloods" that, according to Ann Laura Stoler (1992: 514, 549–550) "encode métissage as a political danger predicated on the psychological liminality, mental instability, and economic vulnerability of culturally hybrid minorities."

Yae's parents were also expressing pragmatic concerns for their daughter's future competitiveness in the marketplace. Their concern about Yae's imperfect English ability and desire for her to have a solid grounding in Japanese *jyōshiki* indicate that her parents were aware of the importance of cultural capital in both Anglophone and Japanese contexts. Since her partial enculturation into Anglophone culture would be a disadvantage in Anglophone contexts, they insisted on the importance of nurturing her ability to navigate through a Japanese work environment. Yae wanted to eventually work for a multinational corporation in Japan, and her parents explained that it would be easier to find a job in Japan as a graduate of a Japanese university. Even if English were used in multinational corporations, Japanese would still be necessary. They said that Yae's limited knowledge of formal Japanese and *kanji* (Japanese/Chinese characters) would disadvantage her, even though she insisted that she would study *kanji* while in the United States. "'All things considered, you know too little about things which you can only learn by living in Japan, such as the Japanese *funiki* [atmosphere], or culture, starting with the Japanese feel for common sense, the *jyōshiki* that comes with being Japanese. These are things that you can't learn through a book in America.' That's what they told me," she said. Yae believed it had turned out well because she was now taking an English-based course popular among *kikokushijos* at a well-known Japanese university where she could use both languages.

David

Jeong Tak, who went by the name David, said that his parents wanted an international education for him due to "all the advantages" that would equip him in an increasingly globalized world. David said of his father's views:

> He wants me to speak English. He wants me to have a broader scope, broader mind, but he doesn't want me to be an American. ... So, he wants me to have all the advantages, I guess, about the broader scope, international friends, and English, all that. In education here, he can really see, for example in science. In Korea, science is like memorizing rather than understanding concepts and do experiments. Well, they do experiments, but not as much as they do here. Here is sort of like a discussion education, where the teachers ask questions and they're sort of like, "Isn't it this? Isn't it this?" Give idea and we understand later. And the teachers analyze it, "Blah, blah, blah, blah." In Korea, it's not like that. So I guess my dad wanted me to get more, like, a creative science, I guess, of education.

David's parents wanted David to have the educational and cultural capital that TIS offered, such as "broader scope, international friends, and English." At the same time, they had concerns that David's exposure to TIS's school culture could potentially turn him into "an

American" when they wanted him to retain his Korean identity. "I'm open-minded, but I'm still more to the Korean thoughts, and beliefs, and so on. ... I think they [his parents] educated me sort of like that. 'You're a Korean, you're a Korean. Although you're going to an international school, you're a Korean.'" David explained that his father impressed upon him that Korean cultural capital was also important for his future economic success:

> It's not that swinging [on a] chair is really bad [something I saw him do in class on several occasions while interacting casually with his teachers], or American beliefs are bad, but then it's just different from Korean beliefs. Since he wants me, and I want it too, to work in Korea, live in Korea for the rest of my life, it's better to have Korean beliefs rather than American beliefs. ...

> Being educated in American school, be part of American teachers, international students, I think he [dad] was ... not scared, but he was worried that I'll have those American sort of system of thought, international beliefs, which I don't think they're bad, I just think they're different.

David's parents felt that it was a combination of "international" and "Korean" capital that would help David "work in Korea."

David conflated educational advantages with "international" or "international beliefs," which he in turn conflated with "American" or an "American sort of system of thought." This conflation indicates that international schools are seen as providers of high-quality education that reproduces cosmopolitan capital in their students, but also that cosmopolitan capital overlaps with Western capital. For David, becoming "international" ran the risk of becoming "American." As a result, his father was concerned about his Korean cultural retention. "He wanted it [international education], but he doesn't want me to be American, have American thoughts and everything, American beliefs and everything. So at home ... I think my dad and mom ... sort of put it into the back of my mind, 'You're Korean, you're Korean.'" David also explained about his fluctuating language ability over the years and his mother's efforts to ensure his fluency in Korean:

> In middle school I thought English/Korean is about the same. My teacher told me that I was—I didn't know what that meant at the time, but then ... he told me that—I was a bilingual. So I was as proficient in English as I was in Korean. But then ... from, like, third grade my mother started to get scared because I was dreaming in English. I was talking in English in my sleep, instead of Korean. ... It meant to her that I was becoming more and more ... lean to the English side rather than the Korean side. So she thought that I might forget Korean.

So she started educating me at home. She bought these textbooks that the kids in my grade would do in Korea, and then she started working on the textbooks with me ... all throughout ... until sixth grade, no, until eighth grade.... Every year she bought these new textbooks for my grade. ... So my Korean education was pretty much settled, I think. So I didn't lose my Korean, I didn't lose my English. But then in high school, Korean education stopped 'cause I was starting to get really busy.

His parents wanted David to retain his Korean language skills because they knew that he would need them in the future.

Cultural capital, whether cosmopolitan, American, Japanese, or Korean, are embedded within national and transnational socioeconomic structures. Parents see TIS as a site for reproducing the necessary cultural capital—such as education, language, access to universities, and so on—in their children to ensure their future success. Parents are dedicated to seeing that their children acquire the "right mix" of national and cosmopolitan capital. This mixture varies depending on where they want or can afford to send their children to study for university. Some parents may perceive their child's hybridity as an advantage, while others may not.

Whether students and parents perceived the school's ideal cosmopolitan practices as "international," "Western," or "American" depended on their proximity to Western cultural capital. At times, parents' best intentions for their children ran contrary to TIS's goal of producing global citizens who by default are westernized to some degree or another. As a result, those who did not practice the dominant form of cosmopolitanism were deemed to be inauthentic cosmopolitans. This perception of inauthenticity was particularly strong with regard to the way the Indonesian students were perceived, as I discuss next.

Postcolonial Elites Meet the Transnational Middle Class

> The Indonesians, they're filthy rich. They pay the school fees,
> but then the school pays a lot of taxes on that, and 90 percent
> of the taxes go back into their [parents'] pockets.
> —Aaron, an American student in eleventh grade (reconstructed)

Aaron said this to me as we sat in the cafeteria with two of his friends during the first couple of weeks into my fieldwork. He and his friends were interested in my research and were offering information about the campus. The hyperbole of his words aside, "filthy rich" was a common description used by non-Indonesian students to refer to the socioeconomic background of Indonesian students at TIS. Sometimes it was said matter-of-factly, and other times mockingly. "Filthy rich" was contrasted with the assumed middle-class normality of the other students. Aaron's friend Catie, for example, explained that while she may be better off than the average Indonesian outside TIS, back in the United States her family is just part of the regular middle class. "Filthy" also suggests that the financial status of the Indonesian students was perceived as lying outside the norm and was gained through unlawful means. While this echoes the political discourse in Indonesia as a result of the nation's chronic corruption issues, it also reflects the unease that emerges when socially constructed class or cultural boundaries are transgressed. There is a perception that Indonesians should be poor, as befits a Third World country, while middle-class Western expatriates are normal. Wealthy Indonesians disrupt this structure.

Given the expensive tuition fees, only the elite and upper classes among the local population in Third World countries are able to access international schools. By enrolling their children in international schools, they are able to convert their economic capital into cultural capital. International schools become a site where different classes of people with varying senses of entitlement to cosmopolitan capital converge—the middle classes from overseas meets the upper classes from the local Indonesian population. The former generally consist of children of professionals working in transnational companies and organizations, while the latter are often children of large business owners and government ministers. The middle classes from developed countries are better positioned to access the cosmopolitan capital necessary to operate in a transnational context than those of developing countries due to the global economic hierarchy. Those with Western cultural capital are particularly well positioned because they have a "natural" claim to cosmopolitan capital.

Mark Allen Peterson (2011: 89) describes a similar dynamic in his study of the Egyptian elite in an American school in Cairo whereby economic capital and cultural capital do not overlap: "For Americans, the primary purpose of the school is to provide an American education such that their children's acquisition of educational capital is not impaired by their parents' relocation to Egypt. For Egyptians, a primary purpose of the school is to provide students with a 'quality' education far removed from the Egyptian system. These purposes combine to create a system in which middle-class Americans set social standards for Egyptians of the highest elite class." Likewise, Western cultural capital has been and still is important in constructing the upper classes in Indonesia since the later part of the Dutch era, as previously discussed in chapter 2.

In Indonesia, the upper classes and upwardly mobile top-end middle classes pursue Western cosmopolitan capital in the form of "transnational goods" and "Western educations" (ibid.: 7). It is common practice for the upper classes to send their children overseas for higher education, particularly to Western countries, but also to Singapore. In order to facilitate the transition into higher education in the West, Indonesian parents choose one of a few options for secondary education for their children, including: a local private school with some English-medium classes, such as those formerly known as "national plus" schools (which may be supplemented by an extra year or two at a transitional institution at the destination country); a local school that offers international education and internationally recognized accreditation; the local international school; or English-language-based education in Singapore or the destination country. Western higher-education credentials can also be attained through private institutions established locally or through international joint ventures that offer Western accreditations. Many education options are available, but the more "authentic" they are as sites of Western cultural production, the higher the status. Both locals and foreigners engage with this discourse of authenticity.

A British woman I met at a conference illustrated this clearly. At the time, Sarah was living in Spain with her family, where her children went to a British international school. Sarah commented that the Spanish locals sent their children to the school because it was perceived as elite, whereas the British did the same because it was the normal thing to do. She spoke of it as though it was curious, possibly laughable, that the locals considered elite what in her mind was merely "normal." There was a gap between Sarah's and the local elite's perception of the school due to their different positionality vis-à-vis cosmopolitan capital. The school represented high-quality education and a site for acquiring cosmopolitan capital for the local elite. It was something out of the ordinary. For the British, it represented an educational quality comparable to that back in the United Kingdom and a site for the reproduction of British capital. The overlapping nature of British (and by extension Western) cultural capital and cosmopolitan cultural capital normalizes its pursuit among the British, like Sarah. Similarly, for those who consider Western culture as part of their identity, TIS would appear to be a natural choice for their children's education. Because the dominant school culture greatly overlaps with their own, it normalizes their choice and renders their pursuit of cosmopolitan capital invisible. It does not make them appear like overdressed "new money."

This normalized pursuit becomes visible, however, when parents are asked whether they are willing to relinquish access to Western cultural capital that is reproduced through educational institutions. I asked Vianny, a mother of one of the students at TIS and an Indonesian woman married to a white American man, about her children's education. I asked whether it was important for her children (US citizens of mixed heritage) to attend university in the United States, and whether she would consider Indonesian universities as an option. She was in clear favor of the United States: "They have a good education there [in the United States] and their father is American. It's better opportunity to tell the truth, right? Just being realistic about it. Much better opportunity for them." Because her children were American citizens by descent, it made the choice of sending them to an English-language-based international school, as well as university in the United States, appear normal. Those with a Western background can choose to place their children in international schools as though it were the most natural choice, while in effect reproducing cosmopolitan capital.

In contrast, those for whom Western cultural capital is not a part of their everyday family life appeared to transgress social boundaries in their pursuit of the same cosmopolitan capital for their children. Indonesians and Koreans, especially, were seen as (mis)using the school. One staff member said of them in passing, "They just want to get into American universities," suggesting that their motivations were not genuine, that they were not committed to becoming international. They were seen as "wannabes" or ambitious upstarts.

Students participated in this discourse. Non-Indonesian students alleged, in the form of rumors, that the Indonesian students gained entry into TIS because their parents had paid a lot of money in addition to the regular tuition fees—in other words they had bought their way into TIS using what was assumed to be unlawful economic capital. Indonesian students, particularly the Chinese Indonesian students, were cast as illegitimate students in these rumors.[2] Although it is difficult to verify the rumors or determine the motives for non-Indonesian students in spreading these rumors, what is significant is that they chose to draw on a discourse that naturalized their own claim to cosmopolitan capital, and thus reinforced the school's ideology of being international that privileged Western cultural capital.

Authenticity was partly constructed based on the identity of the person or body that paid the tuition fees. A large portion of non-Indonesian students had their tuition fees paid for by their parents' employers, such as a government agency, multinational company, or transnational organization (e.g., diplomatic agency, Nike, or the Red Cross), after they had relocated the family to Indonesia. The employers paid for the tuition fees to ensure that the education of their employee's children was not compromised by the relocation. These parents did not make significant financial sacrifices to enroll their children in TIS. Some of their employers also provided high-end condominiums or houses with pools to live in as part of the expat package. But these luxuries were not constructed as "filthy" or "rich" because they were provided for by their employers and therefore considered "lawful"; their lives would presumably return to middle-class normality when they repatriated. In contrast, some students had their tuition fees paid for out of their parents' own pockets. Although these students were from a diverse range of nationalities, Indonesians were among the most conspicuous of this group because many were from wealthy families. For these students, enrolling at TIS required the effort of converting economic capital into cultural capital. This (economic) effort, or lack thereof, acted as a measure for determining authenticity.

Some of the students who hung out in the English-speaking groups were also from wealthy families and were chauffeured to and from school in a Mercedes Benz or equivalent, but the term "filthy rich" was still reserved for Indonesians who hung out in the Indonesian-speaking groups. The Indonesian students stood out due to their visible markers of wealth. A teacher commented that her non-Indonesian students said the Indonesian students were "glamour-loving," in reference to the designer clothes and bags that Indonesian-speaking students sported, as well as their preference at the time for Blackberry phones over iPhones (the latter was preferred by the English-speaking students). Indeed, it was common to see Louis Vuitton and other branded bags lying around the Indonesian hangout area. Also, talk of Indonesian students having bodyguards peppered the conversations I had with students. While I did not observe any students with bodyguards on or near the campus, I did see a number of men who appeared to be bodyguards congregating near the entrance of a beer garden frequented by international school students. One Indonesian student, whose father was a high-ranking government official, said that his father used to assign a bodyguard to follow him around when he was off campus, but he did not like it and managed to convince his father to stop. Students also hired bodyguards on occasion for show. Dae Sik, the Korean student who hung out with Indonesians and at times identified as Indonesian, spoke of hiring bodyguards when he went clubbing. Bodyguards served as a symbolic marker of wealth and power. Indonesians and non-Indonesians alike used such markers for different reasons to construct the Indonesian students as different from mainstream students.

Most of the Indonesian-speaking students who were considered "filthy rich" were also Chinese Indonesians, and often referred to as "Chindo(s)," a term that was not yet in popular use outside the school at the time though it did gain traction later.[3] While some Chinese Indonesian students used the term to describe themselves, others avoided it. Although "Chindo" did not carry a derogatory connotation, it did indicate that the Chinese Indonesian students were singled out as different from other Indonesian students. Staff and alumni sometimes blamed Indonesian students as a whole for having negatively changed the culture of the school and giving the school a bad reputation with their lack of academic diligence and tendency to go clubbing and partying. This was despite the fact that many other students, especially students from the English-speaking groups, went clubbing too. Sometimes the blame was placed more specifically on Chinese Indonesian students rather than Indonesians as a whole. One teacher specifically differentiated between the behavior of indigenous and Chinese Indonesians. She believed the former studied hard, while the latter did not.

The negative perceptions toward Chinese Indonesian students have remained consistent over the decade and a half since Indonesians were allowed to enroll in international schools. An alumnus who graduated in 2003 accused his former "Chindo" classmates of not having "class." A parent whose two children attended TIS' elementary and middle schools in 2017 said, with derision, that "Chindo" students and their parents were acting like "new money" by flaunting their wealth.

It is not the purpose here to determine whether or not a particular group of students did or did not behave in certain ways. The more significant point is that discourses about the inauthenticity of cosmopolitan pursuits by Chinese Indonesian students reflected local discourses about the inauthenticity of the ethnic Chinese minority as Indonesians (Hoon 2008). In Indonesia, the ethnic Chinese were legally differentiated from the indigenous population under the colonial Dutch administration, and subsequently under Suharto's New Order regime. They were allowed to flourish economically, but not politically. Often, they became targets of political scapegoating during times of crisis (most recently in the 1998 riots) as a result of their collective wealth and foreignness.[4] This racializing discourse regarding Chinese Indonesians that was (and still is) present in the national space of Indonesia flowed into the transnational space of TIS.

But among the Indonesian students, the opposite dynamic occurred at TIS. The separation between *pribumi* (indigenous) and Chinese Indonesians was blurred rather than reinforced. This is not to say that these distinctions were forgotten. Shane, who was himself of mixed

British and indigenous Indonesian descent, said of his Chinese Indonesian friends that they are "not Indonesian." Yet, he was close to them and hung out with them constantly, though it did appear that his closest friend among the fellow senior Indonesian boys was Kenji, who was of mixed Japanese and indigenous Indonesian descent rather than Chinese Indonesian. Indonesian students were comfortable enough with their ethnic differences that they were able to casually joke about Chinese stereotypes with each other.

In one of Kenji's Indonesian classes, there were not enough copies of a book that they were supposed to read and so his classmates and the teacher were discussing a possible solution. Michael, a Chinese Indonesian, suggested in Indonesian, and in jest, "One person should photocopy it and sell it!" After some more discussion, the teacher actually did assign Michael to photocopy the book and distribute it to the class. Michael stood there looking slightly confused. The teacher reassured him, "The others will then pay you the cost later." Looking relieved because he thought he had to pay for it all, Michael said, "Oh, okay." So Kenji interjected, "Damn you, *Cina*." Cina was the official translation for China or Chinese, but it had a history of being used as a derogatory term, especially before the political changes that occurred after 1998. There was an unspoken rule in Indonesia about using the alternative term *Tionghoa*, which also means China or Chinese, if one wanted to be respectful when speaking to someone with a Chinese background. By saying what he said, Kenji was acting out a typical reaction to Chinese Indonesians when they are believed to be stingy for not wanting to pay. Then Vincent, who was also Chinese Indonesian like Michael, followed up Kenji's comment by teasing Michael for trying to make a profit out of it. Vincent was playing on stereotypes about the Chinese being business-mongering scrooges. A few moments later, Michael picked up the book in question from the teacher's desk and, as he returned to his seat, chanted, "Profit! Profit!" He accompanied this with a few "hooray" gestures.

Incidentally, Michael is from one of the wealthiest families in Indonesia and his friends say that he usually has bodyguards who accompany him home from school though I never had the opportunity to see this. So, while local stereotypes against the Chinese were used by non-Indonesians as a tool to treat them as different from and their presence at TIS as more inauthentic than indigenous Indonesians, among the Indonesians these ethnic divisions were in fact blurred. They were blurred because at TIS Indonesians of all ethnicities, as well as non-Indonesians who spoke Indonesian, bonded over their sense of not being able to be a part of the mainstream English-speaking groups.

When national and transnational structures intersect, they challenge neatly constructed boundaries because one's economic capital does not always reflect one's cultural capital. It is similar to how "new money" transgresses class boundaries by using economic capital to compensate for lack of distinction, or how the "fallen nobility" feel uncomfortable when they are lumped together with the lower class as a result of their lack of economic capital. At TIS, children of expatriates who would otherwise be considered middle class in their countries of citizenship experience an upward shift as their status is elevated to being culturally equal to or higher than that of the local Indonesian elite. In contrast, the local elite, despite their economic capital, experience a downward shift as they are culturally placed on the same or lower level than middle-class students from overseas due to their lack of a "natural" claim to (Western) cosmopolitan capital. The Indonesian students generally came from families that were financially better endowed than the Western expatriate students.

These positional shifts created a sense of dissonance at TIS. Those who identified with the dominant culture of the school expressed this dissonance by undermining the authenticity of Indonesian students' wealth and right to be at TIS. Dissonance also appeared in the form of competition, particularly among the male students, for the top position in the school social hierarchy, as I discuss in more detail in chapter 7.

In Pursuit of "International" Passports

The pursuit of (Western) cosmopolitan capital takes on a tangible form when it concerns the pursuit of Western passports. Research participants from developed countries never spoke about citizenship issues because they had a "natural" claim to desirable passports. In contrast, participants who were from or whose parents were from developing countries were well aware that passports are valuable assets.

Anaya

Anaya's maternal and paternal grandparents migrated out of India but they maintained their connections to India and returned at various times. Her mother was born in Spain and partly raised there, while her father was born in India and partly raised in Malaysia (Malacca) and Indonesia. In addition to describing her family's transnational engagement over three generations, Anaya emphasized the importance of her mother's Spanish citizenship due to the advantage it provides for her family:

> I was born in Spain. ... My parents realized at that time that they had a very big advantage of getting, of making me be born in Spain considering my mom was born there—that we'd all get European passports. And if you think about it, that's kind of a really, really big advantage. And in the Spanish community you always go with the mother. So my mom has Spanish passport and my dad is really into this, like, "passports," "immigration" [Anaya makes air quotes], and, like, airport stuff, and ticketing. ... So he knows a lot about it, and so he just thought that it would be a big advantage to our future if we all had European passport[s].

> My brother was born here [Jakarta], but he followed my mom and got a Spanish passport. After five years my dad got a Spanish passport as well. And because I was born there [Spain] I automatically got one. It actually is working to our benefit, 'cause now I'm going to university and I have to pay a quarter of the fees that everyone else [who do not have a European passport] has to pay.

Anaya's father thus deliberately sought to acquire Spanish citizenship for his family through his wife's connection to Spain to capitalize on the advantages that it offers.

Anaya's preference for England for her university studies, as opposed to the United States like many of her peers, was not just influenced by the lower tuition fees that she would be expected to pay as a member of the European Union.[5] There were other reasons: "Because my brother's there, and because I have cousins there. And because of my European passport. And because I've always wanted to go there. Because my mom is, like, my mom is very pro-Europe, and she's very ... like, she's always had like this attraction to England. So, it's been instilled, I guess, in me." It is unclear whether her mother encouraged Anaya to go to the United Kingdom (as opposed to the United States, for example) mainly due to her mother's own ties with Europe, family ties in the United Kingdom, or financial considerations. However, it illustrates that even though issues of citizenship may seem like a practical matter, they can also affect a child's emotional preference for university destination (Bourdieu 1986).

Anaya usually hung out in the English-speaking groups that were perceived by the school to be "international." Therefore it could appear as though Anaya's practice of being international was a matter of individual choice. However, Anaya's family's transnational engagement, including that with Europe, began a couple of generations prior to her own. She was therefore predisposed to engage with the dominant culture of the school. According to Bourdieu (1986), "the transmission of cultural capital is no doubt the best hidden form of transmission of hereditary capital, and it therefore receives proportionately greater weight in the system of reproduction strategies." Cosmopolitan cultural capital is hereditary for transnational youth too.

Afra

Afra similarly frames his discussion about passports in terms of tangible benefits. Afra, as I mentioned before, is an Algerian national who was born in the United States. He was living in Korea at the time of our Skype interview, but he grew up in the United States, Mozambique, Turkey, and Algeria. Because his father was a diplomat, he was ineligible for American citizenship despite being born there. Afra explained that the principle of *jus soli* does not apply to children of diplomats.[6] While telling his story about growing up in several countries, he said that at times he would let his friends think he was American because he sounded American, though he felt "guilty" for doing so:

> My parents drew me away from everything Algerian 'cause there was a civil war there and they didn't want me to know those things. So they tried to maintain a house that had no citizenship issues. So we never talked about Algeria or anything. And then I went to Algeria, and I never tried to be Algerian. But now I realize I have this passport and it's a country I don't know. ... And I might have to go back one day, and the only things that I know about the country or I've seen about the country are not good things. So it made me sort of guilty if I told people I'm American, but I'm an Algerian. I'm actually an Algerian citizen. It's like someone saying, "I have a million dollars," but he has a hundred bucks in his bank account. So it's a bit [of a] hard feeling, you know.

Afra uses a monetary metaphor to describe the value of citizenship as a practical asset. In his view, having citizenship in a developing country is like being almost broke, while citizenship in a developed country is the equivalent of being a millionaire. Passports are an institutionalized form of social capital, of having a membership in a network. I kept in regular contact with Afra for several years after our interview in 2009. During this time, he was preoccupied with the strategies he was devising to attain citizenship in a developed country. He spoke often about his efforts to enroll in a university graduate program in a developed Anglophone country, which would enable him to apply for permanent residency, and eventually citizenship.

Deborah

It was the same with Deborah, a Ghanaian national. Deborah was born in Ghana, but moved with her family to Japan, where she studied at an international elementary school. She then moved with her mother and sister to the United States, where she finished her schooling and undergraduate years. Her father remained in Japan and her mother later returned to Japan. Deborah is fluent in English and Japanese. When I interviewed her via Skype, she was working in China as an English teacher. Not long after the interview, her visa to China expired and within two days she had to fly back to Ghana, a country she had left to live overseas when she was two years old and had only visited once when she was six.

In Ghana, she found a job at a Japanese firm on a local salary. Had she had an American passport, her educational qualifications and cultural capital would have earned her a higher salary. Deborah's salary was not enough to pay for the college debt that she had accrued during her studies in the United States. I was in regular contact with her during her three years in Ghana. It was evident that she had difficulty adjusting to life in Ghana and regularly spoke of finding ways to rejoin her family in Japan or, like Afra, applying for graduate school in an Anglophone country. Her visa application to Japan was rejected. So, with the financial support of her relatives, she moved to the United Kingdom to further her studies, then moved to Senegal to find work when her UK student visa expired. After struggling for a couple more years to find regular employment that paid a decent salary, she finally found work at the United Nations in Geneva.

In contrast, those who had acquired citizenship of developed countries as a matter of descent that spanned several generations did not have the same kind of concern for passports. They did not perceive a passport's importance as capital because it was seen as normal in the same way that enrolling at an international school while overseas was normalized for those with Western cultural capital. To those like Anaya, Afra, and Deborah who have to expend effort to acquire citizenship in developed countries, however, the importance of passports was plainly visible.

Pursuing a Cosmopolitan Future

Research shows that parents cite varying reasons for choosing an international or internationalized education: for example, English-language

education, access to university and/or work opportunities abroad, and
an international outlook (Weenink 2008; Amit 2010; Hayden 2006).
Don Weenink (2008: 1099) found in his study of international education in the Netherlands that parents "wanted to prepare their children
for a future in a globalizing world and to stimulate them to engage
in globalizing social arenas." Engaging in these globalizing arenas requires cosmopolitan capital, which overlaps with Western capital. Preparing for a globalizing world thus means different things to different
actors depending on their background and positionality.

TIS offered an education that promised future economic and professional success in both expanding transnational contexts and trans-
nationalizing national contexts. For both contexts, students need to
acquire cosmopolitan cultural capital. For the latter case, students also
need national cultural capital. Indonesian elites see a need to immerse
their children in transnational educational settings like TIS to acquire
cosmopolitan capital that will reproduce their elite status within the
national context of Indonesia as in other developing countries (Peterson 2011). A similar, though less pronounced, dynamic applies to the
Korean and Japanese students.

The pursuit of cosmopolitan capital by those who were differently
positioned due to their cultural background at TIS created a sense of
dissonance. TIS wanted to produce "dedicated cosmopolitans" who
could successfully navigate transnational contexts, whether the international school campus or the world beyond (Weenink 2008: 1094).
For those with the "best passports that money can buy," their pursuit
of capital to become part of the "international cosmopolitan class" appeared natural, dedicated, and authentic (Hage 2005: 470). For those
without them, their pursuit of cosmopolitan capital was constructed
as inauthentic. They appeared to be too pragmatic and failed to fulfill
the school's expectations that they become "international." The dissonance arose from the differing expectations that various actors had
of the school and the shifting class positions that resulted from the
convergence of national and transnational class structures. It is easier
for those who already have Western cultural capital to participate in
transnational contexts. The next chapter will continue to demonstrate
that being international required Western cultural capital within the
context of a Western school culture, but I shift the focus to student
social relations.

Notes

1. The term refers to the common practice of Japanese male heads of household living away from the family for extended periods of time as a result of work-related postings.
2. After I had heard the rumor from several students, I went to the office that handled the school accounts. I asked an Indonesian administrative officer (who incidentally grew up transnationally herself as a child of an Indonesian diplomat) about these rumors. My answer came in the form of a half-hour-long, excruciatingly detailed explanation of the payment process as evidence of the impossibility of bribery. The admissions staff was offended that I had asked about the rumors as though I was the one accusing the school of corruption.
3. At the time of writing, it appears that the term "Chindo" has become more commonly used in Jakarta among English-speaking Indonesians and foreigners. It may have originated among international school alumni, and became popular as an alternative to the English-term "Chinese Indonesian," which is long, and the Indonesian term "Cina," which used to carry a derogatory connotation during the Suharto era when the term "Tionghoa" or "Chinese" (pronounced with an Indonesian accent as "*chai-nis*") was preferred when trying to avoid being derogatory.
4. Ethnicity (and religion) continues to be a political issue as seen in Jakarta's 2017 gubernatorial election when one of the candidates, Basuki Tjahaja Purnama (more commonly known as "Ahok"), became the target of mass demonstrations due to his Chinese Christian background. He had initially led the polls but eventually lost the election and was sentenced to two years in jail—a sentence that even the prosecutors later objected to for being too harsh—on blasphemy charges.
5. This conversation took place before the United Kingdom voted to leave the European Union in the 2016 referendum, which may change the tuition fee structure in the future.
6. A principle that states that a child's citizenship is determined by their place of birth.

CHAPTER 5

The Politics of Hanging Out

Choosing where to hang out and with whom is an important part of school life for young people (Cillessen and Mayeux 2007; Kinney 1993; Lease, Musgrove, and Axelrod 2002). Friendships and social groups may appear to be formed as a matter of choice based on chance meetings. Contrary to popular belief, however, social groups at schools are not formed based on interests or personalities alone, though they do play a role (Ortner 2003). Class and cultural background influence the choices that young people make and the opportunities available to them in forging friendships. Colonial and capitalist discourses intersect at TIS to inform the school social hierarchy and youth practices of hanging out. Students draw on different forms of capital, at times in contradictory ways, as they position themselves in the social hierarchy and determine with whom they prefer to hang out while coping with the effects of mobility on their friendship circles.

Students navigate through and racialize social geographies of power at TIS. Western capital is privileged in many aspects of the school, including student popularity, use of space, perception of the Other, participation in school activities, and student perception of staff. English-speaking groups, particularly the high-status ones, are racialized as "white" (Frankenberg 1997; Dyer 1997). Students who are not part of the mainstream English-speaking groups are perceived as a nameless, faceless "Other." The privileging of Western capital affects students' sense of school belonging. In this context, students compete to become international as a means to climb the social hierarchy in part by acquiring Euro-American cultural capital, which in their words is expressed as becoming "white," "normal," or "Western."

Racializing Status and Student Cliques

Students employed descriptive language that racialized social groups. Students referred to the English-speaking groups as "Western," "white," "*bule*," "everyone," or "normal" (or the "fountain people" in the case of the twelfth graders, because they hung out near the school fountain). The other main groups, as mentioned in chapter 1, were referred to as the "Indonesians" or "Indos" (and often "Chindos"), "Koreans," and "Japanese."[1] The terms they used sometimes ran contrary to the diversity of physical appearances or cultural backgrounds represented in these groups. Instead, the terms emphasized the cultural capital that students had in common. English-speaking students, particularly those in the high-status group(s), were racialized as "white" in reference to their Western capital.

"The White Kids ... are Popular"

During one of the breaks, I chatted to a couple of senior students about cliques and popularity. "So, who are the popular kids?" I asked as we sat in the main outdoor hangout area that had just enough shade for our comfort. It was a sunny, tropical day on the well-landscaped campus, where the lawns were covered with the broadleaf carpet grass that was common to the limited green spaces in Jakarta.

"Well, popularity isn't such a big deal here," Melinda contested. Her answer was typical of the senior students in the main English-speaking groups because their own dominant status was hidden from them. "But I suppose the white kids who like to sit over there are considered popular," Melinda continued as she pointed at the benches near the campus shop. "The 'white kids'?" I inquired suspiciously; I was sure they were not all "white" in the dictionary sense of the term. "Yeah, the white kids," repeated Melinda.

I later took a closer look at the group to which she was referring. Indeed, many of them appeared to be white, but there were also those who appeared to be black, Asian, or of mixed descent. All had a giss that betrayed the Western influences in their lives. "White kids," then, did not refer to physical appearance, but rather cultural competence (Twine 1997). There were also a number of gym bags with the school logo lying on and around the benches, indicating that many of the "white kids" were highly involved in athletic extracurricular school activities.

On another occasion, a couple of male students from the group that Melinda had referred to as the "white kids" helped a few male Korean students set up a tent during a senior sleepover held at school. As they were doing this, one of their friends, Tarson, came over and said, "Hey, the white kids are helping the Korean kids!" There was a pause in the air as we all tried to digest that statement. One of the "white kids" broke the silence: "Dude, I'm Pakistani." The other "white kid" added, as he held on to the tip of the tent he was working on, "Yeah, and I'm Asian. My mom is Chinese ... and, you're half Japanese!" Upon hearing this, the first student chuckled at the inaccuracy of his initial remark and walked away as his friends busied themselves again with the tent.

Student cliques that were perceived as popular were made up of students who were highly westernized in their mannerisms and dispositions. Though many tended to be of European or part-European descent, students were often perceived as white regardless of their physical attributes because whiteness is not always about skin color (Hage 1998). Being "white" was conflated with having Western capital and high social status. Student groups and behavior were racialized.

"The Normal People"

English-speaking groups, though dominant, were not homogenous. If high-status students among the English-speaking groups were referred to as "white," then words such as "normal" or "everyone" were used to refer to other students who represented the majority of the English-speaking students. Jenny, Mee Yon's daughter, whom I have mentioned previously, referred to them as the "normal people" as she recounted her experience when she first enrolled at TIS: "Um, I did have a class with, like, the normal people, but I had, like, a special class with the ESOL people. So I made friends there" (interview, 23 October 2009). The most obvious marker of normality was fluency in English. Jenny's use of the word "normal" reflects how Western capital was made invisible as a marker of distinction among members of the dominant culture, and all others were measured against this normality (Dyer 1997).

By the time I interviewed Jenny, she herself was one of the "normal people." Jenny detailed the social hierarchy by differentiating between the "popular" students, "normal people," and the others:

JENNY: Oh, well there are these kids who go out every night and do drugs and stuff. They're popular people, quote, quote [laughs]. And people who do sports who are in, like, basically in every season ... sports. And [pauses] that's about it. Or [pauses] yeah, yeah that's about it.

DT: And the not-popular ones?

JENNY: You mean, like, the normal people?

DT: The normal people? Are there people [who are] other than normal?

JENNY: Yaaaah [laughs]. The normal people, they're occasionally in sports teams.... They go out once in a while. They [pause], oh, and they're normal-looking. Like, not good-looking, not ugly-looking. I really sound superficial, saying all this [laughs]. Um, and then the not-normal people.... They're just, they're quiet. They don't go out at all, like Koreans. They, like, nobody knows like the mass and individuals [can't tell the individuals from the mass], right? They don't really talk that much ... to foreigners [i.e., non-Koreans].[2] ... Oh, uhm there's this Indo group, they're considered popular, like, dominant because [pause].... First of all they're rich, and like, they're like, in my opinion they're like rebels. 'Cause they go out every night like, they go out and do like rebel things.

DT: What about the other ones? Do they tend to be of particular countries or ...

JENNY: Oh, the sporty ones, they're mostly Australians or like white people. [Pause] So if you're white and good at sports, that's like the very high chance you go out with the popular people group. And [pause] and then the rest is spread out.

DT: Spread out? Like, mix?

JENNY: Yeah.

DT: What about the ... quiet ones?

JENNY: Yeah ... they're mixed too but rarely any white people, I think.

Jenny associated high-status students with going out, participating in sports, and being mostly Australian or white.

Even the types of sports students choose to get involved in contributed to the racialization of popularity. Sports such as rugby, soccer, and basketball are considered high status, while sports such as badminton are considered low status. Jenny commented, "If you're a guy and you're good at sports and you like to go out, you fall into the popular people group. But then it really depends on the sport really." Jenny chuckled as she continued, "If you're in basketball or soccer or rugby, I guess you'll fall into—and if you like to go out a lot—the popular people. But if you're into something like badminton, swimming, or cross-country, and you don't like to go out a lot and you're white

... I don't think you'll [be popular]." I asked her whether some sports are considered better than others, to which Jenny responded, "Yeah, I guess so. 'Cause no one ... falls for varsity badminton." She was suggesting that female students are not attracted to badminton players even if the players make it to the school team because it is not considered high status. As badminton is popular mostly among the students of Asian descent, while other sports have a much higher proportion of students of European descent, its low status has implications for the racialization of the campus whereby "whiteness" is associated with high status and attractiveness, and "Asianness" with low status and unattractiveness.

Indonesians were also considered popular for being wealthy and for going out at night. Indonesians' economic capital made up for their lack of Western cultural capital. Jenny referred to the mainstream English-speaking groups, of which she was a part, as the "normal people" who participated in some sports, went out sometimes, and were supposedly average looking. These students were perceived to be diverse. Finally, low-status groups, such as the Koreans and even groups that were mixed, were perceived as quiet because they did not go out clubbing, and were rarely included among the "white people." High status was associated with either Western capital or wealth, while low status was associated with a lack of both.

Building a White Wall

Students who had native fluency in English and spoke it as their main language of communication at school generally hung out with each other despite their different national, ethnic, and racial backgrounds. Students in these groups were westernized in their mannerisms. The way they sit, walk, talk, move, dress, and wear makeup all betray the Western influences in their lives (Bourdieu 1990). Many of them also exude confidence and a sense of entitlement to social spaces (Burck 2005: 103). These students tended to win the tacit approval of the school as the best practitioners of being international due to the visible diversity within the groups. They were the standard that others were encouraged to emulate and by which others were measured. These students shared a sense of mutual intelligibility with each other based on their Western—especially Anglophone—capital. However, in the same way that, as Hall (Hall and Werbner 2008: 353) notes, liberalism has "never understood its own culture," the shared cultural language embedded within their practice of being international was invisible to these students and the staff.

In contrast, the mutual intelligibility shared by those who had the cultural capital to be international was obvious to those who did not. Mina, the Japanese female student mentioned in the previous chapter, said, "They may seem mixed, but they've basically built a wall around themselves based on being white." The cultural sameness of those in the dominant groups was most visible to those who were positionally marginal to them and struggled to join these groups. Mina said that when she enrolled at TIS as an eleventh grader, she tried to join the English-speaking groups by sitting in their hangout areas. But she gave up after about one week. Mina found that their values and the way they interacted with each other were vastly different from what she was used to. "I tried to do the over-the-top-reaction thing like an American," she explained in Japanese. Mina acted it out for me. She switched to English and expressively said, "That's great! It's beautiful!" as she flung her arms out for effect. "But I wasn't being myself," she reverted back to Japanese. "I thought to myself, 'Why do I have to be the one acting like an American? It's so tiring, I don't like it.' So I quit because school isn't supposed to be a place where you go to get tired." Mina felt as though the onus was on her to make all the cultural adjustments.

On another day, as we crossed paths, I casually said to her in English, "Hey Mina, how's it going?" To my surprise, she spontaneously let out a big sigh and said in Japanese, "I don't get how I'm supposed to respond to that. What are you supposed to say when people say that to you?" She seemed frustrated. In Japanese (and many other languages), it is uncommon to ask about another's well being in casual speech like we do in English. For Mina, the seemingly innocuous greeting represented yet another cultural difference that required her to exert effort to understand and adjust to. The question leaves her wondering whether she is supposed to respond with her real state of mind, or say something else.

Mina had not been trained to respond in a way that creates what Bourdieu refers to as the almost "miraculous encounter" between her giss or bodily hexis, habitus, and the Western transnational environment or field (1990: 66). Drawing on Bourdieu, Amanda Wise (2010: 923) says, "when one encounters a similarly habituated body or bodies they more often than not respond in certain magical or miraculous ways to interactions with our own bodies in given situations." This could be a simple "Hi," a slight change in facial expression, or the process of slightly leaning your body toward someone, being able to almost perfectly anticipate the other body responding by leaning toward you, to which you respond by leaning forward a bit more, ending seamlessly with a kiss or two on the cheeks. Wise (2010: 922) explains, "It is precisely because of their embodied nature that habitus and hexis have the capacity to induce in us affective responses to inter-subjective encounters with those around us and to interactions with our environment." When this magical, miraculous encounter does not happen, then one experiences what the Indonesian students refer to as *"nggak nyambung,"* or "can't connect." Many cited this as their reason for not hanging out in the English-speaking groups.

As a researcher unfamiliar with teenage slang, I experienced a similar sense of dissonance to Mina when I was casually asked by students, "Hey Danau, 'sup? [What's up?]" Male students, in particular, greeted me in this manner. Each time, they would walk past me without waiting for my answer. When they did stop to listen to me detailing my schedule for the day, it felt awkward. The third time it happened, I decided to ask the male student whether there was a standard answer to the question. He told me that it is simply: "Nothing much." I was an adult trying to adjust to a particular type of Anglophone teenage lingo. For some of the boys, these simple greetings turn into complicated rituals. I was following the sport-loving Tarson one day, and every time he passed by one of his male friends from his "white kids" clique in the hallway, whether they were white, black, or mixed, it was accompanied by a bit of fanfare. There was a lot of fist and shoulder bumping, which were too complicated for me to remember and describe without having a step-by-step manual, and a verbal "hey, sunshine" or two, timed with perfection to the rhythm of the physical greeting, all before they would walk on by like nothing had happened. I cannot imagine any of the Japanese or Korean boys who did not grow up in this milieu ever learning these rituals well enough to be able to carry them out with the appropriate giss to create that natural rhythm. Those who are not a part of the dominant culture have to exert effort to understand and adjust to it, and many times fail, sometimes miserably, even with the simplest of greetings. But these efforts are invisible to members of the dominant culture.

Whether the English-speaking groups were considered "white" or "normal" thus shifted depending on the positionality of the speaker vis-à-vis the dominant school culture. Ruth Frankenberg (1997: 1) views whiteness "as ensembles of local phenomena complexly embedded in socioeconomic, sociocultural, and psychic interrelations. Whiteness emerges as a process, not a 'thing,' as plural rather than singular in nature." English-speaking students became "white" in the eyes of the students outside the English-speaking groups even though the latter were able to differentiate between the subgroups within these groups.

They were racialized as "white" due to the Western cultural sameness that the members of these groups shared. In contrast, insiders to these groups and staff members with Western capital perceived the students in the English-speaking groups in general as "international" rather than white. These insiders only labeled the high-status subgroup as "white."

Spatial Practices: Reproducing Status through Hangout Areas

The use of campus space reflected the way groups and status were racialized and gendered. Henri Lefebvre (1991: 27–28) argues that "space embodies social relationships," and it is neither neutral nor "innocent." Rather, he (ibid.: 26) argues: *"(Social) space is a (social) product* ... the space thus produced also serves as a tool of thought and of action; ... in addition to being a means of production it is also a means of control, and hence of domination, of power; yet ... it escapes in part from those who would make use of it." At TIS, this meant that students hung out in various areas following patterns that reflected their social relations. During the common recess time, student cliques congregated in the same area day after day. There were hangout areas that were considered cool and others that were not, reflecting the power relations between groups—relations that reflected the slippage between language, culture, "race," and gender.

Reproducing Racialized Spaces

Jenny, who was an eleventh grader during the second half of my field-work, recounted her changing friendship circles through middle and high school in a way that highlights the link between the racialization of popularity and the use of social spaces. Jenny attended TIS for most of her schooling. When she first enrolled at the school as a second grader, she took classes catering to speakers of English as a second language. But by the time I met her, she considered English her strongest language. She initially hung out with Korean students, but she felt "bullied" by them for being different. Jenny explains, "They just moved from the Korean schools, they had different standards. Like, I don't know the latest fashion or, like, the latest celebrities or anything like that. So they didn't really like me."

In response, Jenny left the Korean group and joined another. "I hung out with the Koreans in sixth grade, and then these people who hang out in the cafeteria," she said, as she gestured with her hand to indicate "these people." I asked whom she meant by it. "You know, like, quiet people who don't really, like … exist that much," she explained. We both took to laughing at her peculiar choice of words as she apologetically added, "I don't mean it that way." Jenny also mentioned that they were mostly of Asian descent and hung out in the cafeteria, a social space that was frequented by all to purchase and eat food, but not considered a choice hangout area for the long term. She continued to explain, "They liked me, they really liked me. But then I felt like, I feel really bad saying this, but 'I could do better than this,' you know? So I went to hang out with the white people."

Jenny's ascendancy in the social hierarchy had its challenges. While the "white people" she hung out with were nice, she said: "I couldn't … I didn't really feel open enough. I felt like I always had to hide myself a bit. I was basically the only Asian in that group, other than one Indonesian girl. So I felt like, if I opened up too much they might not like me, or something like that. I was very insecure. I couldn't, like, act crazy or anything, do anything that stands out that much … do anything that seems to make me look like [pauses] like, you know [laughs], like a loser." I asked what made people seem like a "loser," and she explained: "If I liked someone and if I say, 'Oh, she's kinda …' and everyone's like, 'She's *so* weird.' And yeah, if I say, 'Actually she's not that weird, she used to hang out with me in the cafeteria.' And if I say something like that, they'd be like, 'Oh, oookay' … I think they thought, 'Oh then why is she hanging out with us now,' kind of way." To justify her membership in the group, she felt the need to take on their views as her own and place a distance between herself and the lower-status cafeteria group. When describing the school social hierarchy, Jenny repeatedly expressed her discomfort at making what she felt were "cheap" and "superficial" observations. Yet, as a teenager mired in the politics of school popularity, her perception of reality at the time was such that she made friendship choices according to these dubious criteria. Cultural capital mattered, popularity was racialized, and spatial practices reflected this predicament.

Spatial use of the campus was reproduced from one generation of students to the next. The relatively low status attached to the cafeteria as a hangout area held true for Marco and Ernest's grade, which was a year above Jenny's. During the first half of my fieldwork, I often saw Marco and Ernest, who were still in eleventh grade at the time, hang out in the cafeteria during recess. Most students in their group were of Asian descent, though there was at least one female student of Pacific Islander descent and one male student of mixed (white) American and Asian descent who hung out in the group. The male student was not as westernized as those who hung out in the high-status "white kids" group or the "normal" groups. For example, his accent sounded slightly Indonesian at times when he spoke English. Marco and Ernest recounted that they used to hang out in the cafeteria when they were in grades nine and ten. Then, at the beginning of grade eleven, the group hung out near the main eleventh-grade hangout area. But the area was usually full of the other English-speaking groups, so their group ended up sitting on the benches that lined the hallway adjacent to the main hangout area. They said that they lasted one week there. They felt intimidated and there was not enough space, so they moved back to the cafeteria. This is where I initially often found them and their friends. When I asked Marco and Ernest whether or not the cafeteria was considered a cool place to hang out, one of them replied as he turned to the other for agreement, "I don't think so, we're just known as the Caf people, right?" (interview, 14 December 2009)

When they reached twelfth grade during the second half of my fieldwork, the group moved to one of the new picnic tables that were set up in the main twelfth-grade hangout area. This time, there was enough room for them to hang out near the other English-speaking groups. They called this the "Caf upgrade," which was successful following their failed attempt the year before. The "upgrade" referred to their move from the lower-status cafeteria hangout area to the higher-status main hangout area of their grade. This time, they stayed.

There were a few other groups that hung out in the cafeteria regularly from different grades, and each seemed to have a similar racial makeup and appeared to be of similar status in their respective grades. At least one was a mixed-grade Mandarin-speaking group, but others were English-speaking groups made up of students of Asian descent of various nationalities, similar to Marco and Ernest's group. Social groups that were similarly positioned in their respective grades hung out in similar social spaces.

Toward the end of the 2008–2009 academic year (around May 2009), I saw Andre, an eleventh grader, visiting the hangout area for the twelfth-grade high-status "white kids" group, where the benches that Melinda had pointed to previously were located. Andre was a male student of mixed Dutch and Indonesian descent with a tanned complexion and athletic build, who was also a member of the eleventh-grade high-status "white boys" group. It was as though he was staking out territory for his posse ahead of the new academic year, establishing his entitlement to that hangout area through his association with the older high-status "white kids" in preparation for when they leave. Unsurprisingly, the following academic year (August 2009), Andre and his friends took over those benches. Similarly, in the new academic year the Indonesian-, Korean-, and Japanese-speaking groups of each grade, especially in grades eleven and twelve, occupied the same hangout area that their corresponding upperclassmen had used in the previous year and had vacated. None of these hangout areas had been assigned by the school to particular student cliques. Basically, social relations reproduce social spaces, which in turn reinforce those social relations (Lefebvre 1991).

The relationship between spatial practices and the racialization of status was apparent during the assemblies when students met separately according to their grades once every month or two. The assemblies were held at the same time, but the different grades rotated between four main venues: the cafeteria, the library, and the two theaters. Students were free to sit where they liked, but they chose to follow a particular seating pattern at these assembly meetings. Typically, the "normal" English-speaking students tended to cluster around the center area near the front, with the high-status group nearby. As a result, from the back one could see more students of European descent with light-colored hair sitting closer to the stage. This pattern was more obvious in the higher grades, which is reflective of the greater influence that culture has with age. The other groups, such as the Indonesian-, Korean-, Japanese-, and Chinese-speaking students, tended to sit in different places each time, but never in the front center area, as shown in figure 5.1. When I asked a Japanese student whether or not she would have sat in the front center area had she arrived at the venue earlier than the others, she said no because she felt as though it was not her place.

The spatial proximity of the students with Western capital to the stage symbolizes their cultural proximity to the dominant culture of the school administrators and teaching staff. As in multicultural settings described by Hage (1998: 48–49), cultural affinity with the dominant school culture gave some students a sense of "cultural entitlement," which allowed them to be "spatially dominant" while reinforcing the "spatial exclusion" of those who do not share that same level of affinity with the dominant culture.

Gendered Spaces

The way students used social spaces also indicated that status was gendered. At various levels of the social hierarchy, boys were more dominant than girls in the same group, and some of the all-girl groups seemed like satellites to the core group of their level.

ASSEMBLY SEATING

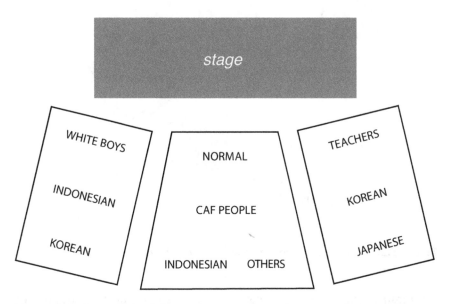

Figure 5.1. An example of the seating arrangement during a student assembly.

During the first semester of fieldwork, the senior (class of 2009) English-speaking students hung out in three spots in the main hang-out area. The "white kids" consisted of both boys and girls, and sat at benches that were placed in a slightly elevated area compared to the others nearby. The largest group is indicated in figure 5.2 as "Normal," to borrow Jenny's labels. This group was diverse (in terms of national-ity), and mixed-gender. Although there were smaller friendship circles within this group, they hung out together in the same general area. The president of the student council hung out in this group. Some English-speaking students preferred to sit at a stone bench located a meter or two away from the larger group, on its periphery. Although this was partly because there was not enough space in the main area, it is notable that those who hung around the stone bench were mostly girls, apart from two boys, one of whom was gay and the other was the boyfriend of one of the girls. These three groups, while they hung out in separate areas, had crossover friendships between the groups. And, though separate, they also had crossover friendships with those who hung out in the Indonesian group. In fact, two core male figures from the Indonesian group were dating Indonesian girls who were part of

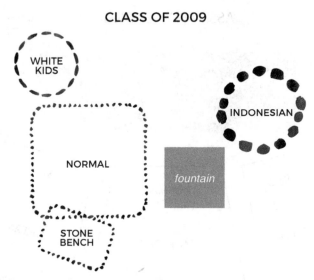

Figure 5.2. Main senior hangout area for the class of 2009.

the main English-speaking group. Both girls had native command of English and I rarely heard them speak Indonesian. The "Indonesian" group was also mixed-gender and culturally diverse but was defined by frequent use of the Indonesian language.

The school administrators introduced small tables to the main senior hangout area the following academic year in a bid to break up the large groupings (see chapter 1). As a result, the new seniors (class of 2010) hung out in smaller groups that were better suited to the new tables. These smaller groups sat roughly according to their social status, as shown in figure 5.3.

The groups that projected a dominant image were the "white boys," "stoners," and "Indonesian" groups. But "white boys" was an ambiguous term. At least one boy, Andre, had an Indonesian parent and a Dutch parent. Nor were the girls "white," according to Jack, who hung out with the stoners. "Those guys, are the white boys," Jack told me as I sat in his hangout area. "White boys?" I asked. "Yeah, they're the white boys," he reiterated.

I looked at the bench along the campus shop wall. There were eight to ten girls with dark hair. Some were of mixed heritage, others were of Asian descent though westernized. There were only about two "white boys." So I asked, "What do you mean by 'white boys'? I mean, look." Jack turned around. "Where are the white boys?" I queried again.

Jack was adamant. "Yeah, well, the *boys* are white boys," he said.

CLASS OF 2010

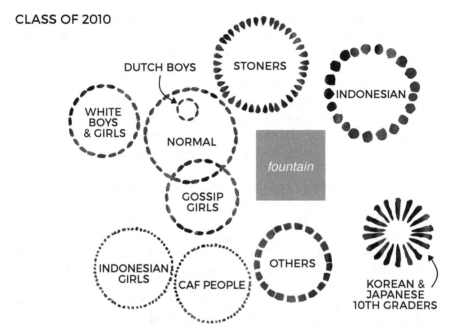

Figure 5.3. Main senior hangout area for the class of 2010.

Although the girls hung out with the "white boys," their presence was irrelevant to the group labels. They were accessories that marked the high-status boys as dominant.

"See those," he continued as he gestured toward the girls, "they care too much about who they're seen with. So they hang out there." He made the same point two or three times in different ways to make sure I understood. "They want to be seen with the popular ones.... They hang out with us outside of school, but in school they're there because they care a lot about what other people say and think." These remarks were made in reference to the fact that the stoners were not considered to be as high status as the white boys.

The girls' popularity was dependent on the boys with whom they hung out. But the girls' choice also affected the boys' status. "We're rivals," Jack said mysteriously of his posse's relationship with the white boys, as though to amuse the researcher with a juicy story of make-believe gang rivalry, since many in the two groups were actually good friends with each other.

The people Jack hung out with were labeled as stoners, but they also referred to their group as the "Black Label."[3] It was an exclusively boys group, though they occasionally had female visitors. They set themselves apart by installing speakers on the ceiling of their hangout area and playing loud music from their smartphones during recess. They projected an image of being tough partygoers. Jack then broke into a cool smile as he said, "And those guys [white boys], they call us the 'stoners.'" Later, some of the girls in the other groups told me that the stoner boys were not as tough as they make themselves out to be, especially when they are on their own. "Divide and conquer," laughed one girl, as she explained that they were more approachable individually. The boys were projecting an image of being powerful by operating as a pack.

The "normal" group was the largest of English-speaking groups. It was mixed-gender. Notably, the president of the student council of the new academic year (class of 2010) hung out, as in the previous year, in this mainstream English-speaking group. The presidents of both years, Daniel (class of 2009) and Rajesh (class of 2010), were culturally versatile and had a nuanced understanding of the sociocultural dynamics among their peers.

Next to that group and further away from the three high-status and main groups was a table that was dominated by girls. Similar to the girls who had hung out at the stone bench in the previous year, they were friends with those who hung out in the main group. Next to that was an all-girls Indonesian-speaking group who generally did not hang out with the main mixed-gender Indonesian-speaking group. The main difference was possibly that these girls did not go clubbing as much and had more crossover friendships with the "Cafeteria" group that sat next to them. Finally, there was an all-white, mixed-gender English-speaking group that sat apart from the others, as they were not considered as "cool." With both batches of seniors, there was a general impression that girls' groups were like satellites to the main mixed-gender groups of equal status. Boys in the higher-status groups projected a sense of dominance. As for the tenth grade Japanese and Korean girls, they were only there occasionally to utilize the empty picnic table because they were unable to find their place in the main hangout area of their own grade.

Not seen in figures 5.2 and 5.3 are the Korean- and Japanese-speaking twelfth graders who hung out at the stone benches tucked under the shade at the side of the main building, away from the more conspicuous senior hangout area near the fountain. It was as though they had removed themselves from the social hierarchy being expressed in the main hangout area to create their own turf, which I discuss in more detail in chapter 6.

Status was also sexualized. It came to the staff's attention that some of the ninth graders in the two major mixed-gender hangout areas of their grade were being territorial by refusing other students entry into their area. I heard that the more popular students had called the other hangout area the "loser hut," and students in the latter had called the other the "slut hut." Teachers took these incidents seriously, though students claimed that the teachers were overreacting. Nevertheless, the way students constructed one another bears analysis. The term "loser" is more gender neutral and could mean that this group was perceived to be less sexually desirable or even asexual. In contrast, "slut" is a gendered term used to describe female behavior, whether imagined or real. While it is a denigrating term, it also connotes the sexual desirability of both the male and female members of the group. Sexual desirability accompanied status. In chapter 7, I will show that Western cultural capital can enhance perceived sexual desirability.

Social Capital: The Power to Make Groups

There were also English speakers who are not shown in figure 5.2 above—boys who hung out mainly in the library and a few girls who hung out elsewhere. These students hung out in places that were out of sight from the others, which, according to one student from another group, was a sign of being marginal. Most did not seem comfortable hanging out with their peers from the main English-speaking groups. One exception was Chaitan, whose parents were Indian, but by the time I met him in Indonesia he had lived in three cities in India, as well as Sri Lanka, Singapore, and China. In China he attended an American school where he believed he had picked up an American accent. "Surprisingly, my gang was all white kids and I was the only Asian," he explained. Though I later found out that Chaitan's friends were not "all white." At least one boy from his group in China was of mixed white and Asian descent, thus evincing the ambiguity of racial categories. As I sat and listened to Chaitan, it became obvious to me that his style of speaking and his giss, or the way he carried himself, were such that they would have enabled him to join the main English-speaking groups with ease. But Chaitan claims he had made a conscious decision not to do that when he was forced to choose between friends in eighth grade: "I was friends with everyone, sort of. Matt and Troy [who were in the main English-speaking group during my fieldwork], and they're like, 'Dude, you're cool and stuff, and you can hang with us. But you gotta stop hanging with them.' That was quite a moment, mindset change you know. I was the guy in middle school, and here I'm like, wowww, I don't wanna be with these people." Their directness had taken Chaitan by surprise: "I mean, really direct. Boom. [Laughs]. ... It just came to me as a shock: choose your friends." Later, Chaitan had to make a similar decision in tenth grade. He was getting close to the Indonesian students, who were considered high status, but felt that he had to abandon his other friends, who he was with when I met him in twelfth grade, in order to be fully accepted—though this time they did not tell him directly. Chaitan said, "There was a feeling that, like you know, 'You can hang with us, but they can't.'" "They" referred to "the guys in the library," to borrow Chaitan's description, some of whom he was already friends with from middle school. Chaitan was instrumental in bringing the guys in the library together with a few others who had been on their own. Chaitan's explanation of how the group came to be suggests that most of them were lacking in what Bourdieu (1989: 23) refers to as symbolic power, "whose form par excellence is the power to make groups."

Members of the dominant groups are often unaware of their own dominance. While Chaitan believes that students were not as cliquey at the American school that he had previously attended in China as they were at TIS, he also recognized his potential bias because he was part of the dominant group there. He recalled: "Maybe because I was on top there, the top dog or whatever, so I didn't feel it as much. Maybe there were equally as many cliques. ... I'm not sure. I wanna believe it wasn't like that. But the thing is, I feel that when you're at the top, you want to make it like everything is happy and stuff." Chaitan's observation echoes the claims that were made by many in the "normal" and high-status English-speaking groups about how popularity was not really an issue at TIS. It was common for them to say something along the lines of "we're just friends," or "we don't have popularity here, we don't care." But when I told students like Marco and Ernest from the cafeteria group about these claims, they looked at me with disbelief and promptly dismissed them: "Huh? Of course there's a popularity thing here. They don't think it exists because they *are* popular!" Those outside the dominant groups were acutely aware of the social hierarchy because it negatively impacted upon their comfort level in various social spaces on campus. For example, Marco joined an extracurricular club that was made up of students learning Spanish who wanted to prepare a performance for United Nations Day. I joined one of their practice sessions and noticed that Dirk, a tall Dutch boy from the main English-speaking groups, would take up a lot of space and end up in the middle of the room as he danced, while Marco ended up squished on the sidelines. Marco's body language indicated that he lacked the confidence to claim entitlement to space.

Although Chaitan's friends were culturally diverse (Italian, Dutch, Indonesian, Indian, and so on), his group mainly consisted of male students. There were female students with whom some were friends, but in contrast to the all-boys "stoners" group, the boys who hung out indoors in the air-conditioned library collectively projected an asexual image while at TIS and they did not have an obvious satellite female group associated with them.[4] In contrast to groups like Chaitan's, the non-English-speaking groups shielded themselves from being relegated to a low status by removing themselves entirely from the English-speaking social hierarchy, as I discuss in chapter 6, and retaining the ability to form a mixed-gender group.

Western capital acted as a measure of normalcy. It was also racialized as "white." Popularity and the use of space was also racialized and gendered. Thus, the ability to be open to the Other is not sufficient for becoming international. In order to become international, students need to also become white and dominant. Those who did not do so felt marginalized both by their peers and the staff.

School Belonging

The sociocultural hierarchy discourages those who are marginalized from participating in activities that promote school belonging. This became particularly obvious when the activities required participants to make light of themselves. The student council organized an annual School Spirit Week for which each day of the week was assigned a theme, such as Gangster Day, Superhero/Nerd Day, Cross-dress Day, and Twin Day, and students were encouraged to dress up accordingly for fun. The week culminated with a Senior Slave Day, where a few twelfth graders were "auctioned" off in front of all their schoolmates during the lunch break. All grades crowded around the school fountain area—the most conspicuous hangout area as well as the chosen hangout area for the popular and mainstream English-speaking and Indonesian-speaking groups—to witness the "slave trade." It involved a lot of shouting and cheering. Typically, a group of students, often the friends of those auctioned, pooled some money to "purchase" one senior, make them dress in embarrassing outfits, and order them around for a day. In one case, a male senior "slave" was made to shave his head by his friends who had "purchased" him, albeit with his permission. Inevitably, some of the "slaves" were dumped in the fountain for fun.

It is an open secret that only the popular kids were ever dumped in the fountain regardless of the event, and watching people being dumped was considered fun to watch only if it involved someone popular. The money from the "slave trade" was donated to charity.

The twelfth graders who volunteered to be auctioned as slaves were from the English-speaking and Indonesian-speaking groups, which are the two groups that competed for status within the school social hierarchy. Only members of these groups volunteered because activities that involve spectacular displays of self-deprecating behavior require the participants to be in a position of power for it to be humorous to both the audience and participants. For those purchasing the slaves, the activity is humorous only if the slaves are from positions of power, and purchasing them offers an opportunity to reverse the hierarchy and poke fun at power. Students who are popular can risk being auctioned off, knowing that they will fetch a reasonable price. Being a prized purchase attests to their popularity, while a low price would indicate lack of interest in the person being auctioned. Therefore, it was easier for members of the English-speaking and Indonesian-speaking groups to participate in this activity as slaves because they did not risk losing face by not being sold.

Cross-dress Day also involved self-deprecating behavior, particularly for males who had to put their masculinity at risk in a heteronormative environment. Only those from the English-speaking groups participated. On that day, there were quite a few people from the mainstream fountain group who were cross-dressed. In the morning, I was sitting on a bench with Thea, John, and Michael near the campus shop, where the white kids usually sit, when Priya came up and asked us for fashion advice. He had a bra on underneath his shirt, but we did not notice it until he took the black shirt off in front of us, and put on a tight-fitting cheerleader shirt instead. After a quick look, Thea told him to wear the black dress that he also had, so he did. Nearby, Monica and Jurgen compared waist sizes by standing back to back. Then they went away and changed into each other's outfits. Craig and another girl had also casually traded outfits. Shivani, on the other hand, had come totally prepared. She even drew a beard on her chin with a marker, and was sporting a red baseball hat to go along with her "sexy" boy look. A few others from the English-speaking groups were also cross-dressed. All the while, they interacted across the genders with ease, and seemed confident that their sexuality would not be compromised by the activity.

But none of the students outside the fountain group cross-dressed, except Joon, a male Korean student. I saw Joon through the window as he passed by the library, where I was interviewing Maki on the library couch. Joon was wearing a strapless outfit with a big bow in the middle, where one would normally see cleavage. I smiled at him and he noticed, acknowledging me with a slight nod. However, when I saw him later he was dressed in his usual male outfit. I asked why he had changed out of his female outfit. "I was too embarrassed," he explained.

In contrast to the English-speaking groups, in which female and male students were casually swapping clothes and enjoying Crossdress Day, Joon tried to participate but felt uncomfortable enough to quit halfway through the day. Joon did not have the cultural capital necessary in the TIS context to engage in behavior that was out of the ordinary without the risk of embarrassing himself or compromising his masculinity. Koichi, one of the male Japanese students, explained this dynamic: "If someone who is always quiet says something that doesn't fit their style, then it just seems totally out of place." The English-speaking groups were not "quiet." They were far enough from being categorized as "losers" that they could break the rules and pretend to act like losers without becoming one. Participating in Crossdress Day reinforced their dominance.

The different uptake of the other three days also reflected the social hierarchy. Like Senior Slave Day, Gangster Day was popular among the English-speaking and Indonesian-speaking groups. Many came dressed like rappers, donning a baseball cap tilted to one side and large golden chains around their necks. Gangster Day was about looking tough and dominant. Meanwhile, Twin Day, which was more about being cute, was popular among the Korean and Japanese female students, but not the English-speaking or Indonesian-speaking students, or any male students for that matter. Superhero/Nerd Day was generally unpopular. I only spotted three seniors who dressed up for it. Dong Gun (from chapter 4) went all the way and dressed like a nerd from America circa 1950 with large, black-rimmed glasses, a white shirt, a bow tie, trousers pulled up high to his waist but not long enough to cover his ankles, and a pair of shiny black leather shoes. One of Dong Gun's many friends dressed up as Superman. She was an Indian girl who generally hung out in areas that were out of sight from the main hangout areas. Finally, a Korean boy painted his face like the Joker from the Batman movie *The Dark Knight*. None of the students who identified with the dominant groups participated in Superhero/Nerd Day. School Spirit Week is not innocent, neutral, or innocuous—it is political. Students perform the events in ways that reflect their relations of power.

Cultural Affinity with the Staff

Cultural affinity with the teaching staff and school administrators plays an important role in campus dynamics because it provides students with access to social capital (Bourdieu 1986). As authority figures, the mostly Anglophone teachers are in an influential position to reinforce the dominance of Western capital, particularly in classrooms (Hall 1996; Lears 1985).

Discomfort at "Being Preferred"

Although Dong Gun complained about teacher attitudes toward Korean students (see chapter 4), he was not the target of the teaching staff's frustration himself because he spoke fluent English, was more westernized than the majority of Korean students, and had friends in almost every major group. By his own admission, Dong Gun said:

> I have no personal experience because the teachers don't think that I'm Korean enough [laughs]. Like, they never see me as a stereotypical Korean just because I don't hang around with them. When they [teachers] go around, they never see me there [where the Koreans hang out] and stuff because I'm always around with different-culture people. So I'm not a part of that issue. These are the things that I hear. Even in class you know, they're just [pause] I don't know, I can't explain it. It's just a feeling. A feeling that you have when you see what's going on.

Dong Gun was a model student for the school's ideal of internationalism. At the start of my fieldwork, a staff member singled Dong Gun out to me as a student who had a typical "K-pop [Korean pop]" look (in reference to his slightly dyed, permed hair) but was well integrated into the larger school community, unlike the other Korean students. Dong Gun was what I call a "floater," because he did not hang out with the Korean groups or any other particular group for long. Instead, he moved between groups with ease and was well liked by peers and staff alike.

Other students who, like Dong Gun, had the cultural capital that made it easier for them to move between English- and non-English-speaking groups articulated similar sentiments of feeling uncomfortable with the fact that they were preferred by members of the dominant culture, particularly teachers, over their Korean peers. Young Sik, another male Korean student who spoke fluent English, said:

> Teachers, I just feel it, like, they're more for Americans, more for the white guys or the guys who speak better with them. … If you ask Koreans, they would offer a list of people who are prejudice [sic] to them. But

as the, the more like international guy, I don't get as much as these guys [pointing to the twelfth-grade Korean hangout area]. I get less, yeah, yeah, I think so. [Pause] When teacher comes, like, I don't know, I feel like they're more, nicer to me than Koreans ... especially these guys who are really struggling now [with their English]. Yeah, they're, teachers kind of yeah, are not too nice.

I also asked Young Sik whether he felt that the teachers were nicer to the *"bules"* than him. Young Sik said, without missing a beat, "Yeah, for sure. That's for sure." Both Dong Gun and Young Sik were westernized and fluent in English, which made them more accepted within the international school context (e.g., Foley 1996: 82).

Ben, or Hyun Bin, another Korean student who spoke fluent English and went by his Anglicized name when interacting with non-Koreans, described similar experiences in relation to his Western peers.

There are people who almost can't speak English. It's like, really bad saying it, but who can't speak English as well ... and have a hard time speaking fluent English ... and there are those who are really fluent speakers. And fluent speakers get along with Westerners easy. But others, Westerners kind of push them aside, that kind of thing. Like, when you have to make groups in class ... those more fluent speakers would be, would have an easier time making groups with Westerners. And if they have to make like a large group, then some Koreans would be left out, that kind of thing.

Ben articulated a sense of discomfort with the privileges that Western cultural capital afforded him that his Korean peers who spoke English as a second language were not able to access. Ben cited this as one of the reasons why he hangs out mainly with his Korean peers.[5] "Some Koreans have better English than others. So for those people, like if they hang out with English speakers, the less fluent English speaker would get, like, a little secluded kind of thing. 'Cause they'll feel like, 'Oh there's so many English speakers, they're hanging out with Westerners,' ... and then there'll be, like, division within Koreans." Even though he felt comfortable speaking English, he chose to do most of his socializing in Korean with his Korean peers because he did not want to participate in making them feel marginalized.

For example, when I joined one of their classes, a teacher pointed out to me the two Koreans who always sat together at the back of her classroom; she shrugged her shoulders as though disappointed with them for self-segregating, especially David (Jeong Tak), who should know better due to his fluency in English. But upon closer look, I noticed that David, one of Ben's friend, was sitting with a Korean girl who everyday, in every class, would first and foremost set up her electronic dictionary on the desk to help her survive the class. She, who remained nameless even to me, always sat quietly and expressionless, while David would occasionally lean over to translate words for her in-between participating in the class, rather loudly in some classes when he was on his own. More significantly, this girl was not quiet all the time, but only when she felt linguistically and culturally uncomfortable. In contrast to her behavior in the classes taught in English, I saw that she would speak up and participate in the Korean class where she could speak in Korean to both her classmates and the teacher.

Rapport Building: with Western Capital

It was easier for teachers and the administrators to build rapport with westernized students because of their shared sense of mutual intelligibility, as a white Australian teacher acknowledged to me. The rapport he referred to was evident in some classrooms taught by other teachers, as well. On my first day in one of the social studies class, the teacher, Dr. Davies, held a lively discussion in which he bounced ideas off the students, one after another, to keep the discussion going. Dr. Davies constantly engaged with the westernized students, who were sitting mostly in the front row, while he engaged the back row only on rare occasions, such as to ask Aisha, a female Malaysian student, for clarification on an issue relating to Islam.

Aisha was called upon to represent her culture to the others and be an expert on Islam. This is a responsibility that is often placed on members of minority groups. Aisha was the only female student among hundreds of high school students who wore a conspicuous religious headdress, the Muslim *jilbab*, as it is commonly called in Indonesia. It is a headdress typically worn by Muslim women in Southeast Asia and elsewhere. It is a scarf that covers the head, particularly the hair, but reveals the face and is often held in place with a pin, broach, or needle. In Indonesia, some women wear it all the time, while others wear it only on formal occasions or not at all. Aisha always wore a *jilbab*, except on United Nations Day when she took it off to perform a dance as part of the Japanese club. Apart from her, there was only one other student who wore a religious headdress, a male student who wore a Sikh turban. Ironically, the jilbab made her a visible minority within the international school, even though just outside its security gates lay the world's largest Muslim country.

When I sat in on Dr. Davies's class on another day, his approach was more subdued, which created a different student dynamic where all students were equally engaged in the class discussions. I suspect that Dr. Davies had allowed the westernized students to dominate the discussion in the previous class because I was present (for the first time) and he wanted to perform an animated discussion for the outside observer. It still stands, however, that the ease with which students with Western capital were able to relate to authority figures naturalized their position as culturally dominant within the school (Hage 1998; Brown 2006).

Students with Western capital actively sought teacher attention, received it, and thereby asserted their dominance. In another example, Mr. Sawyer's math class was culturally diverse, and he appeared to have a good rapport with all of his students regardless of their background or English ability. Despite this, it was the four students from the mainstream English-speaking groups, all of whom were female, who were the loudest and demanded the most attention from Mr. Sawyer.

During this class, my field notes focused on how the four girls looked, sounded, and acted. Appearance-wise, the use of eyeliners set them apart from their other female classmates. Although on various occasions students told me that appearance did not matter at their school, girls who wore eyeliners almost invariably sat next to other girls who wore eyeliners in class. All four dressed in a way that I labeled "dressed up" and "girly" in my notes. Nadia was British and had long, straight blond hair. She was wearing a colorful flower-print top and black tights that came just below the knee. Lauren appeared to be African American and had straightened black hair. She had large round earrings, and wore a low V-neck top that frequently showed her black bra unless she sat up with her back straight. Alyssa had an American accent, though she was Malaysian by nationality and appeared to be of mixed descent (though she may not have been). She wore full makeup and a bra of such bright red that it showed through her opaque white top. Simone, who appeared European, generally spoke with an American accent but sometimes pronounced words in a way that indicated that she was not a native speaker of English. She wore a tight pair of jeans, a flower-print top, and flat red shoes. The clothes the other girls in the class were wearing appeared plain and asexual in comparison. The four girls had a giss that also set them apart (field notes, 30 January 2009): "The fourth girl [Simone] is resting her legs on the bar underneath the desk in such a way that you can see her knee popping out above the desk.... Alyssa has one leg straight on the bar underneath the desk, and one foot on the chair so that her knee also sticks out higher than the desk height. Lauren's knee is also sticking out because she has her legs crossed.... Everyone else is sitting normally with their legs below the desks. The other girl is slumped over the desk." The four girls embodied a spatial presence that was different from and, in this case, more dominant than their classmates; they took up more space.

The other students were relegated to the sidelines in my field notes partly because the four girls were closest to where I was sitting, but also because they were the loudest. While working on a math exercise set by Mr. Sawyer, Lauren yelled out, "Who's finished?" But she did not seem to care about getting an answer and did not even look up. She said it as though to seek attention. Nadia often joked with Mr. Sawyer. When Mr. Sawyer told them to put their pencils down because he wanted their full attention, Nadia retorted that girls can multitask. Mr. Sawyer played along: "Yeah, but boys can't. Reikichi can't." Mr. Sawyer looked briefly in Reikichi's direction, then resumed waiting for the girls' attention. Lauren took a long time to put her pencil down and look up from her work. So then Mr. Sawyer teased her and said, "Everyone is now looking at ya." Finally he got to explain something for a few seconds before the students all start getting lively again.

All four loved talking to the teacher, though Alyssa was not as loud and Simone at times appeared as though she found it difficult keeping up with the other three due to her nonnative English. This is not to say that the other students apart from these four did not have a good rapport with Mr. Sawyer. They did: Mr. Sawyer joked with some of the other students too. Midori, a Japanese girl stood up and casually walked around while doing her work. Reikichi, one of the few Japanese students who preferred to hang out with his English-speaking friends, such as Marco and Ernest, approached Mr. Sawyer to ask a question while listening to his iPod with one earphone. Mr. Sawyer confiscated a mobile phone from one of the Korean girls who responded with a teasing, "Sooooo mean." Finally, two of the Korean girls played around with Mr. Sawyer's computer after class and he did not seem to mind. Nevertheless, it was the four girls who dominated the classroom space by filling it with their voices and body language, and thereby reinforced their connection to the dominant school culture.

Cultural dominance inside the classroom feeds into a sense of "school belonging" outside the classroom. Student affinity with the teaching staff signifies social capital and access to power. Social capital represents what Bourdieu (1986: 248) refers to as "a durable network of more or less institutionalized relationships of mutual acquaintance and recognition" through which one is able to access the pool of capital possessed by others. Students who already have Western cultural capital can enjoy a "multiplier effect" by drawing on the cultural capital that the teaching staff has (ibid.: 249). Their shared cultural capital reproduces social capital through an "unceasing effort of sociability, a continuous series of exchanges in which recognition is endlessly affirmed and reaffirmed" (ibid.: 250).

The cultural affinity between students with Western capital and the teaching staff is evident in the way Kenji conflated his schoolmate's Western capital with authority. I was following Kenji around one day, with his permission, to get an idea of what his school day was like and with whom he hung out. Kenji's father is Japanese and his mother is Indonesian. He is a native speaker of Japanese and Indonesian, and speaks English as a second language, though he is fluent. At one point, we were in the computer room as Kenji worked on his homework and played computer games. There were a few students working behind him. One of them was Darren, who was of mixed decent and hung out with the fountain group. Darren said something in English to his friends while Kenji had his back to them. Immediately Kenji turned to me and asked in Indonesian, "*Guru ya?* [Is it a teacher?]" I turned to look, and told him no. Kenji then proceeded to explain in his usual mixture of Indonesian and English, "*Kadang bule kalo ngomong kayak guru* [When white guys talk, sometimes they sound like teachers], and I'll be like," Kenji turned around and put on a look of surprise as he pretended to find out instead that it was a student, "*anjing* [damn]."[6] Kenji associated the speech patterns of native speakers of English with authority.

Rapport Building: without Western Capital

Studies on multicultural education conducted in the United States show that teachers from minority backgrounds serve as "cultural translators and cultural brokers" for minority students (Irvine 1989: 57). These teachers help minority students "navigate the culture of the school, which is often contradictory and antithetical to their own cultures" (Villegas and Irvine 2010: 185). These teachers are able to act as mediators because they share a sense of mutual intelligibility with the minority students and, at the same time, can engage with the dominant school culture as authority figures. A similar line of argument can be applied to TIS where teachers who do not come from Western or Anglophone backgrounds serve as cultural brokers for students who are unable to identify with the dominant school culture.

Japanese students were often dead silent in the regular classes taught by Western teachers, but became vocal and participative once they were in a class with a Japanese teacher who spoke their language and shared a sense of mutual intelligibility with them. The first time I sat in a twelfth-grade Japanese class for native speakers, the students chatted and joked rather loudly. It started with Koichi sitting in the teacher's chair and announcing that John, the American-born Japanese who was known as Akira among his Japanese friends, now has a girlfriend. Then Koichi whined that all the (Japanese) girls are now taken; and on and on he wailed, shedding fake tears, dramatizing his sorrow at his singleness. He enjoyed the attention; we enjoyed the entertainment. It was a relaxed, friendly atmosphere.

Once Koichi and the others, who had been butting into the soap opera from the sidelines, had had enough, the Japanese teacher, "Kubota *sensei* [teacher]," as they called her, welcomed me to her class and facilitated a casual chat, accompanied by much joking, about the students' diverse cultural experiences.[7] Kubota *sensei* had an assertive feel to her, and something about her giss and the way she dressed seemed slightly atypical of Japanese women to me. I later found out that her partner was a European man. Kubota *sensei* was interested in my research and what I had to say about her Japanese students, who were, in her eyes, Third Culture Kids. The way Kubota *sensei* perceived them ran contrary to the way Western teachers perceived the Japanese students—as being stuck in their Japanese world.

After about forty-five minutes, the fun and jokes culminated in four of the five male students going up to the front of the class to demonstrate, to great hilarity, the physical warm-up exercises they had been required to do at their former Japanese school in time to music that traditionally played on the morning radio in Japan. Then they went back to their seats to focus on the Japanese article they were reading for class. The students became extremely quiet and switched straight into serious study mode. Their behavior in this class stood in stark contrast to their behavior in the mainstream classes.

When their cultural capital is not affirmed as normal in the classroom or other settings, they experience an absence of a sense of entitlement to not only physical, but also verbal space. Though it was unusual to spend forty-five minutes of class time chatting, the relaxed atmosphere itself was similar to that of other Japanese classes for native speakers taught by another Japanese teacher, as well as Chinese-language classes taught by a Chinese teacher and where most of the students were of varying Asian backgrounds. The students who were silent in other classes were more at ease in classes where they had some degree of mutual intelligibility with the teacher. Similarly, an Indonesian teacher said of her Indonesian students who had been at the international school since they were young: "They relax in this class. Even though English is their language, it's still tiring for them [out there]. At least that's how I see it." The students feel as though they are part of the norm in Indonesian classes and do not have to exert effort to negotiate cultural dissonances. Cultural affinity facilitates student-teacher rapport, which in turn promotes a sense of being part of the norm, of belonging in that social space. But in the case of students who are not familiar with Western capital or speak English as a second language, their sense of normalcy is confined to particular classrooms (or hangout areas). They lack the social capital that links them to the authority figures who hold the power to shape the dominant school culture.

There were times when some of the Japanese students turned to me, an adult, as a cultural broker. I had both the linguistic and cultural competence to communicate with Japanese-speaking students, English-speaking students, as well as the teachers. One of the first classes I observed was a college-prep English class for nonnative speakers. The Japanese students were keen to speak to me once they found out that I was fluent in their language (see chapter 2). In another class, Erina, a Japanese student, was similarly keen to talk to me. Erina was very quiet and at times seemed to tense up during group work, when she seemed unable to voice her opinions freely due to her discomfort with her linguistic and cultural differences. However, Erina was by no means shy, considering that she later became the president of the Japanese club. She simply struggled to be herself in the regular classes. I had introduced my research and personal background, including the fact that my mother was Japanese, at the beginning of Erina's class and then sat behind her. When the bell rang to signal the end of class, the first thing Erina did was to turn around to face me and ask, in English, whether I could speak Japanese. Once I said yes, in Japanese, a look of relief came over her face. She switched to Japanese: "I was really curious about that the whole time." Japanese students relished finding an adult, in other words someone in a position of power, who shared a sense of mutual intelligibility with them.

Some non-Anglophone students shared in interviews that their inability to speak English when they were younger resulted in frustration due to communication issues with the teacher. I interviewed Ayumi, another Japanese alumnus who, like Yae, was visiting the school and still had a lot of friends among both the Japanese- and English-speaking groups. Ayumi had enrolled at a Japanese university that offered courses in English. She said that when she attended an international elementary school in Vietnam she felt that the Australian teachers were nicer to the "Western" kids. When she first enrolled at the school, she could not understand how the canteen ticket system worked. So she went to a teacher for help to get her food, but Ayumi could not speak

English well. Instead of treating her nicely, six-year-old Ayumi felt that her teacher bombarded her with English that she could not comprehend. Out of frustration, Ayumi yelled one of the few things she did know in English: "Shut up!" The teacher took offense and walked off. Ayumi panicked and hid herself. There were also at least two boys who told me that they once punched their classmates while in elementary school out of being similarly frustrated that they could not communicate their thoughts to their classmates in English.

In high school, none of the students responded physically to language issues, but there was one student that had come to TIS late in their high school career and said that they had nightmares for the first several weeks due to the stress of not being able to communicate or understand. Another was perceived as rude by one of his Anglophone teachers even though I had seen him behave politely with his Korean teacher. The lack of rapport with teachers is stressful for students when coupled with the lack of language skills.

Likewise, Ali was the only student in his grade with a Palestinian background, and it was important for him that Dr. Briones, who was also originally from the Middle East, was there to ease his adjustment process when he first joined the school. Ali speaks of the fieldtrip he went on during the orientation program for new students (interview, 25 November 2009):

> I went to orientation before and I didn't really like it that much, didn't really connect. I felt like I tried, that actually I tried connecting, but somehow it took a lot of effort and there was no positive result. Like, I tried to talk to a person, like, "What are we doing," and "Why are we doing this?" And I tried to make a joke, but still, like, you know, it's really hard. I just didn't really connect well.

> But I connected with a really good teacher, Dr. [Briones]. You know him? He was there and I connected with him very, very well. We just talked over time and stuff. So he was my savior in the trip.

"Connect" and "connection" were commonly used expressions to describe a sense of mutual intelligibility. It included a shared sense of humor, as illustrated by Ali's reference to his failed attempt to use jokes to connect with his peers. Students frequently cited humor as crucial to establishing a sense of connection with others. Although Ali did not specifically refer to Dr. Briones's shared cultural background, it is clear that Dr. Briones's presence was important for Ali. Dr. Briones acted as a cultural broker for Ali. Later, Ali hung out with the Indonesian-speaking group in his grade. He claimed that it was because he shared their sense of humor.

Student-teacher rapport can also cut across racial lines. Before my fieldwork began, Mrs. Taylor's classroom used to be frequented by students who ate breakfast and lunch or just hung out there whenever she was not teaching. It was "quite a phenomenon" said Mrs. Taylor, and her colleagues corroborated her statement. Later, a white Australian alumnus spoke fondly of Mrs. Taylor, saying that she was a great teacher. While her classroom was not as popular during my fieldwork year, I still noticed that students of Asian descent liked to hang out in Mrs. Taylor's classroom during recess, including Ernest and Marco, who were in the English-speaking group that used to hang around in the cafeteria. The students who liked to hang out in Mrs. Taylor's classroom were different from those who hung out in Mr. Davies's classroom. The latter tended to be from higher status groups than the former. "We feel comfortable with Mrs. Taylor because she understands us and know what it's like to be a teenager," commented Ernest. They did not know that Mrs. Taylor, who sounded American, looked like a white American, and was an American, was raised in Hong Kong when it was still a British territory. She confessed, "I feel safest when I am surrounded by Chinese [sic]. I feel least safe when surrounded by Americans." While Mrs. Taylor appealed to a diverse range of students, it was not just her personality that contributed to rapport building. A shared sense of mutual intelligibility based on her transnational upbringing and familiarity with Asia also contributed to rapport building.

Power of Normalcy

In his application of Gramsci's concept of hegemony on ethnicity, race, and racism, Hall (1996: 424) writes that it has a "multi-dimensional, multi-arena character." The dominant culture of TIS and the way it reinforces the ideology of being international is similarly multidimensional. It does not merely impose itself on the dominated. Hegemony is naturalized and the dominated are complicit. This is because, as Paul Willis (1977: 171) writes, "macro determinants need to pass through the cultural milieu to reproduce themselves at all." Furthermore, racial categories are ambiguous and shifting in transnational settings depending on the positionality of actors in relation to each other (Lindegaard 2009).

Transnational educational spaces are not neutral spaces. Students' sense of belonging is affected by the school culture. At TIS the school ideology of being international privileged Western capital, making it easier for students who were westernized to integrate into the dominant groups. An analysis of student popularity reveals that Western capital was normalized as seen in the use of the label "normal" to refer to the main English-speaking groups. Western capital was also rendered high status and racialized as "white." Westernized students had an easier time building good rapport with teachers because of their sense of cultural affinity. Students who did not have sufficient Western cultural capital felt marginalized, as seen by their contrasting behavior in mainstream and language classes.

"There is no more powerful position than that of being 'just' human," writes Richard Dyer (1997: 2). The normalcy of the English-speaking groups renders their whiteness invisible. There is power in this invisibility to construct being white or Western as being international, a theme that will be revisited in chapter 8. Consequently, self-segregating on the part of the non-English-speaking groups is not merely about students' unwillingness to be international. It is a response to the social hierarchies that privilege Western capital. The next chapter shows that students form separate language groups to ease their sense of marginalization.

Notes

1. Although historically the term "Indo" or "Indos" referred to those who were of mixed European, often Dutch, and indigenous descent, in the TIS context it was merely short for "Indonesians."
2. This was a common use of the word "foreign" among Koreans and Japanese to mean someone who is not Korean or not Japanese, rather than not Indonesian, even though they were in Indonesia. This usage may partly be a function of their language, where word choices are sometimes made in Korean and Japanese based on the situation at hand and the perspective of the person being referred to rather than the broader context.
3. There were other subgroups that used the names of hard liquor to label themselves, for example "Absolut." These group names often came to the fore when those in the group organized parties where they hired out a club and charged a cover cost in an attempt to make a profit.
4. This image did not last into college, according to Chaitan, with whom I caught up about six months after he graduated from TIS.
5. I discuss other reasons in chapter 6.
6. The term "anjing" literally means "dog" in Indonesian and is often used as a swear word. Male Indonesian students often used it casually on each other as well as others.
7. "Kubota" is the teacher's surname and "sensei" means teacher in Japanese. In Japan teachers are called by their surname followed by "sensei."

Invisible Diversity

The process of becoming international is characterized by a sense of ambivalence inherent in hybrid identities. Cosmopolitanization is a social strategy that TIS students use to mediate their positionality within a transnational space. It is a process of negotiating boundaries, sometimes by blurring them and at other times by reinforcing them. I propose that becoming "Western" and becoming "Asian" are both mutually constitutive with becoming "international," as they represent ways of practicing cosmopolitanism that emerge out of the cultural inequalities embedded in transnational and national structures.

The previous chapter demonstrated that the students who were perceived to be international and therefore perceived to be practicing cosmopolitanism had Western capital. They were constructed as "normal." This chapter shows that students who did not acquire sufficient Western capital were constructed as Other and homogenized. The different ways in which students experience a transnational space produces diverse ways of practicing cosmopolitanism. Students respond to cultural hierarchies by reinforcing boundaries of difference to create home turfs into which they can retreat and find relief from feeling marginalized. Students form groups based on language as a response to losing their social network because of a high rate of student turnover. They also gravitate toward these groups as they mature due to the increasing importance of culture with age. Students who feel their transnational upbringing has led to a lack of exposure to their parents' home culture compensate for this lack by immersing themselves in the corresponding language-based groups. I argue that Asian students respond to processes of socialization, mobility, and blurring of boundaries by practicing a form of cosmopolitanism characterized by a form of pan-Asian cultural competency and identity.

Changing Names, Changing Identities

As discussed in chapter 5, students from non-Anglophone backgrounds acquired Western capital in order to integrate into the dominant school culture. Some students experienced this process of acculturation as a change of identity. Students cited name changing as a potent example of the process of accepting an identity change. Sometimes the students themselves initiated the name change, and sometimes it was imposed.

Jenny said that she used to go by her real name, "Hae Jin." But some of the non-Korean boys teased her by deliberately mispronouncing her name. Jenny explains, "I was in elementary school, in sixth grade; they kept calling me 'Hey Jean, Hey Jean' intentionally, so I felt really bad." So she changed her name. Jenny laughingly explained, "I just told them I'm Jenny now, and they're like, 'Okay.'" She had picked the name of her favorite character in a novel for herself. Another Korean student whose Korean name was "Jae Soo" went by the name "Jay (Jae)." When I asked how he got the name, he said that his fifth-grade teacher kept calling him "Jay," so he has been just "Jay" ever since.

A few female students shared similar stories. We were sitting at one of the new picnic tables in the main senior hangout area one typically sunny day when a casual chat turned into an animated discussion about identity. There were two students who were Indian nationals, and they were both named "Vandana." One of them joined the conversation after the rest of us had already been chatting for about half an hour. When she joined, I tried to double check with her whether I was pronouncing her name correctly, and this simple gesture triggered a discussion about the subtle ways in which the dominant culture requires its participants to assimilate.

"Van*da*na, is that how you pronounce ... ," I began to ask, as I pronounced it like I would "bandana" and stressed the second syllable.

Before I could finish my question, Vandana cut in with a firm, "Actually, no! That's a wonderful place to start! First of all, you pronounce my name *Van*dana." With a big smile, she stressed the first syllable, as it would be pronounced in Hindi. The "V" sounded a little like a "W"; the first vowel like "one" than "ban" or "van"; and the last two vowels were pronounced lightly: *V uh n* – d uh – n ah.

"*Van*dana?" I repeated after her.

Once I pronounced it correctly, she said, "Yes, and that's, I mean, that's probably the *basis* of my confusion! Like, I have no idea where I come from. I honestly don't, 'cause I was born here. I've lived here my whole life, and I've gone to an international-based system, school since I was five."

"So, kindie?" I asked.

"Huh, like prep senior, yeah, kindergarten," Vandana continued. "And when I walked into my classroom my teacher goes, 'Oh, so your name is Van*da*na?'" she said, as she imitated my initial pronunciation of her name. "And I don't say anything! I'm like, 'Yaaah.'" She put a blank look on her face. "That's meeee."

We all burst out laughing at her vivid narration as the other Vandana chimed in, "Oh my god, that's so true."

"Yeah, right! I knowww, like." The two Vandanas started to finish each other's sentences. They were caught up in the excitement of knowing that they could empathize with the other's experience.

"And then after that I started introducing myself as Van*da*na," continued the second Vandana, while the first piped in to finish her own explanation: "As, as 'Van*da*na!' Exactly! *Total* identity change, right there! It, it was crazy!"

Although the (mis)pronunciation of a name may appear trivial, it is symbolic of the power of the dominant culture to shape identities. As Vandana impressed upon me, even a change in the pronunciation of a name can result in an instant and *"total* [her emphasis]" identity change. Both Jenny and Vandana hung out in the mainstream English-speaking groups. But even among those who did not socialize with the mainstream English-speaking groups, many still used name changes as a means to connect with the English-speaking world at TIS.

Names can serve as a gateway to another world, another fragment of a person. Daniel (see chapters 1 and 5), whose parents were Danish and American, gave an example of this when he spoke of his two Korean friends, with whom he spends a lot of time in class, but rarely outside of class. Outside of class he hangs out with the English-speaking groups while his Korean friends hang out with other Koreans. Daniel explained:

> Another interesting thing is their names. I always call them David and Lisa. I've never gotten this impression that they seem to mind that. But if ever, like, "Jeong Tak" and "Ye Ryun" [their Korean names]—they sound so foreign. Those sound so foreign when I'm saying them, not the actual way they sound, but foreign to my tongue, that, I really don't associate it with the same person. It's like if all of a sudden I started calling David "Jeong Tak," I would have to like, meet him all over again, and it's really strange. [We both laugh.] But, 'cause I've often considered, you know, "Why do I always call him David?" That's how he introduces himself to the teachers, but that's 'cause most teachers can't remember Korean names.

English names make it easier for other English-speakers to relate to Daniel's two Korean friends, but they also construct boundaries be-

tween Daniel and his friends. The Korean and English names compartmentalize the Korean-speaking and English-speaking cultural worlds
that David and Lisa operate in, similar to the way Indian and American
accents compartmentalized the cultural worlds that the South Asian
boys operated in and demarcated the line between insiders and outsiders (chapter 2).

Those who are not socialized into the dominant culture in the home
environment can acquire the necessary cultural capital, including
name changing, and learn to operate in the dominant culture. Some integrate into English-speaking groups and thus enrich the international
appearance of these groups. The visible diversity that these students
bring to the English-speaking groups renders the Western cultural capital that they share invisible. Those who cannot or refuse to acquire the
necessary cultural capital may separate themselves from the dominant
English-speaking groups. This is often interpreted as ethnocentrism
on the part of the non-English-speaking groups without regard for the
complexity of factors that contribute to the formation of these social
groups, such as the way they are constructed as a homogenized "Other."

A Nameless, Faceless "Other"

As discussed in the previous chapter, the students in the main English-
speaking groups maintained their cultural dominance by defining who
or what kind of behavior was considered "normal," in the same way
that the staff defined who was considered "international." The more
normative a student's behavior appeared, the more they were perceived
and engaged with as individuals. The notion of "normal people" was
reinforced through the presence of those who lie outside the norm.
Those who fell outside the norm became part of a nameless, faceless
Other in the eyes of students in the English-speaking groups.

One day I followed the team-sports class out onto the field, and was
standing around watching them under the hot sun. When it came time
to select the team members, Chris and Naomi, the team captains for
the day, started taking turns picking their team members. Both Chris
and Naomi usually hung out in the English-speaking groups. "Max,"
said Chris. "Juan," said Naomi, as she squinted in the sun. One by one
the students went behind the team captains as their names were called
out. Toward the end, only the Korean students, all of them male, were
left. It was Kyu Sik, DJ (short for Dae Jeong), and Jay (short for Jae
Soo). The names of the latter two had been Anglicized to make it easier
for English speakers to pronounce. But instead of calling them by their

names, Naomi, hesitatingly, said, "You and, you," as she lifted both arms to point at each of the Korean students she was referring to. She could not remember even their Anglicized names and seemed slightly embarrassed about it. Kyu Sik, DJ, and Jay looked a bit unsure as to which one of them Naomi was referring to. "Yeah, you," Naomi added as she pointed again. While those who are part of the norm are recognized as individuals with names and personality, the "Other" becomes a nameless mass.

In addition, cosmopolitan practices are situational. Naomi is a Japanese national who speaks fluent English and hangs out with the English-speaking groups. She was also a member of the UN Day Japanese club and she was quite vocal in criticizing the club leadership (see chapter 8). She regularly complained after club practice that they were being insensitive toward the non-Japanese members of the club by refusing to speak English, the common language, and insisting on speaking in Japanese, which many of the members could not understand. In objecting to the leadership's Japanese-centric management of the club, Naomi aligned herself with the school's ideology of being international. However, once she was outside the Japanese subcontext and in the larger context of the school, she unwittingly conformed to the Eurocentric view that marginalized the students who were not part of the English-speaking groups, such as the Korean boys in her team-sports class. Naomi was committed to engaging with difference in one situation, but reinforced cultural dominance in another.

This incident echoes what Jenny noted in her interview: "I don't think anybody outside the Korean group really knows the Koreans individually. So if one of them comes and, like, tries to hang out with the mainstream people, they would be nice and all but they wouldn't be friends." Later, I asked Ashley, a white American, and Anton, an Indonesian student who spoke English better than Indonesian, whether or not they knew the names of the Korean students. Ashley hardly knew any and was amazed when Anton rattled off the names of Korean students from their grade. I asked Anton why he knew them by name when the others did not. Anton shrugged his shoulders and said, "They don't try I guess."

Daniel, the student council president, gave a nuanced account of cultural racism. He argued that while growing up in a "third culture environment like TIS" would encourage people to be more "open to meeting other people and [be] much more tolerant," it does not "cure people from having prejudices and stuff." He thought that many other factors, such as parenting, come into play in shaping our views. "I still see people who are, you know, I definitely wouldn't say racist, but prejudiced against certain people. Stereotypes," he said. Daniel then continued, "I mentioned that some of my friends happened not to really know any Koreans, but some of them, well some of the people I know at least, I feel, kinda, actually just don't want to meet them 'cause they're [the Koreans are] stereotyped as uninteresting people." The "Other" was constructed as devoid of individuality, "uninteresting," and therefore not worth knowing. Similarly, an alumnus I spoke to even claimed that the ESOL program did not exist back when she was a student because she could not recall any ESOL students from her grade even though there were many enrolled at the time.

The lack of interest in the "Other" hinders the development of free and easy social relations. Yoo Mi recounted that she found it difficult to make "foreign" friends when she first joined TIS as a tenth grader. She explained (interview, 28 April 2009):

> It was frightening. I came here ... I mean I had, like, blond friends when I was young, but when I first came here there was an outing [for orientation] and then I would see people with blond hair and blue eyes and I'll be like, "Oh my god. It's a foreigner there." It was like, it was new. Seem[ed] like I never been to international school before.

> My English wasn't that fluent, 'cause I was spoken Korean, so my English wasn't that good. So, then, just play with my Korean friends I guess. And you know how this school really doesn't like Koreans? You know how they, how they, the impression that Koreans always studying and 'cause Koreans never go parties, and they always study, they always good students, so the impression isn't that great.

Yoo Mi was racialized as "Korean" despite her transnational experiences that were not typically Korean. Yoo Mi was born in Korea but moved to Kalimantan, a large Indonesian island, when she was five years old because her father worked for a mining company. They lived in a remote area in Kalimantan. "It was a forest. I would see orangutan," said Yoo Mi. After living there for two years, she relocated with her family to Surabaya, a city on the densely populated island of Java, where she attended an international school. Yoo Mi did not know what "A, B, C" was but quickly learned English and made friends who were from diverse backgrounds. Then the family repatriated to Korea where she studied at a local school from grade five to ten, during which time she lost her fluency in English. These diverse experiences did not add much to her cultural capital when she moved to TIS in spite of its ideology of being international. In the eyes of the dominant culture, Yoo Mi was simply "Korean."

Despite having had "blond friends" when she was younger, the adolescent years she spent in Korea instilled in her a perception that "blond hair and blue eyes" were superior and, therefore, intimidating. Colonial discourses remain a powerful force that constructs racial imaginaries that are reinforced through contemporary global hierarchies. It perpetuates a gaze that sees the West as at once desirable and intimidating.

Yoo Mi felt that Koreans were not perceived in a positive light. She said: "[After school started] I approached some, some foreigners and I say hi blah, blah, blah but they, they didn't really welcoming 'cause I was new, and they didn't know me and I was Korean. I mean, they say, 'Hi,' and say only service talk, you know what I mean? Like, just like, 'How's the weather?' Not like deep, deep talk. So I couldn't join that group." "That group" was in reference to the mainstream English-speaking group(s). There was a lack of mutual intelligibility between Yoo Mi and students with Western capital that could facilitate further connections. After two to three weeks of trying to join them, she gave up and started befriending other Korean students with whom she had a sense of mutual intelligibility. "After that, I realize that I started playing with my Korean friends, and I felt comfortable you know, how the language, it was much easier for me and they understood me, like how the Western people don't understand, 'How come you don't party and stuff?' But then in Korea society [laughs], not partying [is] good." I asked Yoo Mi to elaborate on the differences between conversing with Korean and Western students: "Asking school homework is the easiest thing.... If I ask Korean friends, 'Oh, what is the school homework,' they tell you and they talk about other things: talk about teacher and how the other teachers that doesn't give this homework but our teacher does and blah, blah, blah.... But if I go to the Western people then they'll just tell me the homework, you know what I mean? And finish that talk." In addition to a lack of mutual intelligibility, Yoo Mi was implying that there is a lack of interest among the students in the mainstream groups toward the others, which negatively affects the flow of conversation and creates a sense of dissonance. The Other is perceived through stereotypical images. The Other is differentiated from each other by their nationality labels "Korean," "Japanese," "Indonesian," etc. Otherwise, the diversity within these groups is invisible. Cultural dominance is maintained by constructing the Other not as individuals, but as nameless, faceless, uninteresting, homogeneous groups.

Invisible Diversity

The seniors who hung out in the Indonesian-speaking group during the first semester of my fieldwork were culturally and ethnically diverse. I regularly found two Filipinos, two Koreans, two Taiwanese, and a few others who were only partially of Indonesian descent in the group. The Filipinos and one of the Korean students were not fluent in Indonesian, and admitted that they could not understand all that was said by their Indonesian friends. Nonetheless, they chose to hang out with the Indonesians. Those who were of part-Indonesian decent were also part British, Japanese, or Thai. Even those who were Indonesian by nationality were of varied ethnic backgrounds. Most were ethnically Chinese, while some were indigenous Indonesian or of Indian descent.[1] Many of these students said that when they were younger they hung out with peers who were of different nationalities, but their social groups changed as they got older, which I discuss later. Many factors contributed to the formation of a (diverse) Indonesian-speaking group, who just as equally use English in their conversations.

The Indonesian in-group diversity was invisible to the staff and many students from the dominant culture. A student from a high-status English-speaking group spoke of the "Indonesian" group as though it were made up exclusively of "Chindos" even though when he spoke of individual members of that group, he was in fact aware that there were a handful of indigenous Indonesians, Filipinos, Taiwanese, and Koreans. But when he thought of them as a group, their diversity became invisible. He racialized them as "Indonesian."

I pointed out to a staff member that the senior Indonesian-speaking group was also diverse. In response, she said that Indonesia was a diverse country anyway. She dismissed the diversity of the Indonesian group as nothing out of the ordinary. I said, "But it is not common to see indigenous, Chinese, and Indian Indonesians form friendships with each other the way they do here." The effort the Indonesian-speaking students made to overcome their differences was not recognized as "international." It was simply seen as being "Indonesian." The diversity in the English-speaking group could have just as easily been dismissed as, "The United States (or the United Kingdom) is diverse anyway." But it was not. The diversity of the Indonesian-speaking group was second class because it did not conform to the school's ideology of being "international," which emphasized *racial* diversity and Western capital.

Creating Home Turf

Linguistic and culturally based groups that were separate from the English-speaking groups provided protection from dissonance for those who did not have Western capital. For those who do not have the necessary cultural capital (e.g., speaking fluent English or a having a Western giss), the Korean- and Japanese-speaking groups provide some degree of shelter from the discomfort of having to engage with the dominant culture.

"English-Infested Society"

Dong Gun, as previously mentioned, floated from group to group instead of being entrenched in the Korean-speaking groups. But Dong Gun spoke at great length defending his Korean peers' choice to remain within the Korean-speaking groups: "So it's natural and it feels more comfortable for Koreans to just be with Koreans in an English-infested society, I guess, in [TIS]." He chuckled at his own choice of the word "infested." He then continued to explain why the Korean students liked to hang out with other Koreans: "They try to survive, live through the day. They need it because they just need to belong somewhere. And if it's not with their culture, then with who, right? But the teachers who always argue that this is an international school, you have to speak English, you have to get along with the people. I mean, that's ideal, but Koreans are, what can you do when one doesn't feel comfortable in that way? So I feel very sad and sorry for the Koreans ... because they're always getting the teachers' fingers pointing at them" (interview, 20 April 2009). Dong Gun's comments suggest that some Korean students experience dissonance due to their lack of fluency in English. Others are fluent in English, but their cultural capital is not sufficient for them to feel a sense of belonging within the larger school community due to a lack of mutual intelligibility.

David (Jeong Tak) described Koreans as "family." David had been at TIS since elementary school, was fluent in English, and said that he used to have "international" friends. Even then he hung out almost exclusively with Koreans as he progressed through school. David says, "It's like all the Koreans are my family." He claimed to feel "way closer to Korean people." The sense of closeness is derived from a sense of mutual intelligibility of experiences that he shares with other Korean young people at TIS.

In the previous chapter I explained that marginal English-speaking students remained marginal because they were unable to mobilize their social capital to form groups. Unlike the marginal English-speaking students, Korean students formed groups with clear linguistic boundaries that were separate from the dominant English-speaking groups. Like the South Asian boys in chapter 2, choosing to speak in Korean enabled Korean students to reclaim the power to draw the boundaries between insider and outsider, and thereby position themselves as insiders. Although they were marginal vis-à-vis the dominant school culture, at least within these linguistic groups they were "normal." As can be seen in figure 6.1, I will show in the next section that the situation was similar for the Japanese-speaking groups.

CREATING HOME TURF

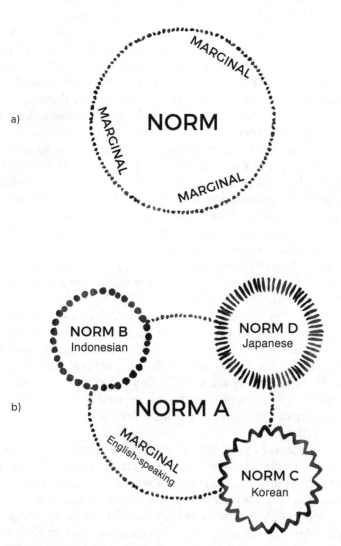

Figure 6.1. Creating home turf.

From Cultural Hybrid to Being "Japanese"

Koichi or Tomioka-kun, as he was commonly known by his Japanese peers, found that moving from the Japanese school to TIS negatively affected his social status.[2] Koichi claimed that he used to be a central or popular figure among his schoolmates back at the Japanese school. His friends corroborated this claim. Moreover, Koichi was a cultural hybrid, but his hybridity was not recognized as being international at TIS since he hung out almost exclusively in the Japanese hangout area. Although both of his parents are Japanese, his family moved to Indonesia when he was in grade two and he grew up mostly in Indonesia. He was a native speaker of Japanese and near-native speaker of Indonesian. I have reproduced an extract of my interview with Koichi in the original languages, accompanied by an English translation, to give the reader a visual picture of his cultural fluidity. The part written in the English alphabet is in Indonesian and the other parts are in Japanese. In explaining how he learned Indonesian at the Japanese school in Jakarta, Koichi switched between the two with ease (interview, 1 April 2009).

KOICHI: 俺の友達でも、俺より長い奴とか俺よりもできない奴もいるんだろうと思うんだけど。(Even among my friends, I'm sure there are guys who've [lived here] longer than I have but can't speak as well as I can.)

DT: Kenapa? Kok bisa? (Why? How come?)

KOICHI: インドネシア語ってこう、なんか面白いなって、「こういう風に色んなことがあるんだ」って。で、だんだん興味持ち始めて、、、だから、[ケンジ] みたいにインドネシア語話せるとこにも入っていくわけ、自分自ら、わかんないけど最初は言葉、「こいつは何言ってんの？」って言って、、、(So, I thought, Indonesian is kind of interesting, like, "Oh, so it's got all sorts of stuff like this." And I started getting more and more interested…. So, I chose to join the kids who could speak Indonesian, like [Kenji]. I dunno. At first it was the language. I was like, "What's he saying?")

DT: Apa, maksudnya di sekolah, apa … ? (Huh? You mean at school or … ?)

KOICHI: Maksudnya di sekolah, dan teman Indonesia ngomong-ngomong. Ini tuch pikir, ini kayak [sic] bagus. Belum keluar kata-katanya juga mau ngomong, gitu. Ya gitu, jadi, "Ini ngomong apa?" Jadi tanya-tanya. "Ini apa? Ini apa? Ini apa?" Gitu. それで、こういう意味だよ、こういう意味だよって 言って、Oh, gitu. Gini, gini. Ya udah, 面白くなって。(I mean at school; like, my Indonesian friends were chatting. And I thought, this seems cool. So I couldn't say anything yet, but I wanted to talk. Yeah, that's how. So I was, like, "What are you saying?" So I kept asking. "What's this? What's this? What's this?" Like that. So then, they would be like, "It means this. It means that." "Oh, really?" "Like this, like this." So yeah, I got interested.)

Koichi explained that he also learned Indonesian from the maid and driver who worked for his family.[3] He got along well with the maid when he was a child and, because she did not speak Japanese, learned Indonesian so that he could play with her. "I probably ended up like this because I spoke Indonesian thinking that it's really fun to speak it," Koichi added in Japanese. Learning Indonesian was "fun." At the Japanese school, being Japanese meant that Koichi was part of the dominant culture and therefore positionally higher than his mixed Japanese-Indonesian schoolmates, making it easier for him to join them. Similarly, he was positionally higher than his adult Indonesian maid and driver in terms of both cultural and class hierarchies. He was also still young and impressionable.

At TIS, Koichi's social circle extended from the Japanese group to the Indonesian group. His interest in Indonesia and fluency in Indonesian was unusual for a Japanese, who, according to the regional cultural hierarchy that reflects the economic structure, are considered higher in status than Indonesians and generally not too interested in Indonesia. Even the way he sat sometimes betrayed his Indonesian upbringing. Indonesians were interested in befriending him. Neither did he seem to have problems talking to Koreans, in fact he had dated one before. Koichi said he used to hang out in the Indonesian hangout area when his older Japanese classmates all graduated together and the Japanese hangout area was left empty. But by the time I met Koichi in his senior year, Koichi's recess time was spent mostly at the Japanese hangout area while his Indonesian-speaking friends regularly visited him there and stayed to chat with him. The most regular of these visitor friends were a Chinese Indonesian, a mixed Japanese-Indonesian (Kenji), and a Korean (Dae Sik) and a Taiwanese who had grown up mostly in Indonesia. Koichi engaged with those who were different on a regular basis, but his cosmopolitan practice was not visible to the teachers and administrators because he did not engage with the "Western" students. Intergroup interaction among the non-mainstream groups was common. However, these cosmopolitan practices remained largely unrecognized.

Although he was a dominant figure within the Japanese-speaking group, Koichi was not a popular figure within the school at large due to his lack of Western cultural capital. Koichi confessed that he wished he could join the English-speaking groups, which he referred to as the "Westerners" as he pointed toward the main senior hangout area:

KOICHI: I do wanna join them. I bet it's really fun to be friends with those guys. I do think so. But there's still, like, a part of me that just can't go there [the English-speaking hangout area]. It's 'cause, it's sort of, like, umm, maybe there's still, like, a language barrier, I guess? I haven't tried, but I guess, to be honest about it, I still feel insecure about my English. I'm not sure I can keep up with the kind of conversations that Americans have. So, it's like, it's really hard to break into that group, I guess.

DT: So, you can't join, but you also have a desire to join?

KOICHI: Yeah, I do, I do.

DT: Is it quite strong?

KOICHI: Well, yeah, kinda; it looks like fun, and I've got a few friends there actually. So, if my friends are there, I'll drop by and stuff. When I see them chatting, I think, yeah, it seems cool. I think, you know, it would be kind of cool to be with my Western friends and be kind of like, "Hey look, I'm the only Japanese guy who's hanging out with them" [laughs]. But yeah, there's a part of me that just can't go there.

And it's like, I've got a normal life here [points to the Japanese hangout area that we were sitting in], so I guess I'm not that desperate. Yeah, I'm not desperate. So, it's like, I've got enough friends even if I don't go there. And there's a part of me that's, like, [trying to convince myself] "Well, if I really wanted to go there, I can, so whatever"; but then again, there's another part of me that wishes I could be that guy who could [freely] hang out over there with them *and* hang out over here [with my Japanese friends]. But in a way, I'm not that desperate, so I guess I don't try.[4]

The friends who Koichi was referring to were his baseball teammates. Doing sports together seemed to be one of the few occasions when language and cultural barriers mattered less and students were able to bond despite their differences. The Japanese girls on the softball team would also occasionally have brief, friendly interactions in the hallways with teammates from the English-speaking groups as they passed each other by. But these friendships rarely developed into anything substantial beyond the sports grounds.

As he spoke of his desire to join the English-speaking groups, Koichi gazed toward their hangout area in the same manner that I saw a few others—Korean-speaking, Indonesian-speaking, and low-status English-speaking students—gaze at those groups. Their gaze carried a sense of longing for something unattainable, something out of their reach. A few months later, as he was about to graduate, Koichi wrote in the school yearbook that I had purchased for myself: "It's only been a short while, but of all the Japanese here, I think you understand me the most. I don't really talk much about myself with others, so that says a lot." I believe he was referring to the time when he spoke of how he could not bring himself to join a group that he longed to join. His words caught me by surprise because I had not realized that he had shared with me something that he had felt was too vulnerable to share even with his close friends.

In Koichi's eyes the English-speaking groups became "Western," even "American," in the same way that he became "Japanese" in their eyes. Those without Western capital perceived being international as being "Western" or "American." Similarly, students in the English-speaking groups and staff perceived the cosmopolitan practices of Asian students as being "Korean," "Indonesian," or "Japanese." Despite his desire, Koichi felt unable to join the English-speaking groups for fear of rejection. He thus remained within the Japanese group where his cultural capital enabled him to feel as though he belonged. Even though he was interculturally competent and practiced cosmopolitanism with other Asian students, Koichi became Japanese at TIS. However, fear of marginalization was not the only reason students hung out in non-English-speaking groups. Neither were these groupings static. Language-based groups became more and more distinct as students got older, as I show in the next section.

Changing Friendship Circles with Age

Asian students, particularly those who had been at TIS since elementary school, noted a clear pattern of change in student interaction where cultural background mattered more as they progressed from elementary to middle to high school. In elementary school, they interacted regardless of cultural background. In middle school there was a vague sense, at least retrospectively, that Asian students hung out more with other Asian students and Western students with other Western students. By high school, student groups became more distinctly based on nationality or language. Patterns of friendship change because having a sense of mutual intelligibility becomes increasingly important with age. It is also a result of student mobility.

Kumar joined TIS in the third grade and initially struggled due to his inability to speak English. But he remembered being friends with children of various cultural backgrounds. As he progressed to middle school, he was mostly friends with other Indian students but still retained friendships with non-Indian students. By the time I met him in his junior year of high school, he hung out almost exclusively with other Indian students.

David (Jeong Tak), who is Korean, had been at TIS since grade two and tells a similar story.

> In middle school it's international kids that I was friends with. Well, I had friends from my ethnicity, but the ones that I usually hang out with. They were much less Korean. So it was really hard for me to have Korean friend or befriend with Korean because in middle school, it was so tiny percent of the students, the level of Korean, the number of Korean. In middle school, I kind of have half American friends ... not American, but international friends, and half Korean friends. Now in high school, it's like 80 percent Korean friends.

By "international," David meant non-Koreans. Even though he found it hard to befriend Koreans when he was younger, he ended up hanging out with Koreans in high school.

Yun Shin, or Sam as he was known among non-Koreans, followed a similar trajectory in that he had more international friends when he was younger, but hung out mostly with Koreans by the time I met him. Sam had lived outside Korea since he was six weeks old. Initially he lived in Jakarta and attended a Korean school until the 1998 riots forced him to relocate temporarily when he was in third grade. He went with his mother to Brisbane, Australia, where he attended a local school and learned English. A year later he moved back to Indonesia to attend TIS. Sam had a transnational upbringing, but he hung out almost exclusively with other Korean students.

Sam cited mobility as one of the reasons for changes in his friendship circles. Even for those who stayed at one international school, mobility featured significantly in their lives. Sometimes all their friends left at the same time, leading them to lose their whole social network with the turn of a single academic year. As his non-Korean friends left, Sam was unable to replace them with other non-Koreans. He eventually hung out more and more with other Koreans: "People come and go, come and go, most people are like that. All my Korean friends are quite stable here, so I have them as very stable friends." As he grew older, it became easier for Sam to maintain friendships with other Koreans than to make new friends among non-Korean students because cultural capital weighs in more on relationships as a teen than as a young child.

Another Korean, Seung Gi, makes this point more explicit. Seung Gi similarly cited mobility as a reason for the changes in his friendship circles. Seung Gi had friends of many different nationalities and, like Dong Gun, I often saw him shuttle among different groups of friends. But as a senior he hung out mostly in the group labeled "Indonesian."

Unlike Sam, he preferred to hang out with Indonesians as opposed to Koreans despite being only able to understand 70 percent of what was said when his friends spoke in Indonesian.

Seung Gi used to have more "international" friends when he was younger. Many of them came and went. As he became older, Seung Gi found it increasingly difficult to befriend the new "international"—which was often conflated with "Western"—students and ended up hanging out mostly with the Indonesian students. He found that he "can't connect [*nggak nyambung*]" with the newcomers. As he grew older, not only did his social capital to access the "international" group diminish as his friends left, but he was also unable to cultivate the Western cultural capital necessary to relate to the incoming Western students. Having a sense of mutual intelligibility with friends is more important as a teen than it is as a young child. As for his preference for hanging out with the Indonesian students over the Korean students, Seung Gi cited financial reasons—his family was generally better off than the other Korean families. Social, cultural, and economic capital all intersected to affect Seung Gi's friendships.

Ben, whose Korean name is Hyun Bin, moved from Korea to Canada, then back to Korea before moving to England, and then Indonesia. In Indonesia, he already had preexisting family friends from the Korean community that helped him make friends among the Koreans at TIS when he joined in ninth grade.

> BEN: I have family friends here who are Korean. I hang out with them. I was automatically [in] the Korean group. I had several friends, because my dad would travel [to] Indonesia and then Korea, Indonesia, Korea. Sometimes brings friends from Indonesia and they were Koreans here, in TIS. So we become very good friends.
>
> DT: So you mean you knew them from before?
>
> BEN: Yeah. Since, like, seven years old.

Ben's social capital facilitated his friendships with other Korean students. Ben believes they were "welcoming" because they knew what it was like to be new at the school: "Yeah, cause they were all like, some time in their life they have, they came here, right? So they know how it feels to first come to see the different groups and stuff. So they were really welcoming and stuff."

Ben was one of the most westernized among the Korean seniors, but still he felt that a lack of social and cultural capital made it difficult for him to befriend the students in the English-speaking groups. Ben explained:

I don't have really many Western friends because I wasn't here in middle school, elementary school. It's Korean people from middle school and elementary school have much more Western friends. 'Cause in elementary school, like, there's no cultural difference because they're so young and stuff. Even middle school, it's less division. But as you go to high school, there's such a strict and vivid division between cultures. It's so hard to make foreign [non-Korean] friends. If they're not in your class, it's like, almost impossible to just go up to them, and it's kind of like intruder. Like, Western [hangout area], Korean guy going in, just random [Korean] guy walking in, and talking to a random Western person—it's kind of weird. But if I have a purpose, that kind of thing, then I can just talk to them.

Students were generally amicable to each other, and felt able to approach individuals in other groups if they had a specific purpose for doing so, such as asking a classmate about a homework assignment. But they found it difficult to just go and socialize with another group.

As Ben suggested, many of the students who had been at TIS since elementary or middle school used to be good friends with students who were, by high school, hanging out in different language-based groups. Students in all the major groups that had been at TIS since elementary school agreed on this. The groups had distinct boundaries in high school, but the friendship trajectories that students had taken indicated that most of them used to practice cosmopolitanism, according to the school's ideology of being international, in that they were friends with people across racial, cultural, and linguistic differences. As they grew older, however, social and cultural capital grew in influence over their sense of mutual intelligibility with each other, affecting their ability to maintain or make new friendships across these differences.

Initially, Ben wondered why students seemed to form the distinct groups, and attributed it to the different future trajectories they would be taking: "I kind of see why now. But when I first came here, I didn't quite see why [laughs]. I heard that in middle school it's better there. They would mix easily, more. But in high school, I don't see why people would divide up, that kind of stuff. But now I see, because what their ultimate goal, like, university and that kind of stuff, is different—how they study, like their parents and stuff—is different. So they wouldn't really get along [with] forei- [sic], other people." According to Ben, different home environments and post-graduation plans influenced students' choice of friends. This argument appears to run contrary to the fact that many students were interested in studying in the United States or the United Kingdom, including Koreans regardless of their cultural background. I suggest, however, that while their destinations for university may be similar, the path they take to get there and their projected life trajectory after university are affected by their family culture, finances, and country of passport, which I discussed in chapter 4.

Both those who stayed and moved found that their social, cultural, and economic capital had a greater influence on their ability to make friends with various groups of transnational youth as they grew older. Even among the high school students I observed, the boundaries based on language were more pronounced among the twelfth-grade students than they were for those in ninth grade. In contrast, the cliques *within* the language-based groups diminished as students matured and popularity within the groups mattered less. It is too simplistic to dismiss the existence of non-Anglophone groups at the school as the result of "self-segregation" and the failure to practice cosmopolitanism. Various factors intersect to influence the formation of these groups.

Significantly, it was mainly Asian students who cited the pattern. In contrast, students from English-speaking group(s), regardless of how long they had been at TIS, were mostly unaware of the pattern. They almost never mentioned that they used to be friends with some of the Korean or Indonesian students until I asked about it. They did not volunteer this information as the Asian students did. Due to their dominant position, members of the English-speaking groups were rarely aware that they were in a group that shared a sense of mutual intelligibility, because this was perceived as normal, as I argued in the previous chapter.

I Miss Being "Korean"

In addition to the impact of mobility, students commonly cited the transnationality of their upbringing as the very reason for being drawn to their Korean peers. All four Korean students mentioned above spent a considerable time, if not their whole lives, outside Korea. They are multilingual, have a "natural" command of English, and, in most cases, are able to write better in English than in Korean, though some are more comfortable speaking Korean than English. However, apart from Seung Gi, who hung out with Indonesians, they (David, Sam, and Ben) claimed that they hung out with other Koreans at TIS precisely because they had limited experience with Korea and had a desire to know their parents' country. Some had no friends in Korea, which was not surprising given that they had not been living there. However, each imagined Korea in a slightly different way, which was reflected in their practice of cosmopolitanism.

Imagining "Korea"

For Ben, who had extensive transnational experiences, hanging out with Koreans at TIS was a new experience. He had left Korea for Canada during elementary school and spent grades five and six in a Canadian town at a school with only three Asian students—himself, his younger brother, and a Canadian-born Chinese. He had gone to Canada on a study abroad program organized by his school in Korea. Ben and his brother home-stayed with a Canadian family during that time. He then returned to Korea for seventh grade before moving to England to study at a boarding school. This time, his brother stayed behind in Korea and Ben was one of two Koreans at the school. Ben prefers to speak Korean, as he can "express more feelings" in Korean than English, but he speaks English fluently with an accent that sounds mildly North American.

During my fieldwork, however, I noticed that he hung out mostly with the Korean students. When I asked him whether he missed hanging out with non-Koreans, since he had spent some time almost exclusively with non-Koreans while in Canada and England, he responded:

> But like, I had that experience so I like kind of having this experience [i.e., hanging out with Koreans] now. So when I go to college, I'll have a different experience. It's okay with me. It's a chance for me to have that experience.

> But the bad thing is, since I have to move around so much, like, when I was about to get so close to the friends there as friends, when I made that kind of friends, I had to leave. It's kinda, it's hard for me to leave those kinds of people and then settle in a new environment. But, yeah, that's kind of [the] bad part of it. But I can just contact them with MSN or, it's okay, yeah.

Ben only spoke in passing about his difficulty in leaving friends behind. But his experiences echo the existing research on Third Culture Kids. They learn to cope with repeated loss of friendships and social networks due to mobility, but these losses can lead to a sense of "unresolved grief" that resurfaces later in life (Pollock and Van Reken 2009 [2001]: 159).

Meanwhile, David spoke of Korea with a sense of longing for the "home" that has never been, apart from temporary visits home (Baldassar 2001). He was a senior and said he would most likely go to Korea rather than the United States (his other choice) for university, partly due to the lower tuition fees in Korea and partly because he had missed out on living in Korea.

Since I've been overseas for a long time, I would like to go back to Korea, stay there, live there, work there, be educated there, and, for now, I don't really wanna travel around the world. I just want to stay and live in Korea. That's my home, so I just wanna, I've been away from home for such a long time, so I wanna go back and live there. That's home. I think I have enough international overseas experiences. And I have barely, you know, Korean experience, experience in Korea. Maybe, like, twenty years later I'll get sick of Korea and wanna live overseas, but for now I wanna stay. I really feel that I'm secluded from the "Korean experience" [makes air quotes], like, that I was, that I'm kind of missing the Korean experience that normal Korean people should have. So yeah, I wanna go back to Korea.

David made frequent references to Korea as "home" and his strong desire to return there as he spoke to me in fluent English. His parents had played a major role in influencing his identity and orientating him toward Korea, as I discussed in chapter 4.

It was common among transnational youth who had lived overseas for most of their lives to be curious about and even *infatuated* with their parents' country precisely because they had very limited experience of living there. During a dinner event that the Japanese students organized themselves, many, especially the younger ones, enthusiastically related that they want to go to Japan for university. They were infatuated with the idea of experiencing student life in Japan, which was something they had only seen on TV drama series that they rent on DVD from a Japanese-style supermarket in Jakarta or read about in Japanese *manga* (comic books). Furthermore, David's (as well as Sam's and Ben's below) desire to immerse himself in the lives of his Korean peers echoes an identity-development stage common to children from minority groups as well as Third Culture Kids when they seek out a "reference group" with whom they share a sense of mutual intelligibility (Cross 1991; Schaetti 2000).

Using Korean "Roots" to Build International "Routes"

Sam claims that he hangs out with other Koreans because he wants to retain his connection to Korea. Sam articulates his interest in Korea as a need to know his "roots." Sam speaks English fluently, though his accent is not as native sounding as David's. He says that he hung out mostly with Koreans even in middle school and cites language retention as one reason.

SAM: 'Cause it's, well I, I didn't want my Korean, to forget my Korean. Nowadays my relatives say that my Korean is pretty good, but still it's

shaky. 'Cause if I speak Korean, it seems fluent and all—no pronunciation issue—but, yeah, some of the hard, like, words, yeah.

DT: Why is Korean important to you? Like, speaking Korean?

SAM: It's a root. It's like, wherever I go, I won't be considered as, like,
even though how good I am in English and all, my root is from Korea
so I don't wanna lose that. 'Cause I've seen people get like, like, who
miss their countries. I've also seen people who don't actually know
how to speak Korean but they're Korean. So I don't, I don't want that
to happen. 'Cause, I like my relatives [laughs]. I wanna speak with my
relatives.

Maintaining connection with relatives through language retention is
important for Sam in establishing roots. This corroborates the TCK
literature that argues that transnational youth find "home" in relationships (Pollock and Van Reken 2009 [2001]). Even so, Sam said he did
not mind changing his Korean passport to an American one if it meant
he could avoid the compulsory Korean army service. For him, identity
was not about nationality.

Sam believed that knowing his Korean "roots" enhanced his ability
to be "international." The two are mutually constitutive because he became more aware that he was Korean when he was in an international
space. This struck home for him when he joined a summer school program run by one of the top high schools in the United States, which
drew students from a diverse array of countries:

There were like people from all around the countries with like different
accents, different sound talking, different faces, speaking and all. I think
it was great, really great fun. People say if you live in foreign countries,
they say if you go somewhere that is very international, people say that
you become an international person. But I think it's more different. You
actually become an international person, but your origin actually becomes stronger 'cause the fact that, the fact that, oh, how should I say,
you seem to know that you are a Korean *more* in international society. It
seems that you *represent*, 'cause you're in international place, in different
countries, it seems you represent more.

It's not that you lose your roots, but you become more aware of it. But at
the same time you *are* becoming international. The fact that you are Korean speaking English, you still can speak Korean and you're speaking
English, and then you are ... intermingling with other countries—I think
that's what makes it international rather than a person who's actually
born in foreign countries.

"A person who's actually born in foreign countries" is a reference
to, for example, Korean Americans who are born and raised in the

United States and can speak English but not Korean. In Sam's view, "they're just American," and "that's not showing diversity, that's showing America."

Sam articulates becoming "an international person" in terms of bilingualism and biculturalism, whereby one has the ability to mediate between cultures. In order to do this, one needs to know their "root" or "basic" identity, and English is useful insofar as it is a tool to communicate that "root" with others, as opposed to it (English) becoming part of one's identity. Sam said, "you can share *your* basics to other countries in English so that, I think that's what international means." Sam's belief that he needs to speak Korean to be Korean and to establish Korean roots to become international appears to contradict research that argues that linguistic ability is not requisite for claims to identity (e.g., Ang 2001). In light of Hall's (1996: 4) words that it is "not the so-called return to roots but a coming-to-terms-with our 'routes,'" it would appear as though Sam is unable to come to terms with his "routes."

Through his long explanation, Sam, like David and Ben (in the previous and next sections), was critiquing the school's ideology of being international, which did not acknowledge alternative practices of cosmopolitanism. Korean students were well aware of the way members of the dominant culture at TIS perceived them as deviating from the school's model of an ideal student. The dominant ideology made the cultural sameness shared by the English-speaking groups invisible, while celebrating physical diversity. In contrast, for Sam intercultural interaction occurs in the presence of difference where difference is defined based on language as opposed to physical attributes such as "race" or ethnicity. Sam was arguing for a different way of practicing cosmopolitanism—becoming international by first becoming Korean to make up for his transnational upbringing. For Sam, becoming "Korean" is mutually constitutive with becoming international.

Becoming "International" by Becoming "Asian"

Young people who experience a sense of ambivalence in transnational spaces negotiate cultural boundaries through varied practices of cosmopolitanism. For transnational youth of Asian descent, becoming "Western" and becoming "Asian" are mutually constitutive with each other. Asian students who did not hang out in the mainstream and high-status English-speaking groups but were more westernized than the other Asian peers they hung out with expressed greater identification with being "Asian," as contradictory as this may seem.

Ben explained that the reason his Korean friends do not hang out with the English-speaking groups is because they do not understand their culture, such as the practice of "egging" and "how they party" and "prom and that kind of stuff." Indeed, despite the large number of Koreans, only a handful attended the prom that year. But because Ben feels "40 percent Western and 60 percent Korean," he is sympathetic to the various practices of Western teenagers. As mentioned before, Ben appeared to me to be one of the most westernized senior Korean students. Even then, he had difficulty befriending the "Western" students in the English-speaking groups.

In contrast, Ben described a sense of affinity with other Asians, in which the cultural boundaries are blurred. I asked him whether he also found it difficult to approach the Indonesian group. "Indo, I'm fine," Ben answered immediately and assertively. Then he continued:

> BEN: There's like more, I don't know. I think it's easier to go into Indo group. 'Cause, like, it's still Asian. And their culture is a little bit more similar to ours than the Western[ers].
>
> DT: Do you know more Indo people?
>
> BEN: Actually, I don't really know them much. But I have friends who are Indo, and friends who are Cantonese and [slight pause] Italian. But people who are Western, like English-speaking countries, it's harder to make friends with since they have their own group and stuff. I don't know. Even Italians have different cultures from like States, and like English, and so it's easier to hang out with Italians. That's how I find it. I don't know why, still.

Ben acknowledges the Western influence on his cultural identity. His experiences in Canada and England had blurred the boundaries between Koreans and other minorities in Anglophone spaces. His sense of "we" includes other Asians and even Italians, and he considers those who are "Western"—in other words students in the English-speaking groups—as "them." Ben is uneasy about not being able to define the boundaries of being "Asian," especially once he began to explain that he could also relate to Italians. This is because he becomes "Asian" through the sense of mutual intelligibility that comes with the shared experience of being a minority in Anglophone spaces. Being "Asian" facilitates Ben's cosmopolitan engagement with others.

At TIS, Asian students seemed to share a sense of being "Asian" that was subsumed under the students' more specific national or ethnic identities. Yae's interview contained slippages between being "Japanese" and being "Asian." Yae, a recent graduate of TIS, was one of the few Japanese who had no qualms throwing in English words into her speech while speaking in Japanese. She was born in Japan, from where she moved to Thailand, then back to Japan, before moving again to the Philippines, Malaysia, and then Indonesia, where she finished high school. In chapter 4, I discussed Yae's predicament with regard to her future. Her parents wanted her to attend university in Japan, her passport country, to establish her identity as a Japanese and ensure that she would not end up in a liminal cultural space. Yae agreed with this, but in explaining her reasons for returning to Japan, she conflated being "Japanese" with being "Asian":

> For one thing, I don't have a feel for what is common sense [*jyōshiki*] in Japan because I've lived in Southeast Asia for so long. And my Japanese is nowhere near perfect.... They [her parents] said I'm lacking in my Japanese identity. I got told, "You just don't have it in you. And it's not like you speak perfect English either." I totally agree with them, as much as I hated having to admit that. But, yeah, at the end of the day, I am more Japanese, [more] Asian after all. I'm Japanese, and up until now I've always hung around Asians. I am Asian after all. But I am lacking in my knowledge of history and *jyōshiki* as a Japanese.

Besides, she says, "Japan is fun, and it feels safe," and even if she did go to the United States, "I probably would have ended up hanging out with Asians anyway." To capitalize on and consolidate her Asian identity, Yae feels the need to become more knowledgeable in Japanese history and competent in performing and understanding Japaneseness or "*jyōshiki*." Yae often conflated being "Japanese" with being "Asian." She gives her tendency to have Asian friends as evidence of being "Asian after all." Yae's conflation of becoming "Japanese" with becoming "Asian" reflects the sense of ambivalence inherent in hybrid identities. Being "Asian" is an expression of her cosmopolitan engagement with others.

Becoming "Asian" suggests a sense of mutual intelligibility among Asian youth who have a transnational upbringing and share the experience of not being part of the dominant culture of a Western transnational space. It is an expression of cosmopolitanism in the same way that being international represents an ideological expression for the cosmopolitan practice that emerges out of the sense of mutual intelligibility shared among transnational youth with a certain degree of Western capital.

The Diversity of Cosmopolitanism

Cosmopolitan practices are situational. In order to participate in cosmopolitan practices that conform to the school's ideology of being international, students acquired Western capital and accepted an identity change. Students who were unable or unwilling to do this were constructed as a nameless, racialized Other, making their cosmopolitan practices invisible. Although cosmopolitan practices that privilege Western capital were conceived as being international by those who were able to participate in them, these same practices were conceived as being "Western" or "American" by those who were unable to integrate into the dominant school culture. In turn, cosmopolitan practices that deviated from the school's ideology of being international were invisible to the dominant culture and conceived as being "Korean," "Japanese," or "Indonesian." Whether or not cosmopolitan practices are recognized as such depends on how difference is defined.

At TIS, Korean-, Japanese-, and Indonesian-speaking students chose to hang out in their language groups because they felt they could "connect" better with their peers and escape feeling marginalized. By creating separate groups, they went from being nameless to being the norm within these groups. The use of languages different from that used by the dominant group enabled them to construct boundaries between insider and outsider, and in the process reclaim their status as insiders, and the power to be gatekeepers.

Some of the Asian students who were more westernized than their peers in their language groups articulated an ambiguous sense of being "Asian." Their sense of hybridity caused their identifications to slip between being Korean or Japanese and being Asian. Asian students shared a sense of mutual intelligibility as minorities within an Anglophone space. Being "Asian" is an expression of cosmopolitan practices that privilege Asian cultural capital in the same way that being "Western" or "international" is an expression of cosmopolitan practices that privilege Western capital. Being "Asian" facilitated alternative forms of cosmopolitanism. The next chapter continues to discuss the dominance of Western capital in transnational spaces by focusing on (hetero)-sexual attraction among transnational youth.

Notes

1. Most of the Indonesian nationals at TIS were of Chinese descent. Although they are a minority in Indonesia, their financial standing means many of

them are better able to afford the expensive international school fees compared to the majority of the Indonesian population.

2. It is common in Japan to use surnames or given names followed by *kun* to refer to someone, usually male or younger. In this case, they have used Koichi's surname, "Tomioka."

3. Expatriate families typically employed a maid, driver, or sometimes a gardener and/or security guard using their own salaries, or these were provided by one of their employers. Many TIS students said that they learned Indonesian through these employees, particularly maids and drivers.

4. Translated mainly from Japanese.

CHAPTER 7

Race and Romance

In this chapter, I begin by discussing the ways in which those with a transnational upbringing, both young people at TIS as well as young adults outside of TIS, racialized their discussions of sexual attraction as they consider various factors for a potential partner. Gender and cultural capital influence their openness to dating or marrying outside their own ethnic groups. For some, whiteness in a partner is ideal, while others shun it. Indonesian-speaking students took this a step further. They used their wealth to challenge the dominant status of "the West" at TIS by drawing on nationalistic discourses of being "Indonesian," thus emphasizing my point that the national and transnational are mutually constitutive. Transnational youth and adults are conscious of the prevailing stereotypes about interracial couples. I show that relations between expatriate men and Indonesian women bring these discourses into relief. Some transnational youth and adults discussed how they avoid or are subjected to stereotyping. The ways in which transnational youth and adults articulate their own and others' sexual desirability and attitudes toward intimate relations demonstrate that their cosmopolitan engagement with the Other is embedded within existing social hierarchies.

Intimate relations are apropos sites for exploring cosmopolitan engagement. They expose the intersections of race, class, and gender within prescribed social structures. Intimate relations formed across difference blur social boundaries by transgressing them, while at the same time highlighting the boundaries as they are transgressed (Stoler 1992). With a focus on heterosexual relations,[1] I argue that colonial and capitalist discourses of sexual desirability and patterns of intimate relations outside the school gates privilege Western capital and influence the perceptions of transnational youth regarding who they are attracted to and who they think is attracted to them. Discourses about sexual desirability affected social dynamics among students at TIS, which in turn was projected onto their cosmopolitan practices to reinforce the school's ideology of being international, which privileges Western capital.

Racializing Beauty and Attraction

Transnational youth form perceptions of beauty and preferences regarding partners by drawing on the discourses that shape the social structures around them. Many racialize beauty and attraction by drawing on discourses of being international, whiteness, and/or nationalism. This racialization is expressed either as desire for whiteness or rejection of whiteness. The perceptions of South Asian students illustrate that the desire for whiteness influences them to perceive "white" as beautiful and natural. In turn, the perceptions of Japanese students illustrate that their linguistic capital (or lack thereof) influences whether or not they reject whiteness in partners (Meerwald 2002).

Indian Girls Like White Boys, Indian Boys Like White Girls

A group of male South Asian students made explicit their views on the desirability of whiteness. I was in the cafeteria chatting with Mandeep and his friends during their free time. They were all male and South Asian. I spoke to about four of them, though not all four were present throughout the conversation. They were part of a usually larger group of six or seven male South Asian students. We talked about the opposite sex, partly because I directed the conversation toward that topic based on what I had seen the previous day when I attended a meeting of the Indian club. Devraj, the president of the club and a well-built and handsome-looking senior, spoke at the meeting about the dance performance they were preparing to showcase on United Nations Day. The club members were made up mostly of students of South Asian descent, of various nationalities, with a few who were not of South Asian descent. As he spoke from behind the podium, Devraj switched accents depending on with whom in the audience he was engaging. I had noticed that there were not that many male students in the comparatively large club of about forty students. The senior boys in the front rows stood out. Most of them, including Mandeep, were good friends with Devraj, and were clearly physically more mature and better built than their younger counterparts. They carried a presence that comes with being atop the age and gender pecking order among a cohort of young people. They also seemed to attract the attention of a fair few of the younger female students.

I said to them, "There was what, eight to ten senior boys and a gazillion girls? Man, yesterday I wished I was a senior Indian boy!" I was suggesting that they may have been the center of female attention, and they laughed as though they were embarrassed. They believed, however, that it did not make a difference. Some said that they were interested in white girls, others in Indian girls or both. "But not the Indian girls at this school," said Devraj. Jagad explained that the "Indian girls are just full of themselves. They think they're all so beautiful." This seemed odd to me given that in my eyes some of the Indian girls *were* beautiful. But according to them, the Indian girls thought they were as beautiful as the white girls, when in reality they are not. Jagad added that the white girls are more modest in their attitude.

Jagad continued to expound his view. Indian girls change to become someone else. They change their clothes, and they try to speak with a different accent. They think they are attractive, but they are not. They are not themselves. They are actually insulting themselves. Puzzled, I asked for examples. Jagad hesitated, and then named Kavita, who he said had completely changed since last year. Jagad felt uneasy and clarified that he was not trying to gossip about Kavita. He then offered Vandana as a contrasting example. I had noticed that while Kavita hung out with her Southeast Asian friends, Vandana was fully integrated into the mainstream English-speaking groups. Jagad felt that Vandana was being herself. She has been the way she is now for a long time. But Kavita tries to act different. At this point, Akshat (the only one in the group who spoke with a distinct Indian accent) interjected with an explanation, "Like, he [points at Jagad] makes fun of my accent and I'm completely fine with it." Jagad then resumed his explanation saying that the only thing that has changed about Kavita is her clothes.

Like them, I had noticed a change in the way Kavita dressed during my year at TIS, but I had seen it as something positive. She had started to wear clothes that were more "feminine." While they did not comfortably fit her still-somewhat-bony frame, I had perceived it as a sign of her maturing and becoming more "womanly" in her still young, girly way. But Jagad and Akshat were digging at something else.

While Vandana's westernized disposition had been cultivated since she was young (she joined TIS when she was five years old), Kavita was only now trying to cultivate this by changing the way she dressed and spoke (i.e., with an Americanized accent). There was no significant difference between the way Vandana dressed and the way Kavita used to dress. Vandana generally dressed in casual shorts and tight-fitting shirts that were not overly feminine. But she carried herself in a way that that made her appear comfortable with the Anglophone crowd, and confident. It came naturally to Vandana, while Kavita had to exert effort. In the boys' eyes, Kavita had transgressed the social boundary that defined her place. Kavita was guilty of mimicry, which made her look inadequate (Bhabha 1984).

I then asked them, "And what do you think the Indian girls think of you?" "Oh, Indian girls, they're into white guys," Mandeep quipped. "Okay, so this is how it is," he said, as he stood up and acted it out for us in the cafeteria. "They see us, and they say [Mandeep puts on a limp voice], 'Oh, hi.'" He said this as he cast a lazy, reluctant sideways glance toward an imaginary Indian boy. As though uninterested and disappointed, he immediately looked at the floor and then away from the imaginary boy. Then he continued, "But when they see a white guy, suddenly it's [this time Mandeep put on a high-pitched voice], 'Ohhhh, hiii!'" He giggled, twisted his body slightly as he raised one shoulder, tilted his chin down, and with his eyes looked up flirtatiously at the imaginary white boy. We laughed as some of the boys nodded in agreement with Mandeep. The boys felt that the Indian girls were more interested in white boys than they were in Indian boys.

Later that day, I saw Mandeep and Jagad enjoying the company of Jackie, who was of mixed white and Asian descent. She was one of the few non–South Asian students from the "normal" English-speaking group who had joined the Indian club. In the context of TIS, Jackie was "white" because she had Western capital through her descent and disposition. Mandeep and Jagad seemed to be giving her their full attention as they chatted in the cafeteria. The scene resembled what Mandeep had acted out earlier, except the genders were switched. True to their confession, the boys seemed more interested in white girls than they were in Indian girls. Although the interaction between the boys and Jackie appeared as though it was international because they looked visibly diverse in terms of "race," it was an interaction that privileged Western capital.

Notions of unassuming beauty signify the predominance of whiteness in the nonwhite psyche. Beauty is racialized within a framework of cultural hierarchies that reflect global economic structures. The Western disposition of "white girls" was perceived as natural, becoming, and authentic. "White girls" seemed to include Indian girls who acquired the appropriate giss from childhood because being Western was racialized as "white." In contrast, those who pursue it at a later stage in their life were perceived as "insulting themselves." The act of pursuing whiteness or Western capital was seen as inauthentic because it involved effort and transgressed social boundaries.

Asian Guys are Like Little Pebbles

A similar dynamic occurred among the Japanese students. When I began my fieldwork, Mina was the only female Japanese student in her grade among six male Japanese students (including Kenji who is of mixed descent), all of whom had moved either from Japan or the Japanese school in Jakarta within the previous three years. As mentioned in chapter 2, Mina greatly valued speaking in English and readily embraced the school's ideology of being international, though she was unable to integrate into the mainstream English-speaking groups. She felt that that the male Japanese students were not being international. She complained to me that the male students were creating walls around themselves—which she called "Japaneseness"—by refusing to mingle with other students.[2]

In contrast, Mina ventured out of the Japanese hangout area to be with her own set of non-Japanese friends. Mina usually hangs out with them when she is not hanging out with the Japanese crowd. These friends, all of whom were female, included Dutch, white American, Iranian, black Canadian, Indian, and Mongolian students among others. As the only Japanese senior who spoke in English to a visibly mixed group of friends, Mina won the school administrators' approval for being international in a way that fitted the school's ideal. Horie *sensei*, the new Japanese teacher who replaced Kubota *sensei* at the turn of the academic year, said that the principal had asked her how they can push other Japanese students to be like Mina.

Mina's perception of the Japanese boys failing to practice the dominant form of cosmopolitanism was reflected back to her in their supposed lack of interest in her as a potential partner. Mina felt that the male Japanese students did not relate to her as someone from the opposite sex, but more as a "pal" due to her tomboyish nature and, according to her Japanese teacher, because she does not fit their ideal of beauty. Mina said (interview, 23 February 2009):

> Kubota *sensei* told me that the kind of woman the boys in my grade have in mind is the kind whose eyes are *pachikuri*, who blinks her large, cute eyes like this [Mina demonstrates by opening her eyes wide, raising her eyebrows, making two perfect circles with both her index fingers and thumbs in front of her eyes].[3] Her eyelashes don't point downwards,[4] has long hair, and is small like this [Mina gestures]. In a way, she's like a pet. That's the kind of girl they idealize.... So I initially wondered if there

was something wrong with me. They don't see me as a woman at all.…
So I told Kubota *sensei* that they refuse to see me as a woman. And she
said that it's because the kind of woman they picture in their minds is
the kind who represent the old, stereotypical *kawaii* type.[5] "So they're the
ones who are behind the times," she said.… She said, "So you have to
live knowing that they're behind the times and snub them."

Mina was tall for a Japanese girl and had small eyes; her eyelashes
pointed downwards. Kubota *sensei* told Mina that in this day and age
women need to be independent, able to build a career and a family,
and follow through with their own vision for life. Mina seemed fond of
Kubota *sensei* for creating space for her where she did not fit the mold,
and admired Kubota *sensei* for being an "independent woman."

But Kubota *sensei*'s advice to Mina about snubbing the boys played
out like comedy one day when I sat chatting with the male students at
the Japanese hangout area. Mina walked past the Japanese bench in
her usual brisk way, with her green bag slung over one shoulder. As she
passed us, she greeted me with "*A, Danau san konnichiwa* [Oh, hi Da-
nau]." Mina waved at me without slowing her pace. I said "Hi" back to
her in Japanese as she continued walking past us to join her girlfriends
on the other bench. She had completely ignored the three boys who
were sitting on either side of me.

The boys looked at each other in disbelief, whispered something,
and then snickered. I asked what was the matter. Daichi began explaining as Koichi piped in with a word or two every so often and Taka
(a short form of his surname, "Takamura"), a pale, thin, soft-spoken
young man, quietly smiled in agreement. The gist of their discontent
was that Mina had no respect for them. "In her eyes, we're just like
rocks lying on the side of the road! No, not even rocks. Little pebbles!" By this time five other Japanese students, both male and female,
had joined us. Daichi had been sitting on the edge of the bench when
he started talking. But seeing that I was paying attention to him and
his audience was growing, he became more and more animated as he
expounded his analysis: "That's right! We're nothing more than little
pebbles that are not worth a glance to her!" Daichi eventually stood up
as his talk escalated into a full-blown Japanese-style standup comedy
performance of the *manzai* sort.[6]

The audience joined in the game by interrupting Daichi with questions to undermine his argument, "Are you sure?" This, in the *manzai*
spirit of things, gave him further license to rattle off his take on the situation. Occasionally, Koichi jeeringly commented from the sidelines:
"'I've got nothing to learn from the likes of you anyway,' *that's* how she
thinks of us." These comments just gave more fuel to Daichi. "We're

nothing! Worthless in our little corner! Crushed little stones! That's how she sees us!" Daichi elaborated, not just in words, but with his whole being and body. A couple of times Daichi spoke in such a frenzy that he had to stop, or acted like he had to stop, to catch his breath. When one of us said, "Look, he's so excited, he's out of breath," Daichi would feign shortness of breath just a while longer. Daichi enjoyed the effect of his performance on the audience and continued at fever pitch while Koichi quipped, "She's the type who will have a hard time when she gets out in the world where you need to know how to get on with people."

It was clear that the young men did not feel that Mina thought much of them. Initially, I thought the boys were overreacting, but Mina completely ignored the boys again as she greeted me on another occasion a few weeks later. It was not that the boys did not care about Mina as a friend. I had seen them banter fondly with her at other times, even after the above incident. As far as romantic attraction went, however, they were not interested. Perhaps Mina's attitude was brought on by the boys' initial lack of interest in her, which would mean that they have themselves to blame for the way she ignored them. Indeed, some of them dated girls who somewhat fit the "cute" stereotype, but not all.

Contrary to Kubota *sensei*'s theory, Koichi was not interested in "stereotypically *kawaii*" girls:

> People often tell me that I go for looks, and well, I guess that's true. Looks are paramount [laughs]. But if you ask me what kind of girls I get attracted to, well, I don't like the girly kind of girls, you know, the *burikko*[7] type, or the type of girls who are really delicate and demure, I don't really like them. I like it when the girl is a bit feisty, or is passionate, you know, something like that is nice. It's really refreshing to see when they're like that, like a bit masculine or there's a hint of masculinity about them.

Koichi's description of the kind of girls he finds attractive echoes the kind of women Mina admired and possibly resembled. Despite this, Koichi was not interested in Mina. Why?

Another possible reason is Mina's lack of respect for Koichi and the other Japanese boys for not being international. As I explained in the previous chapter, Koichi was a cultural hybrid, but his hybridity was devalued due to his lack of Western cultural capital. Having grown up in Indonesia and being fluent in Indonesian in addition to Japanese, Koichi related to Indonesian and other Asian students with ease. Koichi was also enrolled in the same advanced English class for nonnative speakers as Mina, indicating that their English skills were on the same level. But he was not the (Western) cosmopolitan that Mina admired and aspired to be. Perceptions like these explain Koichi's suspicion that those who are white or drawn to whiteness may not be interested in him, as I detail below.

Preemptive Strike

While the Indian boys highlighted the desirability of whiteness in their partners, others who were not white rejected it. Some put their lack of interest in the "Western" students down to cultural difference. Others, especially those who did not have the cultural capital to comfortably interact with the dominant English-speaking groups, were more explicit about the impact of their position in the sociocultural hierarchy on their lack of connection with Western students. The male students in this latter group assumed that Western girls would not be interested in them. Koichi, who had had Japanese and Korean girlfriends, told me that he was open to girls of any cultural background, until I asked whether that included Western girls. It then became obvious that Western girls had not even entered his mind. "Aaah, Western girls, they're like, really up there…. I bet Western girls look at the Japanese and think, 'Ugh.' Western girls are definitely not into Japanese men, no way. I mean, if you think about it, there's more good-looking guys among the Westerners. I think Western men are better suited to Western women, even in terms of the type of guys they like. And, you know, there's a lot more good-looking Western guys. So, you know, that's how things are. That's the reality. Westerners prefer Westerners." Instead of stating whether or not *he* found "Western girls" attractive, Koichi explained that *they* would not be interested in him. He implied that his lack of interest in them was because Japanese men were perceived as inferior to "Western men."

Men considered as Other to the dominant culture are, for example, infantilized. Shanthini, a female Indian student who hung out with the "fountain groups," spoke of a male Korean student of the same grade in a friendly, but paternalistic, way: "Sae Ryun is so cute. Not in a 'He's hot' kind of way, but in a baby kind of way." Sae Ryun was stripped of his masculinity. This act of infantilizing the Other reflects colonial discourses of subordinate races. Said (1985 [1978]) argues that the Orient is commonly depicted as childlike and feminine. Hence, Koichi believed that Japanese men did not fit Western notions of male attractiveness. Racialization of beauty intersects with the school's ideology of being international, which privileges Western capital, and influences who students find attractive.

Language abilities also limit interaction between groups, which then prevents students from expanding their preferences for partners. I asked Koichi whether he had ever been attracted to a "Western" girl, even though he may not have dated any. He responded: "There have been occasions where I thought a girl was cute or gorgeous, but they never turned into romantic feelings. I guess it's because we don't get to interact much. Let's say there's a Western girl who I might think is cute, but I only ever get to look at them and don't get to speak to them or get to know them. Things would probably be different if we could get to know each other." Koichi did not have much opportunity to interact with "Western girls." In the previous chapter I wrote that Koichi desired to hang out with the English-speaking groups, or "Westerners" as he called them, but was unable to. He put it down to his limited ability to fluidly communicate in English with humor, but he also admitted to feeling uneasy about approaching the "Westerners." In the same way that some students retreat into the groups they feel comfortable with because they have the cultural capital to fluidly operate in those groups, so too do their preferences for partners suggest the use of a preemptive protection mechanism: they may think of "Westerners" as collectively good looking, but they are not attracted to them as individuals due to the anticipated rejection.

A male student expressed this sentiment of preemptive protection in a misogynistic way that turned preemptive protection into a preemptive strike. Like most of the male Asian students who were not from the mainstream groups, this student said he preferred Asian girls. As for white girls, he said that they were attractive, but they are the kind that "you use and dispose of [*pake buang*]." But it sounded as though he was putting on a tough façade. He did not have the means to "use and dispose" of Western girls, since to do so would require him to have first gained their attention. He did not have the cultural capital to do so. He was the only boy who made such comments and therefore may not represent the general attitude of students. I am quoting his misogynistic expression only to highlight a pattern among marginalized men who, in order to protect their own sense of masculinity, denigrate women perceived to be members of the superior group. As Partha Chatterjee (1993) argues, women symbolize the purity of the nation, and therefore desecrating them is equivalent to mounting an underhanded attack on the masculinity of the men in the superior group.

Aya and Kayako explicitly stated that their lack of interest in white guys was a result of the cultural hierarchy. We were at an end-of-year social gathering organized by the Japanese students and held at Chunggiwa, a popular Korean barbeque restaurant in Jakarta. One or

two of the senior boys drank alcohol but the rest did not. Only those
who were Japanese or partly Japanese, and one Korean friend of a
senior Japanese student, attended the gathering. One of the lively
older girls, Ellie, started asking the younger students about their ideal
"types" as a fun conversation starter, so I played along and asked questions too. Aya asked whether I was asking for the sake of my research
and I said yes. I worried that this would make her stop talking about
it, but she did not stop. I wondered if it was because she wanted me to
write about the sense of frustration that they experienced.

Many took their turn, stating their preferences, which varied one
to the other: Japanese, Asian, or *bule*. Aya, who was in eleventh grade
and of mixed Indonesian and Japanese descent, said she preferred an
Asian guy, but not Korean due to what she perceived as irreconcilable
cultural differences. Others like Kayako and Isamu, who were in tenth
grade, preferred Japanese, though Isamu did not mind Koreans. According to Isamu, "Westerners" throw around the words "I love you,
I love you" too cheaply, at least from what he saw of Hollywood mov-
ies. He thus felt they were culturally incompatible. I then asked Aya,
"What about a white guy?" Aya answered with a resounding, "No." She
explained, "Because they look down on us." "Yeahhh, I knowww," Kayako piped in. "Yeah, you can tell, can't you," responded Aya.

Both Aya and Kayako had moved from the Japanese school to TIS
in ninth grade and English was their second language. They explained
that they felt looked down upon when they tried to speak English to
the Western students and were not taken seriously or not understood
during group work due to their inferior English skills. "When they say,
'Huh? Huh?' I just go *gara gara gara gara*." Kayako used an onomato-
poeic Japanese expression that signifies a crumbling sound to describe
how it makes her feel. She supplemented this with gestures of shaking
her head slightly from side to side while moving both hands downward in front of her as she wiggled all ten fingers, as though to imitate
the collapse. Kayako looked despondent. Aya sat in silent but serious
agreement, nodding her head lightly. Their limited English skills prevented Aya and Kayako from speaking confidently, inviting responses
from the English-speaking students, which further discouraged them
and instilled a sense of inferiority. As a preemptive move to avoid feeling rejected, they refused to consider students from the English-speaking groups as potential partners.

In contrast, the younger girls seemed infatuated with white boys.
When asked about preferences, the ninth-grade girls right away responded in unison, "*Bule!*" Most of them were fluent in English. But it
is partly their young age that created a strong attraction toward white-

ness. A study by Kara Joyner and Grace Kao (2005) shows that in the United States, incidences of interracial relationships decrease as people age and the anticipation of marriage grows stronger. A senior Indonesian girl at TIS stated that she was attracted to *"bules"* when she was younger, but not anymore. With age comes a more nuanced view of sociocultural relations, which means one does not merely gravitate toward that which is constructed as superior.

Generally speaking, however, girls were more open to boys in higher-status groups than boys were to girls in higher-status groups (Meerwald 2002). Most of the boys from the non-mainstream English-speaking groups were Asian and they consistently and without hesitation stated that they preferred Asian girls to white girls. Girls, on the other hand, were more open to having a white partner. These patterns attest to a gender hierarchy whereby women marry up (hypergamy) and men marry down (hypogamy).

Endogamy for Transnational Youth?

I have hitherto written about the effects of whiteness in encouraging either obvious desires for white partners or (the reverse) ethnically endogamous preferences that appear to reject whiteness.[8] What then does endogamy look like for transnational youth who are cultural hybrids?

Chinese Southeast Asians

Midori was the only one among the Japanese-speaking students who had an exclusive preference for the ethnic Chinese from Southeast Asia. Her preference was perhaps influenced by the fact that her mother was a Chinese Indonesian (her father is Japanese). During one of her breaks, I was chatting with her and her Chinese Indonesian boyfriend about partner preferences. Midori had a habit of rattling off highly politically incorrect statements one after another without considering the implications. Some friends attributed this to her personality. She determinedly stated her preference for the ethnic Chinese from Southeast Asia. They were the only ones she considered attractive. She did not like Western guys. Japanese guys were uninteresting. As for dark-skinned guys like indigenous Indonesians, "They look dirty," she remarked. Midori's dark-skinned, half-Javanese friend Aya was sitting just a few feet away from us. Fortunately, Aya was engrossed with her Nintendo DS2 and did not hear Midori's comment. "Why dirty?"

I asked, "What about Aya?" Midori immediately backtracked with, "Friends are different. They can be dark. That's okay. But not guys." Some East Asian students were prejudiced against darker skin in their preferences for partners.

Westernized Asians and Asianized Westerners

Then Midori asked me about my preference. As it was only fair for me to reciprocate by answering, I told her that although I had been attracted to people of many different backgrounds (and that my preferences had changed over time), at the time I preferred to be with a westernized Asian or Asianized Westerner because that was the closest match to my own cultural background. Midori betrayed a look of mild shock upon hearing my answer, as though I had crossed over to the enemy's camp by allying myself with the oppressors. She proceeded to ask me a series of questions that put me on the defensive. I explained that being culturally mixed meant that I had to deal with cultural difference every day and therefore wanted to keep that difference to a minimum in my intimate relationships. She did not seem convinced that I was not betraying my own.

This was because the people she had in mind were different to the people I had in mind. For Midori, "westernized Asian" and "Asianized Westerner" referred to the high-status English speakers, and did not include the "cafeteria people" I mentioned in chapters 5 and 6. I tried to clarify: "I'm not just talking about the guys over there [pointing to where the "white kids'" benches were]. But also guys like Ernest and Marco and their group." "But they're dorky," Midori countered. It was my turn to be surprised. I then realized that I had envisioned Ernest, Marco, and their friends growing into confident, responsible, and successful adults. I also had in mind some of the friendlier "fountain people" as adults who would have matured and become more open to people from different social groups. So I assured Midori that Ernest and Marco will grow into fine young men in a few years, and so will many of the others. But Midori could only imagine them as teenagers mired in the cultural hierarchy of the school. As far as she was concerned, I either desired whiteness—in other words I was suffering from internalized racism—or had bad taste.

Indians with Western Accents

I asked Anaya about the kind of guys she gets attracted to. As previously mentioned (see chapter 4), Anaya is a female student who self-identifies as a Spanish passport-holding Indian raised in Indonesia and hangs out with the mainstream English-speaking crowd.

> ANAYA: Indian, definitely. I've never been attracted to *anyone* at the school. All the guys I've ever gotten interested in have always been Indian. But I don't know if it's, I don't know if it's because I know that if I allowed myself talk to like someone outside, it would get me into trouble.
>
> DT: Oh, with your parents?
>
> ANAYA: Yeah. Or because it's like actually I don't have any interest in them.
>
> DT: Are your parents pretty strict on this?
>
> ANAYA: My parents are pretty open. I know in the end they'd be like, "You know what, it's your life." Obviously they're gonna be hurt, they definitely.... Because, I don't know, it's just how it is. That's what I mean, responsibility of like, that's the reality of it: it's that they would be hurt by it. But, in the end of course they're not gonna wanna see me unhappy and they're gonna be like, "Do what you want."

Anaya's reference to her parents suggests that she is aware that she may have been socialized into preferring Indian men. She explained that she feels a sense of "responsibility" toward her parents and other family members to be "a good daughter," which defined her as a woman. But her description of the kind of Indian men she liked suggested that there were other influences.

> ANAYA: Cultural—very, very, very, very open. If I were to be attracted to a guy it would be because ... he was about or as international as me and accepting.
>
> DT: Does his accent when he speaks English matter?
>
> ANAYA: It's funny you ask that. I guess so because none of the guys I've been attracted to, they've all been Indian, but none of them have had an Indian accent. One's had an American, one's had a Spanish accent.... This guy, he was like, he is like, like, oh my God [her face flushes]. He speaks like, okay, he speaks broken English and I speak broken Spanish, and so we communicate with broken English and broken Spanish. And so it's really interesting, but yeah. And, one guy had a British accent.

Anaya acknowledged that her preference was to some extent due to her socialization as Indian and in turn her desire to be a "good daughter." But her transnational upbringing added nuance, as seen in her preference for Indian men with Western accents and who were "international." Anaya herself spoke with an Americanized accent. Each of the above examples shows a preference for sameness ("endogamy")

among transnational youth—a preference that is not defined entirely
by ethnicity, but also by cultural orientation that may encompass being international.

Transgressing Class and Racial Lines

The study of intimate relations can highlight group boundaries, such
as those based on class and "race." Relationships between foreign men
and Indonesian women were highly visible in Jakarta despite being
few in number. The stories told about them sometimes carried moments of discomfort over how sexual unions transgressed carefully
guarded boundaries of class, ethnicity, and sexual morality. These moments of discomfort reinforce boundaries while simultaneously transgressing them. Perceptions, especially stereotypes, about white and
Asian couples impacted upon the way transnational youth and others
in transnational spaces felt about their own attraction to those who
were different.

Nice Girls Don't Hang Out with Foreigners

Vianny, a mother of one of the TIS students, was Indonesian, a former Fulbright scholar, and daughter to Dutch-educated parents who
were descended from Javanese aristocrats. She was married to a white
American man who she met at a Fulbright gathering in Jakarta. Vianny
says of her father's initial reaction to her marriage (interview, 15 June
2009): "My dad wasn't very happy that I was marrying a foreigner when
I was dating him. Because when you're a nice girl, you don't hang out
with foreigners. You don't marry with a *bule* or whatever, or hang out
with a *bule*. If you're a nice girl, come from a nice family, you're a
well-educated person, you come from a nice family—because sometimes in Indonesia when you're with foreigners: 'Oh, what kind of *girl*
[said with a derogatory tone] you are.' You know what I mean?" Vianny
was referring to the perception that Indonesian women who date white
men are morally suspect. Accusing women who marry out for being
sexually loose is a strategy for maintaining ethnic boundaries. Loretta
Baldassar (1999) argues that women are markers of ethnic boundaries,
meaning that women from the out-group are often viewed as morally
suspect, while those in the in-group need to have their purity protected.
     Western expatriates were often surprised that Vianny did not fit
the stereotype of the uneducated, lower-class "gold digger." Vianny recounted conversations she had had with them:

"I never seen Indonesian like you." What do you mean? I don't have five eyes or three noses, you know? "All I see is workers and maids." Excuse me? ... Before, I really don't know how to react. I really still don't know. But I don't think it's my problem. They're stupid, they're ignorance. That's it. And they think, "Oh ya, they want to marry foreigners so they can have a better life." Ladies, I never clean the bathroom, now I have to clean the bathroom when I go back [to the United States]. Do you think it's better life? ... Even my friend was so funny. "How come you speak very good English? Where did you learn it?" Oh, on the flight, from there, here. "And how did you meet your husband?" In a bar [sarcastically], you know?

Vianny felt uncomfortable being lumped together with Indonesian women who were socioeconomically of lower status than her, though she simultaneously questioned her own discomfort since it implied that she too was prejudiced toward the other Indonesian women. She explains: "I feel like it's not supposed to be like that. Everybody's the same. But sometimes it just put me in the defensive."

In Indonesia, stereotypes about relationships between Indonesian women and white men are loaded with political, social, and moral insinuations due to the massive gaps in living standards and colonial baggage of racial discourses. One particular stereotype dominates perceptions regarding sexual unions between foreign men and Indonesian women—that the women are of disrepute and hankering after money. Living in Jakarta, it is difficult not to notice that a portion of the racially mixed couples are made up of older, expatriate white men and Indonesian women who are possibly twenty years younger and economically less well off. Even when there is no age difference, the perception is that many of the women are either former maids or sex workers, with the latter carrying more stigma than the former. There are many elite bars in the business districts of Jakarta where the racial imbalance among their patrons is clearly visible as they are often packed with white men and Indonesian women. The public perception is that the women are looking for clients for the evening.

Given the Jakarta night scene, it is difficult for others to hold judgment when they see a couple that may fit the stereotype. For example, the most conspicuous couples were like the one I saw at an English-speaking church in Jakarta. The church congregation was made up of mostly locals, with a significant number of foreigners, including Westerners. Some of the children from the church attended international schools. There was an old, white-haired man who looked past retirement age. He did not seem approachable. He was married to an Indonesian woman, possibly in her thirties. She had long, wavy hair, wore stiletto heels and red lipstick, and dressed in a sensual way that was different from the other women in the congregation. It was difficult not to notice them, due in part to the seemingly significant age difference and also because of her overall demeanor that stood out from the mostly conventional middle- and upper-class congregation. While they were not in the majority, couples like this were not an uncommon sight.

"I'm Not Like Those Mba-mba"

These sights made university students Dina and Camellia apprehensive about the way people might perceive them when they date white men. Both were Indonesian and Dina had had a transnational upbringing (see chapter 2). Dina and Camellia animatedly told me about their experience of interracial relationships as we chatted over dinner at Sizzler's in one of Jakarta's many posh malls. Camellia, who had gone to Europe as an exchange student in high school, said: "And then like I was, fear that this kind of people will see me like ..."

"You're just an ordinary girl chasing for his wealth," Dina, Camellia's best friend, finished the sentence for her. They tried to explain that many Indonesians, including themselves, have a negative perception toward Indonesian women who marry foreigners.

Camellia continued to explain her frustration with her own feelings of wanting to distance herself from those "other" Indonesian women. "It's like, 'But I'm not like those *mba-mba* am I?' You get what I mean with that *mba-mba?*"

"To be judged on how you judge other people right? Hah!!" added Dina.

"*Mba*" is a Javanese term of deference meaning "older sister," but in places like Jakarta it is also used to refer to younger women or women working as maids and shop assistants, jobs usually associated with the lower class. Dina and Camellia were trying to distance themselves from lower-class women as though to say that if they did find a white man desirable, it was not because he was white. They were conscious that even feelings of attraction are mediated by the notion that "white" is superior and desirable. Sexual desirability is embedded within social hierarchies.

Similarly, Daniel, a TIS student whose father was American and mother was Danish (see chapter 6), had no preference as to the cultural background of those he dated, but he had been reluctant to date Asian girls even if he was attracted to one. He explained:

There's a subconscious or outside forces that influence that. Like, let's say, [in] the past I've liked Indonesian girls, but at times I would be reluctant to start any relationship with them 'cause there's a kind of stigma in Western society or something like that. I'm sure you know, if you walk in [the] mall, and you see a fifty-year-old white guy with a twenty-year-old Indonesian girl, it just fits that stereotype. And so, sometimes I've been afraid of—not so much of my parents—but of what my family in Denmark will think if I send them a photo from prom and [there's] this short little Indonesian girl that I meet. I mean, they probably may even assume that she doesn't even speak English. So, that's kinda made me reluctant at times, but other than that, there's not much preference.

To borrow Stoler's (1992: 551) words, it is in intimate relations that issues of class, gender, and race converge "in a grid of transgressions" that tap into "metropolitan and [post]colonial politics at the same time." Transnational youth find themselves having to navigate geographies of power in their cosmopolitan practice of engaging with the Other in one of the most intimate of relationships. Not only that, some may have to navigate the fact that their own parents fit the stereotype, though I did not meet any during fieldwork who were forthcoming about this.

Becoming "Indonesian," Becoming "Men"

Relevant to this discussion is the way Indonesian-speaking students engaged the school's ideology of being international by using their wealth to challenge it, though in gendered ways. I focus on Indonesian-speaking boys who drew on nationalistic discourses of being Indonesian to establish their elite status, which carries currency in the Indonesian national context, within the transnational space of TIS.

"Visitors Must Have Respect"

In terms of intergroup relations, the mainstream and high-status English-speaking groups got along best with the Indonesian-speaking groups due to a general shared interest in drinking and clubbing, but they were also competitive with regard to status. For example, Shane, a student from the Indonesian-speaking group, said, "Sometimes they're arrogant. They walk around like they own the place. So we put them in their place. It's my country. This is my home. So visitors must have respect. Some of them don't."

Though Shane's mother was Indonesian and his father British, he considers himself more Indonesian than British. "Here in Indonesia, I can make conversation with anyone I see. From Bali to wherever I go, upper class to lower class, even *becak* [trishaw] drivers and the beggars," Shane gestured with his hand as he spoke. "But then when I go to England, it's a different story. I don't really know what to talk about." Speaking of the Western students, he says, "When I hang out with them, I just don't feel that connection. It doesn't feel right. It doesn't feel comfortable." There was no sense of mutual intelligibility.

"And what does the school social hierarchy look like? Who's at the top and who's at the bottom," I asked.

"Indo, *bule*, and then Korean, and Japanese," he answered with confidence.

As previously mentioned, social hierarchies in schools may appear to be about personalities, but Ortner (2003; 2002) argues that it is underpinned by class structures. Among the differences that Shane described between him and the *bule* students, he cited the fact that they usually ride taxis instead of being chauffeured around or driving their own cars like he did. The class difference became clear when I once bumped into Shane and Kenji, among others, during my visit to Splash, a popular teenage beer garden located in an upscale neighborhood and frequented by students from TIS and other international or foreign schools, as well as local elite teenagers.[9] I had gone by taxi with a couple of Australian friends I had met in Jakarta. They were both older than me and due to our age we all felt very out of place as soon as we walked in. Anyone could freely order alcoholic beverages or shisha from the stalls surrounding the wooden tables. From the beer garden we could see an outdoor futsal pitch where two teams of adult Westerners were playing. There were a number of Indonesian men who appeared to be bodyguards congregating near the entrance. They had large physical builds, crew cut hair, and were dressed in *baju safari* (dark navy blue or grey short-sleeved outfits that somewhat resembled Chinese tunic suits). They were standing around and waiting, and later disappeared as some of the customers left.

Shane and Kenji arrived later and sat and chatted with us for a few minutes. It was November 2009 and both of them had graduated from TIS earlier that year. Shane had enrolled at the prestigious University of Indonesia, but he hated it. He could not "connect" with the other students as peers because they were middle class and therefore had a different lifestyle. Later in the night, my friends and I wanted to take a taxi home. I asked Shane for a ride to the main road and he was happy to oblige. We got into his modified, black Mercedes Benz Sport. I sat in the front passenger seat. It was impressively posh. Instead of dropping us off at the side of the main road, Shane dropped us at a hotel lobby. As he drove past the gates, he stopped by the security guard at the entrance, rolled down his window and asked, coolly and casually but with authority, for the guard to find us a taxi. The guard, who was much older than Shane, immediately responded with an enthusiastic, "Yes, boss." Shane carried a great sense of entitlement to place, which he used to shelter me, a woman, and my friends, who were foreigners, from the larger society by mobilizing the services of those who were from the lower class.

At TIS, the contest for the top spot was a competition between the cultural capital of the Western students and the economic capital of students from the local elite. Those who are socialized in Western ways have the advantage of being familiar with the culture of the staff; Indonesian-speaking students counter this by making a show of their economic capital. For example, to host a party, Indonesian students might band together, each student chipping in to hire out an elite Jakarta club (and some bodyguards). One student explained that the actual cost was lower than what the other students thought it was but they leave the others second-guessing that cost to play up their own financial capability.

Defending Girls

Similarly, Dae Sik, who I quoted in the introduction to this book, racialized and constructed the "white kids," or "*bule*" as he called them, as outsiders while claiming to belong to Indonesia despite being a Korean national himself. Dae Sik had grown up in Indonesia, was a native speaker of Indonesian, had a giss that blended in better with the Indonesian than the Korean students, and felt better able to connect with Indonesians than Koreans. The constructs of class, race, ethnicity, nationality, and gender intersected in Dae Sik's expression of an oppositional identity to the *bules* and claim to "my country" (Indonesia), and impacted upon the behavior of the teenage boy. A flashpoint occurred before my fieldwork, which I reconstructed through the stories that students told me. In these stories Dae Sik, who liked attention, and his mates asserted their place in both the transnational space of TIS and national space of Indonesia in a nationalistic, racial, classed, and gendered way.

One of the girls in the Indonesian-speaking group, Sandra, had gone through a family tragedy when the flashpoint in question took place. One story has it that during this time one of the boys from the Indone-

sian group took her under his wing, and together with his friends supported her through the ordeal. Anaya explained, "One of the boys took
[Sandra] as a sister and has been taking care of her and stuff like that
after the whole incident. ... All of the boys have gotten really protective
over her" (interview, 27 April 2009). But one night the students were
out clubbing when one of the white male students jokingly called her a
"slut" for "dancing with one of the guys in a club."

According to Anaya, it was meant as a light-hearted tease, but the
Indonesian students "took it literally" and were offended. I had interviewed the boy in question before and spoken to him on many other
occasions. He impressed me as a very respectful, capable, and friendly
young man, so his comment seemed out of character. But not having
been present on the night, I can only proceed with the stories I had
heard and discuss the nuances in the storytelling as opposed to the actual incident or intent. Dae Sik and his Indonesian friends went to pay
the boy a visit at his home with the company of police officers. I relay
it here in Anaya's words:

> ANAYA: They actually sent people to his house, knocking on his door. His
> mom answered the door and it was like, "We need to speak to Liam." And
> in front of Liam's parents they made Liam apologize to Sandra.
>
> DT: Sandra was there too?
>
> ANAYA: Yeah, this is what I heard. But yeah, and they were like, "You
> better watch out." You know, like, "If you do it again," like, "you know
> what we're capable of doing."
>
> DT: Do you feel the [Indonesians] do that because they seriously are an-
> gry or is it more just like a show?
>
> ANAYA: A show, it's a show they put up. I don't feel like they're actually
> ... they, they don't really have anything [to be] angry about, you know,
> 'cause they have everything that they want. They're like, uhh I wanna
> dog, I get a dog; or I wanna phone, I get a phone; I wanna—you know?
> ... I think it was just to put up a show. And then of course [Liam] would
> go and tell his friends, and then it would be like, "Oh my God, the Indos
> have, like, this power."

"Power" was indeed being put on show through this threatening home
visit. According to another student, the "people" that Dae Sik and cohort "sent" or brought along to Liam's house were hired (off-duty) po-
licemen. Even as teenagers they had recourse to the state apparatus to
make a show of power, which they combined with the use of intimida-
tion tactics. It signified eliteness and the construction of a sense of belonging (to Indonesia) that is born out of a sense of power. There were

other spectacular stories about some of the Indonesian boys using their economic capital to hire police, bodyguards, and security guards to make a show of their power. Ownership of guns was also mentioned though I was unable to verify these rumors.

Dae Sik used the defense of women as justification for his nationalist claims. Ethnic boundaries are maintained by casting out-group women as morally suspect and in-group women as pure, chaste, and therefore in need for protection (Baldassar 1999). Those capable of providing that protection are able to claim insider status, albeit based on a gender hierarchy that gives men power over women. As a Korean who grew up in Indonesia, Dae Sik could not relate to his Koreans peers and his claim to Indonesia was precarious. He also appeared to be an attention-seeker who spoke of having a detached father. By showing himself powerful and masculine enough to provide protection to an Indonesian girl whose reputation was at stake, he was claiming himself worthy to be Indonesian and to be respected. Both Dae Sik and Shane drew on gendered (or sexist), nationalistic discourses to assert a sense of place in Indonesia in the face of the ambiguity of their hybrid identities. They sought to become "Indonesian" by becoming "men," and vice versa.

Tim, who is from the high-status "white kids" group that hung out near the campus shop, felt that the Indonesian students projected an image of themselves as "superior":

> TIM: We'd get into fights with them a lot because we don't know which—well, not me personally, but a few of my friends—because we don't talk as much, we don't know which girls are available, and stuff like that. So someone would go dance with them and then get in a huge fight.

> DT: Over girls?

> TIM: Yeah, and other things. They feel ... I feel like they feel like they're very superior because they have a lot of money and they know a lot of very, like, important people that can [laughs] really do, like, a lot of harm to us.... But I don't know, I guess, I guess it's okay in some ways. [Laughs] 'Cause they're hard as a group to hang out with, like, if there's a lot of them. But a few of them are really nice. There's some that I won't talk to, but there's others that are really nice.

Tim refers to the Indonesian students' wealth and their social capital derived from their links to Indonesia's elite and state apparatus, as factors that make them feel superior. The competition for the top spot is expressed through competition for girls, which, as one Indonesian student explained, is just about boys making a big deal out of nothing just so they have something to fight over (Chatterjee 1993).

In articulating his perceptions of the "white kids," Dae Sik drew on a nationalist, anticolonialist discourse. Homi Bhabha (1994: 44) writes, "It is always in relation to the place of the Other that colonial desire is articulated: the phantasmic space of possession that no one subject can singly or fixedly occupy, and therefore permits the dream of the inversion of roles." It is as though Dae Sik, in taking the initiative to represent Indonesia, is fulfilling the "paranoid fantasy" of "colonial desire" whereby the colonized/dominated (momentarily) inverts the hierarchy and becomes the colonizer/dominating.

Dae Sik took recourse to the Indonesian state apparatus to drive home the point that the "white kids" did not belong in Indonesia. The use of an Indonesian nationalist discourse reduced those who adhered to the school's ideology of being international into a white Other. This stands in stark contrast to the story related by the vice principal in chapter 3 of his disappointment at the failure of the state to protect his children from substance abuse. His lack of access to state protection highlighted the foreignness of Indonesia and the transnationality of his own life, thereby making him *feel* cosmopolitan. In contrast, Dae Sik and his peers used the state to construct the expatriates as intruders, not cosmopolitans.

There are male students in both the English-speaking and Indonesian-speaking groups who chose to express their masculinity by a show of wealth and power. Kenji, a male student whose father was Japanese and mother was Indonesian and hung out with students from many different language groups, said in passing that the *bule* students are "wannabe gangsters" who try to act rich but are in fact not. Although many of the dynamics I have described are common to teenagers under varied circumstances, what is pertinent are the national and cosmopolitan discourses that transnational youth draw upon to express their sense of belonging and place. The way they draw upon these discourses is heavily influenced by the global economic structure that informs perceptions of cultural hierarchy. Dae Sik was clearly aware of this hierarchy and it determined with whom he competed. Dae Sik said, over a casual chat, he did not care if Asians made negative remarks about Korea, but he would be offended if "*bules*" made similar remarks.

I double-checked with him, "All Asians?"

"Yeah, all Asians. They can say whatever. It doesn't matter," he confidently answered.

"Are you sure?" I pressed him.

"Aaaany Asians," confirmed Dae Sik without a shadow of doubt.

So I decided to strike, "Even the Japanese?"

Dae Sik looked like he was caught out and quickly backtracked on his words: "Uh, no, no. Okay, okay, I mean: any Asian except the Japanese. If a Japanese or *bule* say shit about Korea, I'll give them shit. But any other Asians, it's okay. I don't care." Dae Sik broke into a smile as though to acknowledge that he had underestimated my understanding of cultural dynamics.

Clearly, the only opinions that mattered to Dae Sik were those of people who were associated, either racially or by nationality, with countries and societies whose socioeconomic standing was higher than Korea's. I have used Dae Sik extensively as an example due to his exaggerated and clear expressions of how transnational youth draw upon the discourses available to them to negotiate cultural hierarchies. But these same dynamics were at work in more subdued ways with other transnational youth.

Gendered differences

I note, however, that the data focus on male students who tended to express being Indonesian in nationalistic terms. Jason, who was seventeen and of legal age to vote in Indonesia, had voted in the 2009 presidential election that took place a few weeks earlier, which he described (interview, 30 April 2009): "My parents were, like, lazy and everything. But I'm so eager. So I just went myself. I'm always, like, looking at the news and everything, just for the election, to see who will make a good leader and everything, and I base it on that." Jason claimed, "I am sort of a nationalist."

In contrast, female students almost never made overtly nationalistic claims to Indonesia. They tended to express being "Indonesian" indirectly: for example, in terms of how their preference in future partners had shifted from "*bule*" when they were younger to someone who was from the "same culture" by the time they reached the end of high school. I asked Eva what she looked for, culturally speaking, in a partner. Eva, who was Chinese Indonesian, said (interview, 29 April 2009):

EVA: Not *bule*. ... Probably, like, the same culture as me, like *Indo*.

DT: *Kalau bule nggak mau?* (You don't want a *bule*?)

EVA: *Nggak mau* ... [laughs]. *Dulu mau, tapi kayaknya nggak mau deh.* They're sleazy [jokingly], *nggak tau deh.* (No, I don't. I used to want [a *bule*], but nah, I don't think I do. They're sleazy [jokingly], I dunno.)

DT: *Maunya Indo atau* more like Chinese Indo? (Do you want Indo or more like Chinese Indo?)

EVA: Like, Chinese Indo. *Tapi nggak mau yang terlalu,* like, traditional
or whatever *gitu.* Like, has to be ... quite culturally diverse, *biar nggak
norak.* (Like, Chinese Indonesian. But I don't want someone too traditional or, like, whatever. Like, he has to be ... quite culturally diverse, so
he's not *norak.*)

"*Norak*" can mean uncivilized, unrefined, vulgar, or tacky. It implies
being a "country bumpkin" and lower class. In other words, Eva's preferred partner is simultaneously (Chinese) Indonesian ("same culture
as me"), international ("culturally diverse"), and upper-class ("not
norak").

Students of various ethnicities and nationalities became (elite) "Indonesian" at TIS through the process of engaging with those whom
they considered different, especially Westerners. Various factors contributed to the process of becoming elite Indonesian: feeling Othered,
feeling unable to "connect," constructing an oppositional identity to
those considered *bule,* and using wealth to set themselves apart from
the Western students and lower-class Indonesians in gendered ways.

The Color of Desirability

Young people at international schools are expected to be international
and open to difference by virtue of their education and transnational
upbringing. However, the processes involved in becoming international are fraught with tensions because they are embedded within
national and transnational structures of power. Culture, "race," class,
and gender intersect and influence (hetero)sexual attraction among
students who racialized beauty. Some were attracted to whiteness in
a potential partner, while others rejected it as a defense mechanism.
Even when students were open to difference, who they were attracted
to and who they believed were attracted to them sometimes had little
to do with being international. Rather, they navigate around colonial
and capitalist discourses that privileged whiteness, not only in relation to sexual desirability but also in the way being international was
defined by the school. Some students asserted their masculinity, negotiated their hybridity, and became Indonesian by drawing on nationalistic discourses. In the process, they racialized Western transnational
youth as white Others, thus illustrating the shifting notions of being
international.

The intricacies of intimate relations make it at once the most vulnerable and unsusceptible frontier to processes of cosmopolitanization.

The privileging of Western capital in transnational spaces affected perceptions of sexual desirability, attraction, and the range of potential partners, like it does choice of friends. As in the colonial era that Stoler (1992: 552) studied, the cosmopolitan practices of intimate relations were "worked through a psychologizing and naturalizing impulse that embedded gender inequalities, sexual privilege, class priorities, and racial superiority in a tangled political field." In the next chapter, I analyze more closely the ambiguous, shifting nature of racialized categories and young people's ambivalence toward cosmopolitan practices.

Notes

1. Data on other relations were insufficient.
2. The original term she used for "Japaneseness" is *"Nihonjin to iu kabe,"* which literally means, "a wall called being Japanese."
3. Kubota *sensei* is Mina's Japanese literature teacher.
4. She is referring to the fact that many East Asians have straight lashes that point downward.
5. *"Kawaii"* literally means "cute." When used in reference to young women, it implies doll-like and helpless in nature, and manga-like in appearance.
6. *Manzai* refers to the Japanese standup comedy usually performed by a team of two comedians where one plays a character who makes ridiculous comments on various matters and the other plays a rational character who tries to bring his friend into line by interrupting him (*"tsukkomu"* in Japanese) with questions. The questioning often does not work as it simply encourages his/her friend to say more ridiculous things.
7. *"Burikko"* refers to girls or women who habitually perform an exaggerated form of cuteness, such as using a high-pitched voice, or in their style of speech.
8. In this section, I am not writing about marriage, but I use the word "endogamy" to explore the way transnational youth may feel attracted to others like themselves.
9. This beer garden has since closed down.

CHAPTER 8

Whose United Nations Day?

Cosmopolitan practices are situational and characterized by ambivalence. Although Western capital is privileged at TIS, the experience of cultural marginalization is shared by transnational youth. They experience it at different times in different ways depending on their background in terms of culture, "race," class, and gender, which affect their positionality or status in any given social hierarchy. Those who are of mixed European and Asian descent occupy a racially ambiguous space where they situationally shift between being white and Asian. Similarly, students of mixed Japanese and Indonesian descent find their identities shift between being Japanese, Indonesian, and international, and they use these shifts to subvert relations of power. Becoming "Asian" and becoming "Western" are mutually constitutive with becoming "international," thereby establishing the notion that cosmopolitan practices are situational and embedded within national, regional, and global structures. It is within this context that I revisit the main ritual that showcased the school's ideology of being international—United Nations Day. The Western nature of the school's ideology has an impact on the way students and teachers perceive and manage UN Day clubs and performances. Students compete with each other to become "international."

Becoming "White," Becoming "Asian"

Due to their racially ambiguous physical appearance, transnational youth of mixed Asian and European descent shift in status, depending on the context. This section discusses two students as examples: one from the "normal" English-speaking groups (Maura) and one from the high-status "white kids" group (Tim). In the West they were perceived as Asian and felt marginal; in Asia they were perceived as white or Western and felt dominant. At TIS, the other students referred to them as "white kids" or *"bule,"* but they self-identified as "culturally Asian."

Shifting Positionalities

Maura's mother is Filipino and her father is Italian American, and her racially ambiguous physical appearance caused her to shift between being perceived as mixed, Asian, and white in different contexts. Maura grew up almost exclusively in Asia, having been born in Indonesia, from where she moved to Thailand, Bangladesh, Philippines, then back to Indonesia, attending international schools for most of that time. According to Maura, she was part of the dominant culture at the international school in the Philippines because it was made up mostly of children of mixed heritage (part Filipino) and locals (interview, 28 April 2009):

> The international school in the Philippines [TISP] was really great. It's not really so much an international school, mostly because most of the kids are like me, mixed half Filipino-half American kids. So that's like, the majority of the population are Filipinos mixed with, like, a white. Yeah, with a Caucasian. Like, my best friends were Swiss-Filipino, Singaporean-Filipino, American-Filipino.... So all our moms would be Filipino and then our dads would all like yeah ... across the world. [Laughs.] Yeah, mainly white.

> So then that's why like [TISP] didn't really feel like an international school because we all spoke Filipino. We are all like, you know, we all knew Manila really well. A bunch of us ... we kind of all grew up together you know, I have friends there who I have been friends with since I was literally six or seven.

In Maura's view, the local elements of the international school made it less "international." As I showed in chapter 3, proximity to the local compromises the international feel of the school. The local enhances "felt cosmopolitanism" insofar as it provides a backdrop for being international, but it detracts from the internationalism once the distance is diminished and the boundaries between the local and international are blurred (Calhoun 2008: 106). The lack of mobility (i.e., she had long-term friends) also detracted from the sense of being international.

The family backgrounds of Maura and her peers in Manila evinced a gendered hierarchy to the cross-cultural marriages represented at her international school. The parents from the local population were mostly mothers, while the foreign parents, who were usually from a more developed country and white, were fathers. This was typical also of cross-cultural couples in Jakarta and among parents of TIS students. Even when the mother was not Indonesian, she would often be from a less-developed country than the father.

Although Maura was part of the norm at TISP, her positionality was situational. When she went to the United States, her passport country, Maura shifted from being normal to "Asian" and therefore marginal to the dominant culture, while in Asia (outside of TISP) she became white.

MAURA: In the States I kinda look like some of the people, well [thinks and changes her mind] ... no, not really ... I dunno.

DT: Do you feel more comfortable there?

MAURA: Oh, I hate being in the States. Whenever I go to the States ... I always go through Chicago, so I walk into the Chicago airport I have like cultural shock 'cause everyone's like white. It freaks me out. I've lived in Asia all my whole life, so then it's like I'm used to seeing Asians everywhere and like walking into an airport and being the tallest person in the airport. It's when I'm in Asia I feel like, I guess 'cause I'm white I feel like ... no, it sounds bad, never mind.

DT: Go on.

MAURA: If you're white in Asia you have the sense of power because you're *white* in Asia. Do you get what I mean? So yeah, then when I'm in the States, everyone else is white. I am the same as them. So then, not only do [I] feel, like, intimidated, they scare me, they're louder than Asians, they're ruder than Asians, they're yeah, I kind of have an Asian mentality.

In Asia, Maura was perceived by locals as white, which gave her a "sense of power" because she could draw on colonial discourses of race that construct "white" as superior and contemporary capitalist discourses that continue to construct "the West" as superior. She internalized this power relation, which made her feel insecure in the United States, where she was intimidated by whiteness. In the United States, her own whiteness does not set her apart and mark her as privileged and more powerful than others. She felt that she had an "Asian mentality" and later claimed, "I'm an Asian," despite the fact that students from the non-English-speaking groups at TIS considered her and her friends as white. Being Asian, white, or international is situational.

Tim, whose mother is Taiwanese and father is white American, was similarly ambivalent about his positionality. Tim was born in the United States; when he was four he moved to Jakarta; then to Kalimantan (Indonesia) in second grade where he studied at a small international school that only had seventeen students; back to Jakarta for fourth grade; back to the United States where he was enrolled for seven months of fifth grade at a public school; to Japan for grades five through eight; back to Jakarta to finish eighth grade at an international school that was smaller than TIS; he then moved schools and enrolled at TIS in ninth grade. Tim claims, "I say I'm from the States. But my mom is Taiwanese. That's usually what I do. But, to me, I actually don't feel like I belong anywhere, like, home to me is where my family is." The impact of mobility on his sense of home echoed that described in the TCK literature (Pollock and Van Reken 2009 [2001]).

Tim found it difficult to fit in when he moved "back" to the United States in fifth grade (when he was about eleven years old; interview, 4 May 2009):

TIM: I really, for some reason, didn't want to be Asian. I wanted to fit in like an American student. I think that really affected me in some ways. Just because I look different and … I didn't want to because I felt like people were looking at me seeing how I was different sort of, yeah. It made me self-conscious. It would be really hard for me to join games and stuff that they were playing because I felt like I wouldn't be accepted just because of the way I looked. It would be hard for me to talk to them because I'm scared they would judge me and be like, "Oh, you're stupid," or whatever. So that affected me in that way.

DT: Does it still affect you?

TIM: No. I haven't really thought about it, so it's so hard for me to explain. [Laughs.]

DT: [Laughs.] Okay. Moving to Japan, what was that like?

TIM: I remember going to school and it was really strange because in the States, I felt like I was Asian. But then when I went to Japan, I felt more Western on the way people were treating me. And I felt more welcome, like all the kids wanted to talk to me, and wanted to know where I was from. And like they tried really hard to be my friends and I really liked that.… Moving there was really nice 'cause the school, there were about forty-five kids per grade, and everyone sort of hung out with everyone. There was no, like, cultural difference.

DT: No cultural difference between … ?

TIM: There were a few other American students, or Caucasian students, and we mixed all with the Japanese kids. Like, they would talk in Japanese sometimes to each other, but most times you could go over there and ask, "Hey, what's up?" And they'll be like, "Oh, so and so," and they would tell us. It wasn't like the States where I felt afraid to kind of go up to people and ask about stuff like that.

In the United States, Tim felt he was "Asian" and was perceived as Asian, which made him feel unaccepted. Whereas in Japan he felt "more Western," "more welcome," and his peers "tried really hard" to be his friend—they were interested in getting to know him. He did not feel intimidated about approaching his peers. As with Maura, Tim's positionality shifted upward as he moved from the West to Asia due to the perception that those with Western capital are superior to those without. Tim also internalized this perception, which affected his sense of confidence in approaching his peers in the United States. Like Maura, Tim identified as Asian. He said, "Culturally, I consider myself more Asian than Western" because "I've lived overseas, basically my whole life, in Asia, and I feel I look more Asian." Tim cited his physical appearance in comparison to his white peers in the United States as one of the reasons for identifying as Asian. Tim's own identification stood in stark contrast to how he was perceived by other students at TIS, where he was seen as one of the popular, high-status "white kids."

Maura said, "When I think of hierarchy, the only reason they're higher than us is because they think they are, and we let them." "We let them" indicates that cultural hierarchies are internalized as habitus—ways of acting, thinking, and feeling that are in line with the external social structure but are experienced as second-nature (Bourdieu 1990; Ortner 2006). They are also constructed in relation to economic hierarchies. Tim and Maura grew up in environments where colonial racial discourses of white superiority intersect with capitalist structures in visible ways. Tim said: "One of the things that I find really strange is when I'm here [in Jakarta], most of the workers like in McDonalds, in all these restaurants are Asian, and then going back to the States and having, like, giving orders to someone who is white or Caucasian is really strange to me. I feel it's, it's really weird. I don't know why. It's just something about it is strange to me." Growing up in an environment where class division overlaps with racial difference visibly reinforces the notion that Western capital is superior and above working-class service jobs. Transnational youth internalize the conflation of racial whiteness with class superiority, which affects their perception of themselves and others, and consequently their social interaction with others.

Friendships based on shared interest?

Although both Maura and Tim claimed that their friendships were forged based on shared interests, they tacitly recognized that cultural sameness and hierarchies may have a role in shaping with whom they became friends. Maura said: "In my group we're international, 'cause we have Australian, Canadians, and Americans and yeah ... oh, that's actually the three we have [laughs]; oh, there's an English; oh, a French. Yeah, but we're all, like, white except for Lila [laughs], but, who's basically white. Like, her mentality and stuff. I mean, I guess it's kind of, like, racist. Well, not racist, it's just being really, you know ... when it all boils down to it, we're all friends, really." Lila was of African descent but adopted by white Canadian parents when she was still young. While Maura claimed that her friends were "international" and were simply "friends," her reference to Lila's "mentality" as "basically white" indicates that she recognized they shared a cultural sameness. The fact that Maura feels intimidated around those who are "white" suggests that she was aware that cultural hierarchies make it difficult for those in a marginal position to approach those in a dominant position. Yet, when Maura described her own friendships, these hierarchies mattered less because "when it all boils down to it" they were just "friends."

It would be naïve, however, to assume that Lila's friends were completely colorblind and that her physical appearance had no bearing on the way they interacted with her. During the limited time that I spent with her, I noticed that her friends would make references to her dark skin in the form of a friendly joke about her being "black." Although TIS students did generally seem comfortable joking frequently about race among friends, whether it was about being "Asian" or "white", and did not subscribe to extreme political correctness, the interaction I observed with Lila seemed a little awkward. It was as though her friends were going out of their way to demonstrate that they think nothing of race and are comfortable enough with her to be able to joke about it. Lila would at first be confused, as the comment seemed to come out of nowhere. Once she understood, she would laugh it off and skillfully counter their jokes with a witty come back. After observing a couple of interactions like this, I asked Lila how often her friends refer to her skin color. She said it occurs about three times a day, everyday. Lila was one of a handful of black students at TIS. While she seemed to take no offense at the comments, the frequency with which they occurred suggests that the way students experience the school's social space was racially nuanced.

As with Maura, Tim cited "interests" multiple times as the reason underlying why he gets along with some and not with others. However, as he explained his inability to connect with Americans, he slipped between talking about diverging interests and about differences based on physical appearance and culture. "Well, I didn't fit in for one. I didn't really have a lot of friends, just because everyone … I don't know what it was. I think it was just how I grew up was different from them and I just couldn't fit in. I didn't have the same interests as them. I don't think the students really liked me, I look different for one, 'cause everyone was American there. And then I was Asian. So I guess they didn't really accept me for that." While he recognizes that differences in their upbringing meant that his interests diverged from his American peers, he was also aware that his physical appearance affected his sense of marginality and led him to feel that they did not "accept" him. As for his friends at TIS, Tim says, "I found that we had more or less the same interest, and I started going out to like Splash [a beer garden] and all those places with them. And it was really cool. I started to fit in." Outside his immediate circle of friends, Tim feels that "the Indonesians, the Chindos," and "the more-white people" go out while the Korean students "stay and study"; and thus he says of the Koreans, "I feel like we don't really mesh like that. Like, we'll just go different ways." But when he speaks of TIS's social hierarchy, these differences and his lack of interest in the Korean students overlap with his perception that they are "lower" in the hierarchy: "I feel, on the top of the food chain, would be the Chindos. And then after that, I don't know, I don't really hang out with the Koreans very much, so maybe I *feel* like they're lower." While diverging interests contribute greatly to the formation of social groups among transnational youth, these divergences are moderated by perceived cultural hierarchies through which value is attached to various interests. Going out (i.e., drinking and clubbing) is seen as interesting, while studying without going out (since some do both) like the Koreans is not.

Cultural hierarchies are nuanced, and a sense of ambivalence permeates the experiences of transnational youth. For Maura and Tim, their positionality shifts depending on whether they have more or less Western capital compared to the dominant majority in the given context. Their racially ambiguous physical appearance affects the way others perceive and treat them as well as how secure they feel in different contexts.

Becoming Not-Indonesian

The experiences of transnational youth and their cosmopolitan practices are mired in the structures that shape their habitus. Levi spoke to me at some length about his ill feelings toward Indonesia over a chat in the presence of another student, Maya, who was working on her laptop (reconstructed from field notes, 29 September 2009). We sat at a table near the fountain that was usually occupied by the "normal" senior English-speaking groups, of which Maya was usually a part. Levi, also a senior, occasionally visited these groups, although he usually hung out with the "stoners," known as the partygoers. Ironically, Levi was not a regular partygoer because his father had come to Indonesia as an American Christian missionary. Levi was not usually allowed to go clubbing, and had to spend time serving the community and going on mission trips.

I asked Levi about his background, and he told me that he was American. I double-checked with him because I had heard that he was partly Indonesian, but he denied it. He reiterated that he was American. As I sat there looking confused, Maya interjected, "Yes you are. You are half Indonesian." At this, Levi conceded that his mother was Indonesian, but he added that he does not like Indonesia. "Don't say that," retorted Maya, whose mother was Indonesian and father was a Filipino raised in Indonesia. But Levi continued, "I hate Indonesia. I don't like anything about it—the food, the place. I can't wait to graduate and get out of here." Levi also stated that he was not Asian, and that he did not like being called Asian. At this point, Maya made a clear stand. She told Levi that he was being racist and asked him to stop. When he continued, Maya declared she could not listen to him anymore, closed her laptop, and left.

Levi used to go to national plus (see chapter 1) and other local schools, and was fluent in Indonesian. But he insisted that he was "just American," and planned to go to a military college in the United States, where he had hardly ever lived, because he wanted to do his duty and "serve the country." Levi wanted to leave Indonesia and never come back, though he would have to return at some point since his grandparents were still in Indonesia. Levi said his mother came from a poor Indonesian family. He could not understand what his father had seen in his mother to want to marry her since Levi believed his mother was unattractive. Levi also disliked it when his Indonesian cousins say that he is rich. "Because I'm not. We're middle class," explained Levi. In his view he was middle class by American standards, and therefore normal.

It is difficult to determine the exact reasons behind Levi's negative views toward Indonesia—views that he stated he would not repeat should I interview him formally with a recording device even though he was happy to make them plain to me otherwise. But we can infer that Levi's desire to distance himself from Indonesia, figuratively and geographically, reflected an attempt to navigate around social stereotypes and the perception that Indonesia is inferior. Levi wanted to be a normal, middle-class American, not a poor, ugly Indonesian. Levi referred to his interest in attending military college in his attempt to identify with his father's American background. Regardless of whether or not he eventually attended such a college, Levi's use of nationalism (in the sense of providing physical protection) to express his identity was common to male TIS students whose hybrid identities were precarious and needed to be constantly asserted. Transnational youth, like Levi, are not the embodied beacon of a "happy hybridity": they embody the burden of social hierarchies that reflect national and transnational economic hierarchies (Lo 2000: 153).

Becoming "Japanese," Becoming "*Haafu*"

Levi's desire to distance himself from Indonesia was shared by those who were of mixed Japanese and Indonesian descent. Ellie and Aya, whose fathers are Japanese and mothers are Indonesian, used their shifting positionalities and drew on TIS's ideology of being international to subvert national hierarchies. Ellie and Aya used to go to the Japanese school in Jakarta, where the dominant culture was represented by those who were "pure" Japanese. Being only "half" Japanese, they performed "Japaneseness" and downplayed their "Indonesianness." They did this to gain access to the dominant (Japanese) culture and escape being marginalized. But at TIS, where diversity was celebrated, Ellie and Aya used a different strategy—they used their mixed background to subvert the hierarchy that privileges "pure Japaneseness."

"Southeast Asians Are ... Just a Factory Outlet"

Early on in my fieldwork, I learned that Ellie, Aya, and their friend Midori spoke fluent, native Indonesian, but I noticed that they never spoke it in school. Even when Indonesian students spoke to them in Indonesian, they responded in English, a language in which they were not entirely comfortable. There was also a time when I went to a mall near TIS with Ellie and her Japanese friend. When Ellie ordered her frozen yoghurt, she spoke to the shopkeeper in broken Indonesian with a Japanese accent. It seemed odd to me. Several times I asked Ellie and Aya why they did this, and each time they avoided answering my question by walking away as though they did not hear me—that is, until we were in an enclosed room where they were sure that no one could hear them.[1] Once it was obvious that we had privacy, they were more than eager to talk.

"I want to blend in as a Japanese, so I don't speak it," explained Ellie on not speaking Indonesian. "It's turned into a habit, so now I can't speak Indonesian at all anymore, sort of."

"Yeah, yeah, I know what you mean," Aya piped in. "I hate it when they [the Japanese] say, 'You're mixed, aren't ya?' because it feels like they're putting up a wall between us."

"Yeah, it feels like they're looking down on you," said Ellie. Then she continued as she put on a cold, condescending tone, "It's like, 'Oh, so you're a *haafu*,[2] an Indonesian *haafu*." Ellie and Aya were finishing each other's thoughts, attesting to the similarities of their experiences of the perceived superiority of "Japaneseness."

Ellie provided a sketch of the cultural hierarchy that is in large part dependent on global economic hierarchies and intrudes upon the social dynamics among students. She believes that the Japanese think of white people as, metaphorically speaking, "branded goods." While apologetic for her metaphor, she continued to share the rest of the picture: "The Chinese are, like, locally made," she contended.

"At the end of the day, it's all about skin color," Aya noted.

"And Southeast Asians are ... let's see. ..." Ellie pondered a little and declared, "just a factory outlet!" I burst out laughing at her description as Ellie quickly added, "Seriously, like, *kaki lima* [street-food seller] or something."

The school is a site of reproduction for global economic hierarchies that are internalized as cultural hierarchies, true to Bourdieu's (1986: 252) claim that "economic capital is at the root of all the other types of capital." But Bourdieu (ibid.) goes a little further, positing, "these transformed, disguised forms of economic capital, never entirely reducible to that definition, produce their most specific effects only to the extent that they conceal (not least from their possessors) the fact that economic capital is at their root." Aya's comment about "skin color" and Ellie's capitalistic metaphor suggest that economic and racial hierarchies intersect. Ellie's observations suggest that the Japanese believe in the superiority of the West and inferiority of Southeast Asia, including Indonesia, in relation to Japan. The economic root of racial hierarchies that were constructed during colonial times is perpetuated without the full knowledge of those participating in its perpetuation.

Ellie and Aya chose to distance themselves from Indonesia by rejecting the use of their Indonesian cultural capital in order to naturalize their belonging with the Japanese in the same way that Levi tried to distance himself from Indonesia in order to identify as American. Cultural and racial hierarchies based on economic hierarchies have a profound influence on the subjectivities and behavior of transnational youth, as they need to navigate around these constructions.

Subverting National Hierarchies

However, Ellie and Aya's positionality shifted at TIS, where their mixed background turned into cosmopolitan cultural capital. Ellie explained that when she told Western students she has a mixed background, "They say to me, 'Oh, half Indo?' It's like, it's easier for me to make friends than for the pure Japanese." Being mixed meant that others were more interested in getting to know her. Ellie, whose mother is Batak Indonesian and who, by Indonesian standards, would be considered light skinned, was keenly aware of her newfound cultural capital, where the ideology of being international, as opposed to ethnically pure, prevailed.

In contrast, her friend Aya did not feel as empowered in the new environment. Aya had darker skin and, unlike Ellie who had epicanthic folds, Aya had double-fold eyelids. These features made her appear more Javanese[3] than Japanese. While Ellie could somewhat pass as a Japanese, Aya could not. But Aya, whose middle name is Rachael, did agree on some points and added, "Oh, yeah, yeah. I know. [It's better] when I say I'm a *haafu*. Also, my name, they'll suddenly change their attitude towards me when I tell them my name is Rachael."

"Do you get it?" says Ellie to me. "It's like, seriously, I thought, 'Oh, so Koreans and Japanese are really looked down on here, it's the reverse [compared to the Japanese school].'"

Aya nodded in agreement as she said, "Yeah, yeah … I suppose in that sense it's kinda better here."

"Seriously, to be honest, to be quite blunt, it's like, 'Sorry folks.'" By "folks," Ellie was referring to her Japanese friends and implied that it was now her turn, as a *haafu*, to feel closer to the dominant culture while the "pure" Japanese were more marginalized. Then she added, "This is just between us, yeah," to indicate that it was not something she would talk about openly with her Japanese friends who were not of mixed descent. "So, because of that, I can make friends [here]. And it's like, I think for the first time in my life I feel proud to be a *haafu*." Aya and Ellie, being mixed Indonesian and Japanese, found that their *haafu* identities carried more currency in the international school than at the Japanese school.

At the same time, Aya and Ellie felt that the cosmopolitan capital from their hybrid identity would not have currency in Japan, in the same way that Tim's cosmopolitan capital did not have currency in the United States. Aya, for example, claimed that she chose to remain in Indonesia to attend TIS for high school due to her mixed background instead of going to Japan as many of her Japanese schoolmates did. "I thought that maybe if I went to high school in Japan it might be the same as the Japanese school here, and I didn't want that. I wanted a change, like, in terms of life, you know, like the way they discriminate against *haafus*. ... It's bad enough here in Indonesia—I figure it would be worse in Japan." But she planned to go to university in Japan because, she said, "University students are already adults, so I have this image that they probably won't be as cliquey. ... Plus I want to experience what it's like to study in Japan at least once." Many transnational youth were infatuated with their parents' home country, which was also often their country of passport (see chapter 6). They wanted to experience life, particularly as a student, in that place they had heard so much about and visited but never actually lived in as a local. Even so, some, like Aya and Ellie, were aware that they would experience various social spaces differently from their peers due to the perceived currency of their cosmopolitan capital.

The dominant culture has the power to define the rules of the game, while others must either play by those rules or contest them in their attempts to decrease their sense of marginalization. Ellie and Aya (though more so Ellie than Aya) were able to subvert the Japanese hierarchy when they moved to TIS at the start of high school by drawing on the discourse of being international. Different aspects of transnational youths' hybrid identities become available to them as tools to diffuse their sense of marginalization at different times depending on the dominant culture of their social environment. Ellie and Aya still felt marginalized compared to students who were more westernized, but they had a better feel for the cosmopolitan game than their "pure" Japanese friends. Neither transnational educational spaces nor cosmopolitan practices are neutral. Both intersect with global, regional, and national structures to cause variability in young people's experiences of a transnational upbringing.

Competing to Become "International"

Students drew on the discourses of the school's ideology of being international to enhance their own positioning not only as individuals, but also collectively. In this section, I bring together various themes covered in this book through an analysis of how the UN Day clubs were interpreted and managed. "Being international" is not just an ideal; it is a strategic positioning of oneself within a complex intersection of hierarchies.

Diversity Made Visible and Invisible by Race

Some of the teachers I spoke with had the impression that the Indian club had the most diverse membership among the "national" clubs that performed. As evidence, one of them noted that they clearly remembered at least one of the performers being white. They also felt that the Japanese and Korean clubs seemed most ethnically homogenous. Another teacher pointed out that he had observed the Japanese club practicing and had heard them giving instructions in Japanese, thus concluding that they were all Japanese. But the leaders (mainly Erina, the club president, and her two close friends) in the Japanese club were not giving instructions in Japanese because the members were all Japanese; rather, they were adamantly refusing to use English for reasons that were not made clear to me (I return to this point later).

The staff members I spoke to were taken by surprise when I told them that approximately 20 percent of the members in the Indian club were of non-Indian descent, while as much as 40 percent of the Japanese club was either of non-Japanese descent or only of part-Japanese descent. I posit that the diversity in the Indian club was more readily apparent to the audience because they had two students who were white and two who were of mixed white and Asian descent. Meanwhile, the Japanese club looked homogeneous because their members appeared "racially" similar, as they were all of Asian descent, though from different nationalities, ethnicities, and linguistic backgrounds. The nationalities they represented included Vietnam, Laos, Philippines, Indonesia, Malaysia, China, and India. While the Korean club was indeed made up of members who were all of Korean descent, the Chinese club was also diverse linguistically and in terms of nationality. Most were of Chinese descent, but they were of different nationalities, and spoke different languages as their native tongue: Mandarin, Indonesian, English, and Tagalog. Their main language of communication during practice was English, which was the only language they spoke in common. However, as with the Japanese club, the cultural, linguistic, and national diversity of the Chinese club remained invisible due to the "racial" semblance of its members. Diversity is most visible when it crosses difference that is constructed through colonial discourses of race, which W. E. B. Du Bois (2007 [1903]: 3) refers to as the "color-line."

Cosmopolitan Hierarchies Recurring Like Fractals

Although the staff perceived the Japanese club as homogenously Japanese, the club members' perception of themselves was more nuanced.[4] I hung out with them through many of their practice sessions, some of which were held in the Japanese teacher's classroom. These sessions ended with long casual after-school chats about anything from club activities and relationships to "expats" in the red-light districts of Thailand. The Japanese club had a reputation for putting on excellent performances, and it was clear from their conversations that many of them perceived the Korean club as their main competitor. They were competing with the Koreans on two fronts. Firstly, as a matter of national pride, they competed for performative excellence. Many non-Japanese students in the club said that they joined because they were impressed by the club's performance in previous years. The Japanese club's popularity, as well as the popularity of Japanese-language classes among Asian students, reflected Japan's cultural power that is derived from its position in the economic hierarchy in the region.[5] Secondly, the Japanese students competed with the Korean students to be more international, as defined by the school's ideology. Some of the members of the Japanese club who were either of full or partial Japanese descent spoke accusingly of the ethnic homogeneity of the Korean club, who allegedly were not allowing non-Koreans to join the club and were excessive with their practice schedule. The former was a false allegation—the Korean club did not have a formal policy of excluding non-Koreans—and the latter was subjective.

It is significant that the Japanese students were conscious of the ideology of being international. Whether or not the Japanese club was in fact more inclusive is a secondary matter. Many of the Japanese students marked the ethnic homogeneity of the Korean club and constructed it as parochial. This enabled the Japanese students to feel as though they were more international in the way they managed their UN Day club compared to the Korean club. At TIS, ethnic homogeneity acted as "a marker" of the quintessential Other. Hage (1998: 57) argues that in Australia, Aboriginal Blackness acts as a marker that "allows various non-Blacks an access to Whiteness. All the cappuccinos, macchiatos, and caffe lattes of the world that are neither black nor white, skin-colour wise, can use the Blackness of the Aboriginal people to emphasise their non-Blackness and their capacity to enter the field of

Whiteness." At TIS, ethnic or national homogeneity represented blackness within the ideology of being international. The Japanese students,
particularly the club leadership, distanced themselves from the ethnic
homogeneity of the Korean club to access a degree of cosmopolitan
capital that was otherwise out of their reach due to their limited fluency in English and Western capital. The Japanese students accepted
the legitimacy of the ideology of being international and submitted to
its symbolic power, which Bourdieu (1991: 164) explains, "is that invisible power which can be exercised only with the complicity of those
who do not want to know that they are subject to it or even that they
themselves exercise it." This reinforced the Japanese students' sense of
superiority vis-à-vis the Korean students, a sentiment that reflects the
rivalry for economic and soft-power dominance as well as the history
of Japanese colonialism in the region. The practice of being international that privileges ethnic, national, and racial diversity becomes a
badge of distinction.

Notwithstanding their attempt to compete to be "international,"
the Japanese club leaders reinforced Japanese normativity within the
club. As I mentioned earlier, the leaders were adamant about using
Japanese to give instructions even though a large portion of the members could not understand Japanese. Some of the other Japanese students, particularly those who were better able to make friends outside
the Japanese-speaking groups, were as puzzled as I was by the leaders' choice of language. I asked Satoshi, who was of mixed Japanese
and Indonesian descent and regularly hung out with students from the
Indonesian-, Korean-, and English-speaking groups, about it. He just
muttered, with a look of resignation, "Yeah, those guys ... I dunno."

Some of the Japanese-speaking students took turns to translate
the Japanese instructions into English, but they did not always do so.
Sometimes the non-Japanese-speaking students could not keep up
with the dance routine as they were not always clear on what they were
supposed to do. There was a core Japanese-speaking group who held
offices in the club, were dedicated to choreographing and practicing
the routine, and were responsible for teaching it to the other members, namely the non-Japanese-speaking and younger Japanese-speaking members. This contributed to the variable quality in their ability
to dance the routine. Although they all took turns dancing in the front
row, the non-Japanese-speaking students were relegated to dancing
mostly in the back rows for the performance while the better dancers—
the older Japanese speakers—danced mostly in the front rows.

The leaders seemed ambivalent about the non-Japanese-speaking
members, whose presence was beneficial for the club's image of be-

ing international and thus tolerated, but not accepted (Brown 2006). For example, Midori, who often made impulsive comments, casually said that she wished Aisha's Muslim *jilbab*, or headscarf, would fall off while dancing. Although this was said only in the presence of Japanese-speaking members and Aisha knew nothing of it, on the day of the performance Aisha voluntarily removed her *jilbab* because she felt it appropriate to do so. Non-Japanese Asian students enriched the international image of the Japanese club, but they were relegated to an inferior position that reflected regional socioeconomic hierarchies.

It may appear contradictory that the Japanese students constructed themselves as international, while simultaneously reinforcing the dominance of Japaneseness. However, this is precisely the same principle underpinning the school's ideology of being international. Those with Western capital construct themselves as international while simultaneously reinforcing the dominant position of Western capital by contrasting themselves with the cosmopolitan blackness, so to speak, of the non-English-speaking language groups. These groups were tolerated and even necessary for enriching the diversity of the school. Hage (1998: 121) argues that the value of minority cultures "lies in their function as enriching cultures." They made the school look "international." But in most cases students had to acquire Western capital (i.e., assimilate) to be accepted. The leaders of the Japanese club were drawing on the school's ideology of being international and reproducing a Japanese version of the ideology within the club like a fractal pattern.

The noninclusive attitudes of the Japanese-speaking leaders toward those who were not Japanese seemed to go unnoticed by those who were the target of these attitudes, or at least I did not hear them complain about it. These attitudes were, nevertheless, a source of indignation to some of the other Japanese-speaking members. Chitchats in Horie *sensei's* classroom, which turned into a Japanese hangout area after school, were filled with complaints about the club's leaders when the leaders were not present. Naomi, who was a native speaker of English and usually hung out with the English-speaking groups in her grade, was particularly vocal about her displeasure with the club's leadership. She is also Horie *sensei's* daughter, and had had more exposure to cosmopolitan cultural capital than her Japanese peers because her mother had also spent time in the 1960s and 70s growing up in Japan, Belgium, Singapore, and Malaysia, where she attended an international school. Despite being critical of the club leaders and their exclusionary practices, Naomi had also been guilty of participating in a similar dynamic. On another occasion, as discussed in chapter 5, I saw her unintentionally reinforce the dominance of the Western school culture over Korean boys by participating in the construction of Koreans as the nameless, faceless Other. Naomi, like the others, reproduced the fractal pattern. In the context of the Japanese club, she marked the noninclusive attitudes of her Japanese peers as cosmopolitan blackness, thereby positioning herself as being more "international." But in another context Naomi reinforced the dominance of Western culture. Cosmopolitan practices are situational both for the leaders of the Japanese club as well as Naomi—they shift between practicing cosmopolitan engagement with the Other and cultural dominance over the Other, depending on the context.

As the performance day approached, the tension over the club leadership exploded during a dress rehearsal. Erina, the club president, and the other dancers were on stage when a disagreement arose over how they would end the performance. The leaders wanted to end it with a bow while saying "*Arigato gozaimashita,*" which is the long form of "thank you." Horie *sensei* felt it was too long and messy. She preferred that they end with the leader shouting "*Rei!* [bow]," then the others would follow with a decisive bow as you would see in martial arts matches and many other events in Japan. I was sitting with Horie *sensei* in the audience watching the rehearsal. Erina and Horie *sensei* argued back and forth for a while until Horie *sensei* suddenly raised her voice and scolded Erina in the presence of all. Erina broke into tears as her closest friends comforted her. Having "hung out" with both Horie *sensei* and Erina, I felt uncomfortable because I did not want to seem as though I was taking sides on the matter by virtue of being near the teacher at the time of the incident.

Horie *sensei* later explained that Erina and her two close friends were too proud, which prevented them from "breaking out of their shell" to mingle with non-Japanese students. Erina was the student who had looked pleasantly relieved when she found out I spoke Japanese the first time we met. I had also seen her face stiffen as she found herself unable to participate in a small group discussion during class. Perhaps this was why she and her friends had been adamant about giving out instructions in Japanese—to exercise agency whenever they could in an otherwise marginalizing environment without revealing their inability to communicate effectively in English (e.g., Foley 1996). Perhaps their pride had been a defense mechanism against feeling paralyzed in a transnational space that privileged Western capital. It was a mechanism to which the Japanese-speaking students, such as Satoshi and Naomi, who had more cosmopolitan capital, did not need to resort.

A New "We are the World"

United Nations Day was as a kaleidoscopic showcase of visible diversity, as I described in chapter 1. It served the purposes of the school's ideology of being international. It was the only designated day on which students of non-Western backgrounds took center stage both literally and figuratively. They were given a license to be something other than "Western." In fact, students from Western countries struggled to find ways to express their "culture" on UN Day that visually compared with the "ethnic cultures." While a handful came dressed as medieval knights or Uncle Sam, their main expression of identity was in the form of T-shirts printed with their national flag or in the color of their national sports teams (usually soccer). On this day, the non-Western—and more generally the non-Anglophone—elements of the school received validation as something "enriching" *for* the cosmopolitanism of the dominant culture (Hage 1998: 121).

However, the UN Day performance clubs that were organized along national imaginaries had several contradictory consequences. On the one hand, they pandered to the romanticization of visible diversity. On the other hand, they reinforced national boundaries. One student claimed that United Nations Day made them (as it did me) feel excluded because they did not belong to any national group. Specifically, the competitive nationalistic spirit between the Japanese and Korean clubs was of concern to the staff, as it was counterproductive to the school's cosmopolitan project of breaking down cultural boundaries. James, a member of the coordinating staff for the performances, related that the staff was considering making changes to the way UN Day was organized.

> We are gonna do something different with the UN Day next year for a couple of reasons. One, we feel that the program has just become kinda stale, because it's been done in the same way for so long. But also there's this, you know, it's actually, like, national identity competition day. [Laughs.] It is. It's like who's gonna be better, the Japanese or the Koreans? And you know, now the Indians have gotten more people involved, right? But it really is. And so our idea is to try to get representatives from each of the groups, and over a weekend workshop—this comes from an ISTA, an international theaters association model—do a festival approach where we collaborate.... So the Korean leaders can say, "We wanna do this section of Korean drumming," but instead of it being only the Koreans that learn it, everybody in an ensemble learns it. So everybody can bring in influences from their culture. But we're gonna ... synthesize and then make a, you know, a blending.... And we all learn to do things from each other's cultures. To us that's much more what [TIS] is really about.

James was addressing the fact that the design of United Nations Day was outmoded. Its emphasis on visible diversity comes out of a multicultural model that is premised on cultures being distinct and designed within a national framework for nation-states to cope with a diversifying society. The model was not designed for a transnational framework where identity is complex and constantly evolving (Hall 1993). James's suggestion for a new way of organizing the performances is an attempt to accommodate the hybridity of transnational youth.

Nonetheless, UN Day was the day when those who were usually relegated to a position of parochial Other were able to express themselves and "exist" in a positive way, to borrow Jenny's words from chapter 5. James comments,

> But I think we're gonna have a hard time selling it to the Japanese and the Koreans and the Indian community because there's so much national pride, and we're taking away an opportunity for them to exhibit their national pride, so I think we're gonna get a lot of resistance. ... What we're gonna say is, this is gonna be an old format ... we're gonna return to performances at lunch when they're doing that on stage outdoors. So they can still have that option but it's not as sexy as the stage [indoors]. You still have the opportunity if that's what you wanna do. So we're not, so people can't say we're taking that away, but we want to take the emphasis off the show in here [the theater], off the nationalism in the show in the [theater] into something that's more, really, truly, "We are the world."

The nationalistic overtones of the performances caused the school to want to rectify the situation by redefining the rules of engagement. In James's view, the national clubs, especially the Korean and Japanese clubs, allegedly failed in attracting wider membership because their practice schedule was too rigorous, which was true of the Korean club but not the Japanese club. The performance was held at the end of November, and James explains, "I think that's partly because the rehearsal schedule is really demanding. I mean, those kids are working on that, I think, from August[6] and they meet on Saturdays. I mean it's very intense and what they do is incredible ... and I watched that, and there's part of me that goes, well we're not gonna get that." The way the Korean and Japanese students practice was not something that "we," that is, the Western staff and students, were going to "get" because it was different from the norm.

Cosmopolitanism is recognized as cosmopolitanism only when it is practiced on the terms of those of the dominant culture, not of those in a marginal position. Hage (1998: 121) contends that this "discourse of enrichment" veils the ability of the dominant culture to assign value to other cultures; the act of displaying minority cultures in a good light "mystifies the deeper division between holding the power to value (negatively or positively) and not holding it." Ultimately, the school held the power to define and change the rules of the game.

Fractal Cosmopolitanism

In line with its ideology of being international, TIS encourages students to engage with difference, but its practices occur within a transnational educational space where global, regional, and national structures intersect. Students draw upon the discourses prescribed by these structures to reinforce their own superior position in the global or regional hierarchies, or subvert national structures. As a result, the pattern through which minority cultures enrich the dominant Western culture by making it look international while it retains its dominance is repeated like fractals in the transnational space of TIS. The pattern set by the dominant culture was repeated on a smaller scale within the Japanese club. Although Erina and her friends did not have the cultural capital to play the cosmopolitan game, they nevertheless internalized the rules of the game, which privileged Western capital. They played by the same rules in their attempt to reduce their own sense of marginalization. Erina and her friends exercised agency within the Western transnational space in ways that reflected the confines of their habitus. The non-neutrality of transnational spaces created a hierarchy among those competing to be "international."

All are complicit in reproducing the structures that support the school's ideology of being international. Students, parents, and teachers are, however, complicit in different ways in different contexts. Transnational youth share a sense of ambivalence due to their experience of cultural marginalization, but experience it differently in different contexts depending on their positionality, which in turn is affected by their cultural background.

Notes

1. Discussions with Ellie and Aya were conducted in Japanese.
2. "*Haafu*" is the Japanese pronunciation of "half" and refers to mixed descent.
3. The dominant ethnic group in Indonesia.
4. A fractal is "[a] curve or geometrical figure, each part of which has the same statistical character as the whole" (*Oxford Dictionaries*, April 2010,

s.v. "fractal." Available at http://oxforddictionaries.com/definition/english/
fractal.)

5. See Nye (2004) for a discussion on the way cultural power is a resource
that can be the basis of a country's "soft power."

6. The academic year starts in the last week of August.

Conclusion
Transnational Youth

There is no simple formula for raising the ideal cosmopolitan who transcends all boundaries, given that new boundaries are constructed even while old ones are deconstructed. In fact, the very notion of an ideal way of being international is flawed, as it is premised on the existence of a hierarchy of cosmopolitanisms that betray the structures that shape it. Like everything else, cosmopolitan practices, that is, practices that facilitate engagement across difference, are shaped by the complex interplay between structural forces, individual choices, and the immediate context. This book neither offers a five-point solution to the issue of self-segregation that so concerned the educators at TIS, nor does it offer a more ideal form of cosmopolitanism. Instead, it contributes to a better understanding of the experiences of young people growing up in a transnational world where cosmopolitanism is institutionalized as cultural capital in all its diverse forms.

To summarize, one of the basic contributions that this book makes to the study of transnational youth is to use an interdisciplinary approach to move beyond the TCK–non-TCK binary. It does so by recognizing that the concept of Third Culture Kids presents a powerful narrative, but that it is most useful as an emic concept, not an analytical concept. Like any population, transnational youth have their own folklores with which they imagine their identities and collective histories. "Third Culture Kids" is one of them.

After the research for this book was done and dusted, I was having a casual dinner with a new acquaintance, who is a former "Chevron kid" and TIS alumnus, and a couple of others, when he said, in his Californian accent, "I sometimes have a longing for home too, but it's not an actual place." Kevin was American by citizenship, and had grown up in the United States, Indonesia, and Australia. Fittingly, I had met him by chance at a think tank focusing on international relations. We were enjoying a sumptuous buffet of international cuisines at the Pullman Hotel in the central business district of Jakarta, with his Australian wife and his boss, when we began talking about "home." Kevin had made the comment in response to a story his boss told about the Navaho reservation in Arizona in the United States. His white American boss had grown up on the Navaho reservation, is married to a woman who is of mixed Lao and Thai descent, and speaks native-sounding Korean due to his professional training. His work had taken him to Perth, where the shores meet the Indian Ocean. But sometimes when he sees photographs that his Navaho friends post on Facebook, he is overtaken, to the point of tears, by a longing for the redness of Arizona's rocks and the magical effect the sun has when it reflects off them. It was magical not so much for its beauty, but because the specific combination of colors and atmosphere was unique to the landscape in which his emotions and childhood memories were anchored.

Both Kevin and I sat there feeling that we could relate to his boss's sense of longing for home (as well as the experience of being culturally mixed), but not the nostalgic picture of a specific geographic location that defines home. It is in this gap that the term Third Culture Kids narrates transnational belonging for those who have experienced multiple geographic and cultural displacements, despite being insufficient as an analytical concept. Therefore, rather than entirely dismissing the existing literature in psychology and education that takes the concept of Third Culture Kids for granted, this study has used an anthropological approach to embed the term, and the individual experiences of those who identify with it, in its broader context.

This book offers an anthropological perspective to previous studies that have not been able to lend themselves to an analysis of mobility that can account for the growing diversity of transnational youth and their relation to socioeconomic structures. It brings the children of expatriates of diverse nationalities and of the local population into one analytical field without losing site of the multiple structures that affect their lives. There is tension between the shared transnational experiences and the different cosmopolitan practices of these young people. The young people I studied all had a transnational upbringing and were equal targets of the school's project of educating global citizens. The shared experience of a transnational upbringing, however, is tempered by factors such as culture, "race," class, nationality, and gender.

TIS's ideology of being international represents a set of ideas and practices about engaging peaceably with others across difference. Being international was characterized by having a global outlook, as well as: a propensity to engage with the Other, who was defined by visible

differences (mainly "race"), speaking (natural) English, being associated with the (Western) expatriate community, distance from the local,
Western capital, and being socialized into the transnational capitalist
class. To be international, students had to have what I collectively refer
to as (Western) cosmopolitan cultural and social capital. The ideology
of being international was a Eurocentric form of cosmopolitanism,
reflecting the contemporary "global currency of whiteness" (Carey,
Boucher, and Ellinghaus 2009: 5).

At TIS, being international was packaged as an ideal that all students should pursue. However, students were differently positioned in
this pursuit due to the diversity of their cultural backgrounds. Some
students were favorably positioned to acquire cosmopolitan capital
because they were fluent in English and had acquired Western capital
through their home or school environment. Others were not. The different positionalities of students influenced the creation of different
language groups among them that frustrated the school's mission of
producing global citizens.

Cosmopolitan practices are thus diverse and situationally embedded within the sociohistorical contexts of global structures of power.
The school's ideology of being international promotes an idea of social
cohesion through which a global community was imagined, but it also
reproduces both national and transnational class structures through
the privileging of Western capital. TIS was a transnational educational
space where multiple national and transnational structures converged.
These structures placed varying demands on students in accordance
with their future aspirations regarding where they would go to college,
work, and live. Some had to maintain a balance between Western cosmopolitan capital and the national capital that would enable them to
work in their countries of citizenship. Students, parents, and teachers
who were part of the dominant school culture perceived the attempts
by non-Western students to acquire Western capital without becoming
international as inauthentic. In contrast, students who did not gain the
school's approval as being international practiced alternative forms of
cosmopolitanism.

Ambivalence characterized the way cosmopolitan practices were
perceived as "international," "Western," "Asian," "Indonesian," etc.,
depending on whose perception was in question, because whether or
not someone is cosmopolitan lies in the eyes of the beholder. Students
become "international" by becoming "Western," "Asian," "Indonesian,"
"Korean," and/or "Japanese," and so on. Many of these processes were
mutually constitutive ways of practicing cosmopolitanism that emerged
out of sociocultural inequalities. James Clifford (1997: 10) states, "what

matters politically is who deploys nationality or transnationality, authenticity or hybridity against whom, with what relative power." The
staff inadvertently exercised symbolic power by tacitly or not so tacitly recognizing as "international" or "TCK" certain students or student groups over others (Bourdieu and Thompson 1991). Those who
had the cultural capital to feel comfortable in the English-speaking
groups were perceived as "international," while those who did not
were perceived as ethnocentric and their cosmopolitan practices became invisible.

There was a contradiction in the school's ideology of being international. The ideology promoted a deracialized, colorblind view of the
world, but its cosmopolitan practices are dependent on the visibility
of racial differences. The cultural sameness of those with Western
capital was rendered invisible by their racial diversity. Jacqueline Lo
(2000: 153) refers to this celebration of diversity as "happy hybridity,"
which pays little heed to the "tension, conflict or contradiction" inherent in intercultural encounters and thereby "masks and perpetuates
structural inequalities." It does not take into account that for those
without Western cultural capital, the English-speaking groups can be
inaccessible. The school's ideology of being international universalizes
a Western construct of cosmopolitanism. It created a hierarchy of cosmopolitan practices. Students competed to be "international" within
the confines of the dominant form of cosmopolitanism as represented
by the school's ideology of being international. Alternative forms of
cosmopolitanism were relegated to an inferior position by virtue of
not being recognized as "international." Hage (1998) argues that being
cosmopolitan, in this Western sense, is an ideal that has to be constantly desired and sought after, though it can never be reached. It is
"by feeling qualified to yearn for such a position" that people are identified as cosmopolitan (ibid.: 58).

Even so, the ideology of being international reproduces class by enabling transnational youth with the "capacity to aspire" in a globalizing
world, a capacity that Arjun Appadurai (2004: 68) argues is more developed in the "relatively rich and powerful." Appadurai (ibid.) writes
that those who are better off "are more able to produce justifications,
narratives, metaphors, and pathways through which bundles of goods
and services are actually tied to wider social scenes and contexts, and
to still more abstract norms and beliefs." It is in this sense that the ideology of being international becomes the vehicle through which socioeconomic structures in both national and transnational contexts are
reproduced. International schools act as one of many sites where this
process of reproduction occurs by institutionalizing cosmopolitanism

as cultural capital. The experiences of transnational youth are thus embedded in a globalizing, capitalist, postcolonial world.

This book has used the shared experiences of a transnational upbringing among the cohort I studied as a starting point to investigate the way young people interact with each other as they make sense of their ambivalent, shifting places in an increasingly globalizing world. The way transnational youth engage with the ideology of being international reveals the complex nature of the whiteness of being international, as well as the way relations of power are reproduced as patterns within a pattern like fractals. More significantly, this study of transnational youth highlights the diversity of cosmopolitan practices.

This book has analyzed the complex set of factors that make transnational youth a heterogeneous group, but an exploration of their differences, it must be remembered, was made possible by first acknowledging their shared experience of liminality in their transnational upbringing. Although they may not hang out together, Maura (see chapter 8) believed that growing up outside of their parents' cultural milieu meant that the American, Indonesian, Korean, and Japanese "kids" shared something: "We all kind of have a collective culture together."

References

Allan, Michael. 2004. "Cultural Borderlands: Cultural Dissonance in the International School." In *Culture and the International School: Living, Learning and Communicating Across Cultures (International Schools Journal Compedium)*, ed. Edna Murphy, vol. 2, 89–97. Saxmundham: Peridot Press.

Amit, Vered. 2000. *Constructing the Field: Ethnographic Fieldwork in the Contemporary World*. London: Routledge.

———. 2010. "Student Mobility and Internationalisation: Rationales, Rhetoric and 'Institutional Isomorphism.'" *Anthropology in Action* 17(1): 6–18.

Anderson, Benedict. 1983. *Imagined Communities: Reflections on the Origin and Spread of Nationalism*. London: Verso.

Ang, Ien. 2001. *On Not Speaking Chinese: Living between Asia and the West*. New York and London: Routledge.

Appadurai, Arjun. 1996. *Modernity at Large: Cultural Dimensions of Globalization*. Minneapolis: University of Minnesota Press.

———. 2004. "The Capacity to Aspire: Culture and the Terms of Recognition." In *Culture and Public Action*. Standford, ed. Vijayendra Rao and Michael Walton, 59–84. Stanford, CA: Stanford University Press.

Ashcroft, Bill. 2001. *Post-Colonial Transformation*. London and New York: Routledge.

Baldassar, Loretta. 1999. "Marias and Marriage: Ethnicity, Gender and Sexuality among Italo-Australian Youth in Perth." *Journal of Sociology* 35(1): 1–22.

———. 2001. *Visits Home: Migration Experiences between Italy and Australia*. Carlton South, Vic.: Melbourne University Press.

Barth, Fredrik. 1994. *Ethnic Groups and Boundaries: The Social Organization of Culture Difference*. Oslo: Pensumtjeneste.

Bashkow, Ira. 2004. "A Neo-Boasian Conception of Cultural Boundaries." *American Anthropologist* 106(3): 443–458.

Beck, Ulrich, and Natan Sznaider. 2006. "Unpacking Cosmopolitanism for the Social Sciences: A Research Agenda." *The British Journal of Sociology* 57(1): 1–23.

Bell-Villada, Gene. H., and Nina Sichel, eds. 2011. *Writing Out of Limbo: International Childhoods, Global Nomads and Third Culture Kids*. Newcastle upon Tyne: Cambridge Scholars Publishing.

Benson, Michaela, and Karen O'Reilly, eds. 2009. *Lifestyle Migration: Expectations, Aspirations and Experiences.* Farnham: Ashgate.

Berzonsky, Michael D. 2005. "Ego Identity: A Personal Standpoint in a Postmodern World." *Identity* 5(2): 125–136.

Bhabha, Homi K. 1984. "Of Mimicry and Man: The Ambivalence of Colonial Discourse." *October* 28: 125–133.

———. 1994. *The Location of Culture.* London and New York: Routledge.

BirdLife Australia. 2013. "Brain Teaser of the Month." *The Golden Whistler* 2(5): 3.

Blommaert, Jan. 2010. *The Sociolinguistics of Globalization.* New York: Cambridge University Press.

Bolon, Anne Sophie. 2002. "At Home Abroad / Third Culture Kids: Nowhere to Call Home but I Like Being a Global Nomad." *International Herald Tribune* (*New York Times*), 26 October.

Bottomley, Gillian. 1992. *From Another Place: Migration and the Politics of Culture.* Cambridge and Melbourne: Cambridge University Press.

Bourdieu, Pierre. 1977. *Outline of a Theory of Practice.* Cambridge and New York: Cambridge University Press.

———. 1984. *Distinction: A Social Critique of the Judgement of Taste.* London: Routledge.

———. 1986. "The Forms of Capital." In *Handbook of Theory and Research for the Sociology of Education,* ed. John. G. Richardson, 241–258. Westport, CT: Greenwood Press.

———. 1989. "Social Space and Symbolic Power." *Sociological Theory* 7(1): 14–25.

———. 1990. *The Logic of Practice.* Cambridge: Polity Press.

Bourdieu, Pierre, and John B. Thompson. 1991. *Language and Symbolic Power.* Oxford: Polity Press.

Brown, Phillip, and Hugh Lauder. 2009. "Globalization, International Education, and the Formation of a Transnational Class?" *Yearbook of the National Society for the Study of Education* 108(2): 130–147.

Brown, Wendy. 2006. *Regulating Aversion: Tolerance in the Age of Identity and Empire.* Princeton, NJ: Princeton University Press.

Brummitt, Nicholas, and Anne Keeling. 2013. "Charting the Growth of International Schools." In *International Education and Schools: Moving Beyond the First 40 Years,* ed. Richard Pearce, 25–36. London: Bloomsbury Publishing.

Bunnell, Tristan. 2013. "The International Baccalaureate and the Role of the 'Pioneer' International Schools." In *International Education and Schools: Moving Beyond the First 40 Years,* ed. Richard Pearce, 167–182. London: Bloomsbury Publishing.

———. 2014. *The Changing Landscape of International Schooling: Implications for Theory and Practice.* Abingdon and New York: Routledge.

Bunzl, Matti. 2004. "Boas, Foucault, and the 'Native Anthropologist': Notes Toward a Neo-Boasian Anthropology. *American Anthropologist* 106(3): 435–442.

Burck, Charlotte. 2005. *Multilingual Living: Explorations of Language and Sub-*

jectivity. Houndmills, Basingstoke, Hampshire, and New York: Palgrave Machmillan.

Calhoun, Craig. 2008. "Cosmopolitanism in the Modern Social Imaginary." *Daedalus* 137(3): 105–114.

Cambridge, James, and Jeff Thompson. 2004. "Internationalism and Globalization as Contexts for International Education." *Compare* 34(2): 161–175.

Carey, Jane, Leigh Boucher, and Katherine Ellinghaus. 2009. "Re-orienting Whiteness: A New Agenda for the Field." In *Re-orienting Whiteness: Transnational Perspectives on the History of an Identity*, ed. Leigh Boucher, Jane Carey, and Katherine Ellinghaus, 1–14. New York: Palgrave Macmillan.

Chatterjee, Partha. 1993. *The Nation and Its Fragments: Colonial and Postcolonial Histories*. Princeton, NJ: Princeton University Press.

Cillessen, Antonius H. N., and Lara Mayeux. 2007. "Expectations and Perceptions at School Transitions: The Role of Peer Status and Aggression." *Journal of School Psychology* 45(5): 567–586.

Clifford, James. 1986. "Introduction: Partial Truths." In *Writing Culture: The Poetics and Politics of Ethnography*, ed. James Clifford and George E. Marcus, 1–26. Berkeley: University of California Press.

———. 1997. *Routes: Travel and Translation in the Late Twentieth Century*. Cambridge, MA: Harvard University Press.

Coleman, John. C. 2011. *The Nature of Adolescence*. London and New York: Routledge.

Coles, Anne, and Anne-Meike Fechter. 2008. *Gender and Family among Transnational Professionals*. New York: Routledge.

Cross, William E. 1991. *Shades of Black: Diversity in African-American Identity*. Philadelphia: Temple University Press.

Delanty, Gerard. 2009. *The Cosmopolitan Imagination: The Renewal of Critical Social Theory*. Cambridge and New York: Cambridge University Press.

Desilet, Gabrielle. 2014. "The Construction of Cosmopolitan Identifications among 'Third Culture Kids' in Two International Schools." Ph.D. dissertation. Canberra, ACT: Australian National University.

Dolby, Nadine, and Aliya Rahman. 2008. "Research in International Education." *Review of Educational Research* 78(3): 676–726.

Downie, Richard Dixon. 1976. "Re-entry Experiences and Identity Formation of Third Culture Experienced Dependent American Youth: An Exploratory Study." Ph.D. dissertation. East Lansing, MI: Michigan State University.

Du Bois, W. E. B. 2007 [1903]. *The Souls of Black Folk*. Oxford and New York: Oxford University Press.

Dyer, Richard. 1997. *White*. London and New York: Routledge.

EARCOS. 2010. *Global Citizenship*. Retrieved 16 February 2013 from www.earcos.org/other_award.php.

El-Zein, Abbas. 2002. "Being Elsewhere: On Longing and Belonging." In *Arab-Australians Today: Citizenship and Belonging*, ed. Ghassan Hage, 225–240. Carlton South, Vic.: Melbourne University Press.

Erikson, Erik H. 1959. *Identity and the Life Cycle: Selected Papers*. New York: International Universities Press.

———. 1968. *Identity: Youth and Crisis*. New York: W.W. Norton.

———. 2008. "The Problem of Ego Identity." In *Adolescent Identities: A Collection of Readings*, ed. Deborah L. Browning, 223–240. New York: The Analytic Press.

Expat Web Site Association. 2017. *International Schools and SPK* in Indonesia*. Retrieved 11 January 2017 from http://www.expat.or.id/orgs/schools.html#International.

Fail, Helen. 2002. "An Examination of the Life Histories of a Group of Former International School Students." Ph.D. dissertation. Claverton Down, Bath: University of Bath.

Fail, Helen, Jeff Thompson, and George Walker. 2004. "Belonging, Identity and Third Culture Kids: Life Histories of Former International School Students." *Journal of Research in International Education* 3(3): 319–338.

Farrer, James. 2010. "'New Shanghailanders' or 'New Shanghainese': Western Expatriates' Narratives of Emplacement in Shanghai." *Journal of Ethnic and Migration Studies* 36(8): 1211–1228.

Fechter, Anne-Meike. 2007. *Transnational Lives: Expatriates in Indonesia*. Aldershot: Ashgate.

———. 2016. "Between Privilege and Poverty: The Affordances of Mobility among Aid Worker Children." *Asian and Pacific Migration Journal* 25(4): 489–506.

Fechter, Anne-Meike, and Katie Walsh. 2010. "Examining 'Expatriate' Continuities: Postcolonial Approaches to Mobile Professionals." *Journal of Ethnic and Migration Studies* 36(8): 1197–1210.

Ferstad, Corrine Freitas. 2002. "A Sense of Home: What Constitutes a Sense of Home and Community for Pre-adolescent and Adolescent Youth Living in International Transition?" Ph.D. dissertation. Cincinnati, OH: Union Institute & University.

Field, Norma. 1996. "Texts of Childhood in Inter-nationalizing Japan." In *Text and Nation: Cross-Disciplinary Essays on Cultural and National Identities*, ed. Laura García-Moreno and Peter C. Pfeiffer, 143–172. Columbia, SC: Camden House.

Foley, Douglas E. 1996. "The Silent Indian as a Cultural Production." In *The Cultural Production of the Educated Person: Critical Ethnographies of Schooling and Local Practice*, ed. Bradley A. Levinson, Douglas E. Foley, and Dorothy C. Holland, 79–91. Albany: State University of New York Press.

Foner, Nancy, and Phillip Kasinitz. 2007. "The Second Generation." In *The New Americans: A Guide to Immigration Since 1965*, ed. Mary C. Waters and Reed Ueda, with Helen B. Marrow, 270–282. Cambridge, MA: Harvard University Press.

Frankenberg, Ruth, ed. 1997. *Displacing Whiteness: Essays in Social and Cultural Criticism*. Durham, NC: Duke University Press.

Frederick, Leah Ruth. 1996. "Balancing the Four Major Influences on Transcultural Students through an Educational Environment." Ph.D. dissertation. Athens, GA: University of Georgia.

Geertz, Clifford. 1960. "The Javanese Kijaji: The Changing Role of a Cultural Broker." *Comparative Studies in Society and History* 2(2): 228–249.

Gellar, Charles A. 2002. "International Education: A Commitment to Universal Values." In *International Education in Practice: Dimensions for National & International Schools*, ed. Mary Hayden, Jeff Thompson, and George Walker, 30-35. London: Kogan Page.

Gerke, Solvay. 2000. Global Lifestyles Under Local Conditions: The New Indonesian Middle Class. In *Consumption in Asia: Lifestyle and Identities*, ed. Chua Beng-Huat, 135–158. London and New York: Routledge.

Goodman, Roger. 1990. *Japan's "International Youth": The Emergence of a New Class of School Children*. Oxford and New York: Clarendon Press & Oxford University Press.

Hage, Ghassan. 1998. *White Nation: Fantasies of White Supremacy in a Multicultural Society*. Sydney: Pluto Press.

———. 2005. "A Not so Multi-sited Ethnography of a Not So Imagined Community." *Anthropological Theory* 5(4): 463–475.

———. 2009. "The Open Mind and Its Enemies: Anthropology and the Passion of the Political." *SlowTV*, part 1. Retrieved 18 July 2011 from http://www.the monthly.com.au/anthropology-and-passion-political-ghassan-hage-2230.

Hall, Stuart. 1993. "Culture, Community, Nation." *Cultural Studies* 7(3): 349–363.

———. 1996a. "Gramsci's Relevance for the Study of Race and Ethnicity." In *Stuart Hall: Critical Dialogues in Cultural Studies*, ed. David Morley and Kuan-Hsing Chen, 411–440. New York: Routledge.

———. 1996b. "Who Needs an Identity?" In *Questions of Cultural Identity*, ed. Stuart Hall and Paul du Gay, 1–17. London: SAGE Publications.

Hall, Stuart, and Pnina Werbner. 2008. "Cosmopolitanism, Globalisation and Diaspora: Stuart Hall in Conversation with Pnina Werbner, March 2006." In *Anthropology and the New Cosmopolitanism: Rooted, Feminist and Vernacular Perspectives*, ed. Pnina Werbner, 345–360. Oxford and New York: Berg.

Hayden, Mary. 2006. *Introduction to International Education: International Schools and Their Communities*. London: Sage Publications.

———. 2011. "Transnational Spaces of Education: The Growth of the International School Sector." *Globalisation, Societies and Education* 9(2): 211–224.

Hayden, Mary, and Jeff Thompson. 1995. "International Schools and International Education: A Relationship Reviewed." *Oxford Review of Education* 21(3): 327–345.

———. 2008. *International Schools: Growth and Influence*. Paris: United Nations.

Hayden, Mary, Jeff Thompson, and George Walker, eds. 2002. *International Education in Practice: Dimensions for National and International Schools*. London: Kogan Page.

Hill, Ian. 2007. "Multicultural and International Education: Never the Twain Shall Meet?" *International Review of Education* 53(3): 245–264.

Hoon, Chang-Yau. 2008. *Chinese Identity in Post-Suharto Indonesia: Culture, Politics and Media*. Brighton and Portland, OR: Sussex Academic Press.

———. 2013. "Multicultural Citizenship Education in Indonesia: The Case of a Chinese Christian School." *Journal of Southeast Asian Studies* 44(03): 490–510.

Igarashi, Hiroki, and Hiro Saito. 2014. "Cosmopolitanism as Cultural Capital: Exploring the Intersection of Globalization, Education and Stratification." *Cultural Sociology* 8(3): 222–239.

Imam, Syeda Rumnaz. 2005. "English as a Global Language and the Question of Nation-Building Education in Bangladesh." *Comparative Education* 41(4): 471–486.

Imoto, Yuki. 2011. "Producing the 'International' Child: Negotiations of Language in an International Preschool in Japan." *Ethnography and Education* 6(3): 281–292.

International Baccalaureate Organization. 2013a. "History of the International Baccalaureate." Retrieved 20 April 2013 from http://www.ibo.org/history/.

———. 2013b. "IB Fast Facts." Retrieved 23 April 2013 from http://www.ibo .org/facts/fastfacts/index.cfm.

———. 2013c. "Mission and Strategy." Retrieved 16 February 2013 from www .ibo.org/mission/.

Irvine, Jacqueline Jordan. 1989. "Beyond Role Models: An Examination of Cultural Influences on the Pedagogical Perspectives of Black Teachers." *Peabody Journal of Education* 66(4): 51–63.

Jenkins, Richard. 1992. *Pierre Bourdieu*. London and New York: Routledge.

———. 1997. *Rethinking Ethnicity: Arguments and Explorations*. London: Sage.

Jensen, Lene Arnett. 2008. "Coming of Age in a Multicultural World. In *Adolescent Identities: A Collection of Readings*, ed. Deborah L. Browning, 3–18. New York: The Analytic Press.

Jordan, Kathleen. A. Finn. 1981. "The Adaptation Process of Third Culture Dependent Youth as They Re-enter the United States and Enter College: An Exploratory Study." Ph.D. dissertation. East Lansing, MI: Michigan State University.

Joyner, Kara, and Grace Kao. 2005. "Interracial Relationships and the Transition to Adulthood." *American Sociological Review* 70(4): 563–581.

Kanan, Hana M., and Ahmad M. Baker. 2006. "Influence of International Schools on the Perception of Local Students' Individual and Collective Identities, Career Aspirations and Choice of University." *Journal of Research in International Education* 5(3): 251–268.

Keeling, Anne. 2016. *Huge Global Demand for English-Medium K-12 Education*. Retrieved 22 August 2016 from http://www.iscresearch.com/information/isc-news.aspx.

Kinney, David A. 1993. "From Nerds to Normals: The Recovery of Identity among Adolescents from Middle School to High School." *Sociology of Education* 66(1): 21–40.

Knorr, Jacqueline. 2005. "When German Children Come 'Home': Experiences of (Re)migration to Germany—and Some Remarks about the 'TCK' Issue." In *Childhood and Migration: From Experience to Agency*, ed. Jacqueline Knörr, 51–76. New Brunswick, NJ and London: Transaction Publishers.

Konno, Ayako. 2005. "Examining the Relationship between Ethnic Identity and Adjustment in Asian International Students: Understanding the Experience of Third Culture Kids." Psy.D. dissertation. Chicago, IL: Chicago School of Professional Psychology.

Korpela, Mari. 2010. "A Postcolonial Imagination? Westerners Searching for Authenticity in India." *Journal of Ethnic and Migration Studies* 36(8): 1299–1315.

———. 2016. "A (Sub)culture of Their Own? Children of Lifestyle Migrants in Goa, India." *Asian and Pacific Migration Journal* (4): 470–488.

Krishnaswamy, N., and Archana S. Burde. 2004 [1998]. *The Politics of Indians' English: Linguistic Colonialism and the Expanding English Empire.* Delhi and Oxford: Oxford University Press.

Kumaravadivelu, B. 2006. "Dangerous Liason: Globalization, Empire and TESOL." In *(Re)-locating TESOL in an Age of Empire,* ed. Julian Edge, 1–26. Basingstoke and New York: Palgrave Macmillan.

Kustulasari, Ag. 2009. "The International Standard School Project in Indonesia: A Policy Document Analysis." M.A. thesis. Columbus, OH: Ohio State University.

Lacroix, Celeste. 2004. "Images of Animated Others: The Orientalization of Disney's Cartoon Heroines from 'The Little Mermaid' to 'The Hunchback of Notre Dame.'" *Popular Communication* 2(4): 213–229.

Lallo, Oren. 2008. "Falafel à la Baguette: Global Packaging for Local Core in International Schools." In *The Production of Educational Knowledge in the Global Era,* ed. Julia Resnik, 169–183. Rotterdam: Sense Publishers.

Leach, Robert J. 1969. *International Schools and Their Role in the Field of International Education.* Oxford and New York: Pergamon Press.

Lease, A. Michele, Karen T. Musgrove, and Jennifer L. Axelrod. 2002. "Dimensions of Social Status in Preadolescent Peer Groups: Likability, Perceived Popularity, and Social Dominance." *Social Development* 11(4): 508–533.

Lefebvre, Henri. 1991. *The Production of Space.* Oxford: Basil Blackwell.

Leggett, William. H. 2003. "Culture, Power, Difference: Managing Ambivalence and Producing Identity in the Transnational Corporate Offices of Jakarta, Indonesia." Ph.D. dissertation. Champaign, IL: University of Illinois at Urbana-Champaign.

———. 2005. "Terror and the Colonial Imagination at Work in the Transnational Corporate Spaces of Jakarta, Indonesia." *Identities* 12(2): 271–302.

———. 2010. "Institutionalising the Colonial Imagination: Chinese Middlemen and the Transnational Corporate Office in Jakarta, Indonesia." *Journal of Ethnic and Migration Studies* 36(8): 1265–1278.

Leonard, Pauline. 2010. "Work, Identity and Change? Post/Colonial Encounters in Hong Kong." *Journal of Ethnic and Migration Studies* 36(8): 1247–1263.

Levinson, Bradley A., and Dorothy C. Holland. 1996. "The Cultural Production of the Educated Person: An Introduction." In *The Cultural Production of the Educated Person: Critical Ethnographies of Schooling and Local Practice,* ed. Bradley A. Levinson, Douglas E. Foley, and Dorothy C. Holland, 1–54. Albany: State University of New York Press.

Liang, Elizabeth. 2017. *Alien Citizen: An Earth Odyssey.* Retrieved 11 January 2017 from http://cargocollective.com/aliencitizen.

Lindegaard, Marie Rosenkrantz. 2009. "Navigating Terrains of Violence: How South African Male Youngsters Negotiate Social Change." *Social Dynamics* 35(1): 19–35.

Linger, Daniel Touro. 2005. *Anthropology through a Double Lens: Public and Personal Worlds in Human Theory*. Philadelphia: University of Pennsylvania Press.

Lo, Jacqueline. 2000. "Beyond Happy Hybridity: Performing Asian-Australian Identities. In *Alter/Asians: Asian-Australian Identities in Art, Media and Popular Culture*, ed. Ien Ang, Sharon Chalmers, Lisa Law and Mandy Thomas, 152–168. Sydney: Pluto Press.

Mahoney, Ellen. 2014. *Founder's Story*. Retrieved 29 December 2016 from http://seachangementoring.com/founders-story/.

Malinowski, Bronislaw. 1922. *Argonauts of the Western Pacific*. London: G. Routledge & Sons.

Martins, Andrea. 2008. "Expat Assignments: Are You Addicted?" *The Telegraph*, 28 August.

Matthews, Julie, and Ravinder Sidhu. 2005. "Desperately Seeking the Global Subject: International Education, Citizenship and Cosmopolitanism." *Globalisation, Societies & Education* 3(1): 49–66.

Matthews, Michael. 1988. "The Ethos of International Schools." M.Sc. thesis. Oxford: University of Oxford.

Mayall, Jyoti. 2010. "National Plus Schools and the Indonesian National Education Policy: Background, Function and Major Issues." Ph.D. dissertation. Crawley, WA: University of Western Australia.

McCaig, Norma M. 2002. "Raised in the Margin of the Mosaic: Global Nomads Balance Worlds Within." *International Educator* (Spring): 10–17.

McDonald, David. 1996. *The Etymology of Jizz*. Retrieved 3 February 2015 from http://web.archive.org/web/19960512210529/http:/home.sol.no:80/tibjonn/jizzdmcd.htm.

Meerwald, Agnes May Lin. 2002. "Chineseness at the Crossroads: Negotiations of Chineseness and the Politics of Liminality in Diasporic Chinese Women's Lives in Australia." Ph.D. dissertation. Murdoch, WA: Murdoch University.

Mitchell, Katharyne. 2003. "Educating the National Citizen in Neoliberal Times: From the Multicultural Self to the Strategic Cosmopolitan." *Transactions of the Institute of British Geographers* 28(4): 387–403.

Morley, David. 2000. *Home Territories: Media, Mobility and Identity*. London: Routledge.

Mysbergh, James H. 1957. "The Indonesian Elite." *Far Eastern Survey* 26(3): 38–42.

Narayan, Kirin. 1993. "How Native is a 'Native' Anthropologist?" *American Anthropologist* 95(3): 671–686.

Nye, Joseph S. 2004. *Soft Power: The Means to Success in World Politics*. New York: Public Affairs.

O'Reilly, Karen. 2009. "The Children of the Hunters: Self-Realization Projects and Class Reproduction." In *Lifestyle Migration: Expectations, Aspirations and Experiences*, ed. Michaela Benson and Karen O'Reilly, 103–120. Farnham: Ashgate.

Ortner, Sherry B. 2002. "'Burned Like a Tattoo': High School Social Categories and 'American Culture.'" *Ethnography* 3(2): 115–148.

———. 2003. *New Jersey Dreaming: Capital, Culture, and the Class of '58*. Durham, NC: Duke University Press.

————. 2006. *Anthropology and Social Theory: Culture, Power, and the Acting Subject.* Durham, NC: Duke University Press.

Ossman, Susan. 2013. *Moving Matters: Paths of Serial Migration.* Standford: Stanford University Press.

Parker, Lyn. 2003. *From Subjects to Citizens: Balinese Villagers in the Indonesian Nation-State.* Copenhagen: NIAS.

Pearce, Richard., ed. 2013. *International Education and Schools: Moving Beyond the First 40 Years.* London: Bloomsbury Publishing.

Pennycook, Alastair. 1998. *English and the Discourses of Colonialism.* London and New York: Routledge.

Peterson, Mark Allen. 2011. *Connected in Cairo: Growing Up Cosmopolitan in the Modern Middle East.* Bloomington: Indiana University Press.

Phillips, John. 2002. "The Third Way: Lessons from International Education." *Journal of Research in International Education* 1(2): 159–181.

Phillipson, Robert. 1992. *Linguistic Imperialism.* Oxford and New York: Oxford University Press.

Phinney, Jean S. 1990. "Ethnic Identity in Adolescents and Adults: Review of Research." *Psychological Bulletin* 108(3): 499–514.

————. 2008. "Ethnic Identity Exploration in Emerging Adulthood." In *Adolescent Identities: A Collection of Readings,* ed. Deborah L. Browning, 47–66. New York: The Analytic Press.

Pieterse, Jan Nederveen. 2001. "Hybridity, So What? The Anti-Hybridity Backlash and the Riddles of Recognition." *Theory Culture Society* 18(2–3): 219–245.

Pollock, David C., and Ruth. E. Van Reken. 2009 [2001]. *Third Culture Kids: Growing Up among Worlds.* Boston: Intercultural Press.

————. 2001. *Third Culture Kids: The Experience of Growing Up among Worlds.* Boston, MA, and London: Nicholas Brealey Publishing.

Resnik, Julia. 2008. "The Construction of the Global Worker through International Education." In *The Production of Educational Knowledge in the Global Era,* ed. Julia Resnik, 147–167. Rotterdam: Sense Publishers.

Rizvi, Fazal. 2009. "Global Mobility and the Challenges of Educational Research and Policy." *Yearbook of the National Society for the Study of Education* 108(2): 268–289.

Said, Edward. W. 1985[1978]. *Orientalism.* Harmondsworth: Penguin.

————. 1994. *Culture and Imperialism.* New York: Vintage Books.

Sander, Marie. 2014. "Passing Shanghai: Ethnographic Insights into Expatriate Youths' Mobile Lives." Ph.D. dissertation. Heidelberg: Heidelberg University.

Schachter, Elli P. 2005. "Erikson Meets the Postmodern: Can Classic Identity Theory Rise to the Challenge?" *Identity* 5(2): 137–160.

Schaetti, Barbara F. 2000. "Global Nomad Identity: Hypothesizing A Developmental Model." Ph.D. dissertation. Cincinnati, OH: The Union Institute.

Schwartz, Seth J. 2001. "The Evolution of Eriksonian and, Neo-Eriksonian Identity Theory and Research: A Review and Integration." *Identity* 1(1): 7–58.

Schwartz, Seth J., James E. Cote, and Jeffrey Jensen Arnett. 2005. "Identity and Agency in Emerging Adulthood." *Youth & Society* 37(2): 201–229.

Sennett, Richard. 1998. *The Corrosion of Character: The Personal Consequences of Work in the New Capitalism.* New York and London: W. W. Norton & Company.

Sklair, Leslie. 2001. *The Transnational Capitalist Class.* Oxford and Målden, MA: Blackwell.

Smith, Michael P. 2001. *Transnational Urbanism: Locating Globalization.* Malden, MA: Blackwell Publishing.

Snyder, Benson R. 1970. *The Hidden Curriculum.* New York: Alred A. Knopf.

Soemardjan, Selo. 1962. *Social Changes in Jogjakarta.* Ithaca, NY: Cornell University Press.

Sparrow, Lise M. 2000. "Beyond Multicultural Man: Complexities of Identity." *International Journal of Intercultural Relations* 24(2): 173–201.

Spears, Richard A. 2004. *Historical Dictionary of American Slang.* New York: Random House.

Stoler, Ann L. 1992. "Sexual Affronts and Racial Frontiers: European Identities and the Cultural Politics of Exclusion in Colonial Southeast Asia." *Comparative Studies in Society and History* 34(3): 514–551.

———. 1995. *Race and the Education of Desire: Foucault's History of Sexuality and the Colonial Order of Things.* Durham, NC: Duke University Press.

Tamatea, Laurence. 2008. "A Practical and Reflexive Liberal-Humanist Approach to International Mindedness in International Schools: Case Studies from Malaysia and Brunei." *Journal of Research in International Education* 7(1): 55–76.

Tanu, Danau. 2011. "Vignettes from Another Perspective: When Cultural Hierarchies Matter at an International School." In *Writing Out of Limbo: International Childhoods, Global Nomads and Third Culture Kids*, ed. Nina Sichel and Gene H. Bell-Villada, 220–231. Newcastle upon Tyne: Cambridge Scholars Press.

———. 2014. "Becoming 'International': The Cultural Reproduction of the Local Elite at an International School in Indonesia." *South East Asia Research* 22(4): 579–596.

———. 2015. "Towards an Interdisciplinary Analysis of the Diversity of 'Third Culture Kids.'" In *Migration, Diversity, and Education: Beyond Third Culture Kids*, ed. Sajia Benjamin and Fred Dervin, 13–34. Basingstoke: Palgrave Macmillan.

———. 2016. "Going to School in 'Disneyland': Imagining an International School Community in Indonesia." *Asian and Pacific Migration Journal* 25(4): 429–450.

Tanu, Danau, and Laura Dales. 2016. "Language in Fieldwork: Making Visible the Ethnographic Impact of The Researcher's Linguistic Fluency." *The Australian Journal of Anthropology* 27: 353–369.

Twine, France Winddance. 1997. "Brown-Skinned White Girls: Class, Culture, and the Construction of White Identity in Suburban Communities." In *Displacing Whiteness Essays in Social and Cultural Criticism*, ed. Ruth Frankenberg, 214–243. Durham, NC: Duke University Press.

Useem, John, and Ruth Useem. 1967. "The Interfaces of a Binational Third Culture: A Study of the American Community in India." *Journal of Social Issues* XXIII(1): 130–143.

Useem, John, Ruth Useem, and John Donoghue. 1963. "Men in the Middle of the Third Culture: the Roles of American and Non-Western People in Cross-Cultural Administration." *Human Organization* 22(3): 169–179.

Useem, Ruth Hill. 1973. "Third Cultural Factors in Educational Change." In *Cultural Challenges to Education: The Influence of Cultural Factors in School Learning*, ed. Cole Speicher Brembeck and Walker H. Hill, 121–138. Lexington, MA: Lexington Books.

———. 1993. "Third Culture Kids: Focus of Major Study—TCK 'Mother' Pens History of Field." In *NewsLinks*, 1. Princeton, NJ: International Schools Services.

Useem, Ruth Hill, and Richard D. Downie. 1976. "Third Culture Kids." *Today's Education* 65(3): 103–105.

Van Reken, Ruth. E. N.d. "TCK Relationships and Grief." Retrieved 14 August 2008 from http://tckacademy.com/class/001/tckclassminicourse001.pdf.

Villegas, Ana Maria, and Jacqueline Jordan Irvine. 2010. "Diversifying the Teaching Force: An Examination of Major Arguments." *The Urban Review* 42(3): 175–192.

Walters, Kate. 2006. "A Story to Tell: The Identity Development of Women Growing Up as Third Culture Kids." M.A. thesis. Langley, BC: Trinity Western University.

Weenink, Don. 2008. "Cosmopolitanism as a Form of Capital." *Sociology* 42(6): 1089–1106.

Werbner, Pnina. 1999. "Global Pathways: Working Class Cosmopolitans and the Creation of Transnational Ethnic Worlds." *Social Anthropology* 7(1): 17–35.

Willis, Paul E. 1977. *Learning to Labour: How Working Class Kids Get Working Class Jobs.* Farnborough: Saxon House.

Wimmer, Andreas, and Nina Glick Schiller. 2002. "Methodological Nationalism and Beyond: Nation–State Building, Migration and the Social Sciences." *Global Networks* 2(4): 301–334.

Wise, Amanda. 2010. "Sensuous Multiculturalism: Emotional Landscapes of Inter-Ethnic Living in Australian Suburbia." *Journal of Ethnic and Migration Studies* 36(6): 917–937.

Wolf, Eric R. 1956. "Aspects of Group Relations in a Complex Society: Mexico." *American Anthropologist* 58(6): 1065–1078.

Wurgaft, Nina. 2006. "Also Known As: An Exploration of Cultural Hybridity." Psy.D. dissertation. Keene, NH: Antioch New England Graduate School.

Wylie, Michael. 2008. "Internationalizing Curriculum: Framing Theory and Practice in International Schools." *Journal of Research in International Education* 7(1): 5–19.

Yeo, Wee Loon. 2010. "Belonging to 'Chinatown': A Study of Asian Boarders in a West Australian Private Boarding School." *International Studies in Sociology of Education* 20(1): 55–66.

Yoneyama, Shoko. 2000. "Student Discourse on Tokokyohi (School Phobia/Refusal) in Japan: Burnout or Empowerment?" *British Journal of Sociology of Education* 21(1): 77–94.

Index